NORTH KOREA'S HIDDEN REVOLUTION

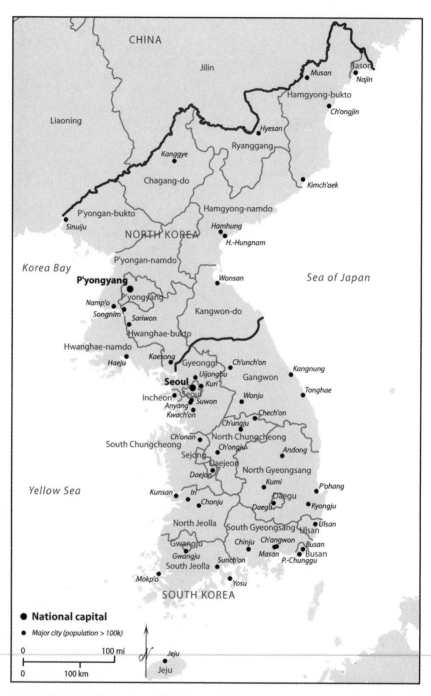

Map of the divided Korean Peninsula

Illustrations copyright © 2016 by C. Scott Walker, Harvard Map Collection

NORTH KOREA'S HIDDEN REVOLUTION

HOW THE INFORMATION UNDERGROUND IS

TRANSFORMING A CLOSED SOCIETY

JIEUN BAEK

Yale UNIVERSITY PRESS

NEW HAVEN & LONDON

Yale University Press books may be purchased in quantity for educational, business, or promotional use. For information, please e-mail sales.press@yale .edu (U.S. office) or sales@yaleup.co.uk (U.K. office).

Set in Meridien type by IDS Infotech, Ltd.
Printed in the United States of America.

ISBN 978-0-300-21781-0 (hardcover: alk. paper)

Library of Congress Control Number: 2016939291

A catalogue record for this book is available from the British Library.

This paper meets the requirements of ANSI/NISO Z39.48-1992 (Permanence of Paper).

10 9 8 7 6 5 4 3 2 1

Both my grandfathers were born in North Pyongan Province and fled south right before the Korean War divided the country. They spent their lives praying that they would be able to reunite with their families in North Korea. Though they passed away with their prayers unfulfilled, their dream of reunification lives on. I dedicate this book to them.

CONTENTS

AUTHOR'S NOTE

In 2007, when I was a junior at Harvard College, I received an interview request from a Voice of America reporter. Voice of America is one of several programs that broadcast daily into North Korea. It is difficult to know how many people are listening, or how long the average listening session is, since conducting in-country surveys is impossible: the North Korean government will not allow independent surveyors unfettered access to its population. But it is clear that increasing numbers of people do listen to these programs secretly, and that the programs do affect some of them. Some defectors have said that they regularly tuned in to Voice of America broadcasts even though they were aware of the risks involved: North Korean citizens who are caught listening to foreign radio programs can be punished with severe interrogations, imprisonment, or even execution.

The interviewer asked me to describe an event that my student organization, Harvard Undergraduates for Human Rights in North Korea (H-RINK), had hosted with a defector. The defector had recounted his escape from North Korea to several dozen undergraduates. I remember thinking about how I could answer the reporter's questions about why I was interested in human rights issues in North Korea, what impact events to raise awareness could have, and why Americans like myself were interested in participating in such student organizations. I considered the stark contrast between the risks that listeners inside North Korea were taking to listen to this program, and the simplicity and safety that enveloped my fellow students and me. If my grandfathers had never escaped from North Korea, I could easily have been a listener from inside the regime rather than in front of the microphone in Cambridge.

Over the past eleven years, I have spent countless hours with hundreds of North Korean defectors in South Korea and the United States. My personal experiences with defectors from all walks of life—from orphans who spent years in political prison camps, to professors, to military and government officials—inspired me to write about the information flowing covertly over the border and how it is changing North Korean society. Through my work, I've been able to continue speaking with missionaries, journalists, activists, members of nongovernmental organizations (NGOs), and academics—as well as students who are not North Korean, but have been inside the country and witnessed the effects that such information has had on North Korean society. Both primary and secondary sources have helped me describe how foreign media and information make their way into North Korea, and how they may be instrumental in someday bringing down one of the most brutal and repressive regimes in modern history. At heart, then, this is a story of the transformative power of media and information, as well as the resilience of the human spirit to survive and find freedom.

The stories of defectors are portrayed as accurately as possible based on my interviews, conversations, and personal relationships with them. Most of their stories have been recorded, and they have given me written permission to retell them. All requests for having names and identifying traits anonymized, altered, or omitted have been honored.

A note about terminology referring to North Koreans who have escaped: the words "refugees" and "defectors" are commonly used to describe them, yet North Koreans do not simply migrate to third countries, and "defector" is becoming an obsolete term in South Korea because of its strong political connotations. The Korean word for North Korean defectors is Tal-buk-ja, or Tal-buk-min, which means "people who fled the North." But new terms are being coined, too: in 2005, South Korea's Ministry of Unification announced the use of Sae-Teo-Min, meaning "people of new land." Buk-han-tal-ju-min, a more recent term, means "people who renounced North Korea." Indeed, some North Koreans did actively denounce North Korea as a government, but others dislike the strong political connotation with their new demographic identity. Some younger North Koreans prefer "former North Koreans," "resettlers," "new settlers," or Buk-han Chool-shin, which means "of North Korean origin." With these considerations in mind, this book is for an English-speaking audience, and I have decided to use the term "defectors" to refer to North Koreans who escaped North Korea.

Please also note that a Korean name consists of a family name followed by a given name. For example, in Korean, my name is Baek Ji-Eun. In the United States, however, I follow the American tradition of using my given name followed by my family name—Jieun Baek. Readers will see mostly the Korean style for names in this book, depending on the context.

This book is intended for a general audience and therefore will use popular English spellings for Korean terms. While writing this book, I tested different versions of romanization of Korean terms with non-academic readers (including Revised

Romanization and McCune-Reischauer), and most overwhelmingly preferred popular English spellings for accessibility purposes. For example, to refer to North Korea's capital city, I use the spelling "Pyongyang" rather than the McCune-Reischauer romanization of the term, which is "P'yŏngyang," or the Revised Romanization of the term, which is "Pyeongyang."

I hope this book will inspire readers to learn more about North Koreans who are taking extraordinary risks to fulfill their insatiable curiosity about the world that exists beyond their own borders.

DRAMATIS PERSONAE

Names marked with an asterisk have been altered. Personages who appear briefly only once or twice are not included.

Jeong Gwang-Seong: Male, twenty-seven years old, from Horyeong City in North Hamgyong Province. Currently a university student in South Korea majoring in political science and diplomacy.

Kim Ha-Young*: Female, twenty-three years old, from Musan City in North Hamgyong Province. Currently a university student in South Korea, majoring in political science.

Kim Heung-Kwang: Male, fifty-six years old, from Hamhung City in South Hamgyong Province. Currently the executive director of North Korea Intellectuals Solidarity (NKIS).

Choi Jung-Hoon: Male, forty-seven years old, from Hyesan City in Ryanggang Province. Currently the director of North Korea People's Liberation Front and broadcasting director for Free North Korea Radio.

Kim Seong-Min: Male, fifty-four years old, from Jagang Province. Director of Free North Korea Radio.

Nehemiah Park*: Male, thirty-five years old, from Musan City in North Hamgyong Province. Currently a businessman in South Korea.

Ji Seong-Ho: Male, thirty-four years old, from Hoeryong City in North Hamgyong Province. Currently the director of non-governmental organization Now, Action and Unity for Human Rights (NAUH).

Lee Joon-Hee*: Male, twenty-six years old, from Hyesan City in Ryanggang Province. Currently a student in South Korea studying political science.

Park Se-Joon*: Male, approximately forty-six years old, from one of the Hwanghae provinces. Currently studying in South Korea and running activism projects related to North Korean information distribution.

Ahn Yu-Mi*: Female, twenty-seven years old, from Hoeryong City in North Hamgyong Province. Currently studying English in South Korea.

PROLOGUE

Ahn walks up to the edge of the Tumen River, on the border between North Korea and China. With his senses on high alert, he scans the border for Chinese guards, whose assignment is to catch people like him. At the narrowest points of the river, where it is only about fifty meters wide, Ahn can easily see North Korea from where he stands. He's being paid a handsome fee for being one of two middlemen smuggling outside goods into North Korea, and he will receive the second half of his payment upon completing the mission.

Certain that he isn't being watched by Chinese security personnel or North Korean border guards, Ahn empties his bags into a plastic bin and wraps the bin in a plastic bag to waterproof it. He then methodically ties this package to a sturdy wire and, gripping one end of the wire tightly, hurls the bin across the river. Silence surrounds him as his eyes follow the arc of the bin in the air. It lands in the water, close to where Ku stands. Ku is the second middleman, who will take these outside goods into North Korea.

On the other side of the river, standing in North Korean territory, Ku has a much more dangerous job. If North Korean border guards catch him engaging in any unauthorized trade, especially possession of this package, he could be beaten or sentenced to a political prison camp.

Ku quietly walks into the river to grab the bucket, which is still attached to the wire that Ahn holds. After grabbing it, Ku climbs out of the river, removes his incriminating wet clothes, and discards them. He changes into a dry outfit and casually makes his way back into a city where he will sell these goods—one hundred USB drives—on the black market to eager North Koreans.

North Korean leaders see these seemingly harmless little USBs—which are filled with illegal content such as foreign films, television shows, South Korean soap operas, and digital books— as weapons against the state, and they invest significant resources in preventing such media from entering the country. Out of fear that foreign information could inspire North Korean citizens to become disaffected with their country, the only legal media are state-sanctioned.

Yet over the past two decades there have been cracks in the state's control over the dissemination of information among citizens. Ahn and Ku's rudimentary method of exchanging information and media is one of many ways in which people are risking their lives to inform North Koreans about the world outside their country, knowledge that many desperately crave. Ahn is a North Korean defector living in South Korea who runs a Seoul-based NGO that works to send information into North Korea. Ku is a North Korean citizen who is paid by the NGO to be the middle-man who acquires the USBs and sells them to North Koreans, who in turn sell them on the black market at a marked-up price. Dissemination of foreign information is a profitable business in North Korea, because the demand is so high.

The flow of information is having a significant social and cultural impact on North Koreans, who support themselves with illicit activities. The country is home to numerous criminal enterprises, with much of its GDP coming from drug production and trafficking, counterfeit money laundering, and skirting of international sanctions. North Korea has not published economic statistics since the 1960s, so GDP numbers produced by the World Bank, the CIA's *World Factbook,* and other sources are all estimates. Illicit networks pave the way for the exchange of information across even the most policed of borders. Brokers don't care about the products they are moving across borders as long as they are receiving a satisfactory kickback for their work. Goods acquired through illegal trade are sold on the black markets that have proliferated across North Korea since the mid-1990s, and those same markets, among other means, allow for the illegal exchange of information.

A motley crew of foreign organizations, defectors, smugglers, Chinese middlemen and businessmen, and North Korean soldiers who turn a blind eye with bribes comprise a sophisticated network that links North Koreans to the outside world. In addition to facilitating the movement of goods like cell phones, laptops, medication, and clothing, this network brings foreign information and media into the country. The accompanying diagram illustrates the interrelated nature of these various actors.

Foreign NGOs that raise funds to create content, fill USBs and DVDs, send shortwave radios, and create ways to get these to smugglers comprise what I call the "compassion-driven network." These goodwill-driven organizations work to bring positive change to an oppressive society. Profit-driven networks are all the smugglers both inside and outside North Korea who help move these USBs and other vehicles of foreign media purely for profit. These actors do not care if the USBs contain audio Bibles or porn. I would also include in this group the marketeers who

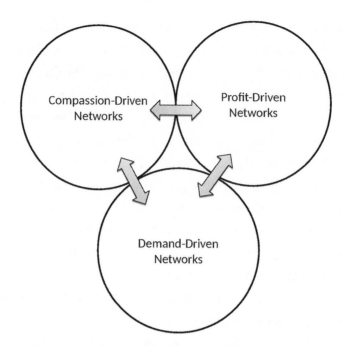

Interlinked networks of actors that jointly push foreign information into North Korea

sell them on the black market. For these individuals and organizations, the profits they earn upon delivering these materials into North Korea outweigh the risk and costs involved. And finally, the demand-driven networks are composed of consumers who watch and listen to the content. These three networks work in concert to push and pull information into North Korea, and make the distribution process robust.

Foreign movies, TV shows, soap operas, books, music, and encyclopedias have been making their way into North Korea illicitly. This active flow of goods and information now plays a central role in the social consciousness of North Korean individuals, and has sparked irreversible changes inside North Korea. One of these changes has to do with media consumers' heightened awareness of higher living standards outside of North

Korea, which has compelled many North Koreans to question why they have to be so poor. It's not that different from what many Russians refer to as the "battle between the television and the refrigerator," that is, the push and pull between state propaganda and living standards. The North Korean government has been pushing as much state propaganda as possible on its people without being able to provide a daily experience that matches this rhetoric. The government even went so far as to launch a "Let's Eat Two Meals a Day" campaign in the early 1990s to encourage decreased food consumption.

ESCAPING NORTH KOREA

North Korea has a population of approximately 25 million. Leaving the country without permission is considered treason and is punishable by death, yet many have tried to leave in pursuit of a better life with more opportunities. (Few people leave primarily in search of political freedom and human rights; the concepts are so unfamiliar to them that most couldn't even describe what they mean before defecting.) Many escaped to China thinking that they would return to North Korea after making and saving some money, but ended up defecting to South Korea after learning more about it. Some children I spoke with were tricked into defecting by their own parents who had already escaped, and who told the children to follow the "uncle" who would take them to their parents, only to find out later that the "uncle" was in fact a paid broker and their parents were not in China, but in South Korea. When one member of a family defects, the others are at risk, because they are kept under close surveillance and are subject to imprisonment in labor camps because of their guilt by association.

Since North and South Korea are separated by a 2.5-mile-wide, mine-ridden demilitarized zone, defectors aiming for South

Korea go through China first. Given the nearly impossible obstacles involved in defection, we can only guess from the numbers of those who do make it that thousands more have tried but failed. Unsuccessful attempts often end in capture, torture, imprisonment, or death. There are no estimates of failed attempts, but many defectors who have settled in South Korea and elsewhere were successful on their second, third, or fourth attempt, and have shared harrowing recollections of other North Koreans being brutally punished for attempting to defect.

Currently, nearly thirty thousand North Koreans have settled in other countries, including 29,900 North Korean defectors who have successfully reached South Korea; approximately 650 defectors who are now in the United Kingdom; and 194 who made it to the United States. There are small numbers of defectors in other European countries, as well as in Canada, Australia, and Southeast Asia. North Korea shares a 17.5-kilometer border with Russia, but this is an irrelevant border when it comes to defectors.

There is a Korean saying that "seeing once is better than hearing something a hundred times." A South Korean government researcher who has been interviewing North Korean defectors since the mid-1990s observes that when defectors cross into China, their minds are opened and their worlds change because they can watch unlimited Korean TV shows and news programs and can see how wealthy China is compared to North Korea. Seeing how people with disabilities and lower incomes are not purged from Beijing and Seoul, but are actually taken care of by other people and by the government, is astonishing to North Koreans. Seeing people dedicate their lives to service and volunteer work, as Catholic nuns, pastors, NGOs, and student volunteers do, alters North Koreans' view of their social order. North Koreans express pleasant surprise at hearing defectors speak on TV and radio. It blows their minds that media outlets are not reserved for the elite.

The majority of North Koreans defect by crossing the North Korean–Chinese border illegally. Due to China and North Korea's Friendship Agreement, established in 1961, China does not recognize North Koreans as political refugees, but as illegal economic immigrants. Chinese authorities find and forcibly repatriate North Koreans back to North Korea, fully aware that upon their return they will face the very real possibility of detention, torture, forced abortions, sentences to political prison camps, and even death. Such forcible repatriations of refugees who face a credible fear of persecution in the home country is a flagrant violation of the 1951 Convention Relating to the Status of Refugees, to which China is a party. Chinese citizens are sometimes given cash rewards for turning in North Koreans. Tens of thousands of North Koreans are estimated to be in China, living and hiding in legal limbo. Given North Koreans' legal vulnerability in China, they are often exploited as sex workers, laborers, or brides for local Chinese men. If a North Korean woman resists sex work or marriage, her illegal status in China may be revealed to the Chinese authorities, who will quickly repatriate her to North Korea. There have been horror stories of women and girls brutalized by their Chinese husbands and brothel owners. Before 2009, more than 70 percent of North Korean women and girls were believed to be victims of sex trafficking, but after that, the numbers seem to have decreased significantly, largely because many defectors now go through brokers and organized groups.

Defections today are often arranged by family members who defected earlier, so compared to the mid-1990s, the length of time between defection from North Korea and arrival in South Korea has decreased. This is because the family members who are already settled in South Korea often pay for brokers to arrange for the secret transit of the defectors through China and across other countries so they can seek asylum at a Korean embassy in a third country. In recent times, then, about 30 to 40 percent of North Korean refugees have reached South Korea with the help of brokers who have been in contact with previously settled family members. The number of defectors who have relatives in South Korea is increasing. Yet simultaneously, the absolute number of defectors entering South Korea annually has dropped dramatically. This is because since Kim Jong-Un came into power, border security has been increased significantly, and consequently so has the amount of the bribe required for defectors to pass. In the past, a $2,000 to $3,000 bribe was sufficient to cover the risks involved for border patrol and all the brokers involved for one North Korean defector. But the ramped-up security and punishments have driven these prices up to near prohibitively high levels of $7,000 to $10,000. Furthermore, the percentage of absolutely desperate North Koreans has decreased in the past fifteen years.

Once North Korean defectors arrive in South Korea, they are interrogated by the intelligence services for approximately two months to ensure that they are not spies posing as defectors. (The duration of this interrogation has varied over the years.) They are then sent to Hanawon, a government-sponsored resettlement and re-education center, where they spend three months learning the basics of democracy, civics, human rights, and capitalism, as well as life skills. There are religious rooms for refugees who are interested in exploring Christianity, Catholicism, or Buddhism. Some refugees take their spirituality very seriously, perhaps because religious organizations played a vital role in their defection process and they want to learn more about the religions that inspire them. Others—especially the young defectors I met—say that they pretend to be "spiritually interested" and attend whichever service provides the tastiest food options. Among the various medical services available, dentistry and internal medicine are in the highest demand. A doctor told me that many North Koreans have been wrongly diagnosed and/or unnecessarily consumed unhelpful medications over the course of their lives.

Each year, the South Korean government spends $70 million for North Korean refugee resettlement. For every North Korean refugee, approximately $100,000 is spent on the investigation and settlement process. Some people receive free housing; others are offered apartments at half the market price. Many NGOs in South Korea help with the resettlement and assimilation process for North Koreans once they graduate from Hanawon.

On a recent visit to Hanawon, I tiptoed quietly into a nursery housing North Korean toddlers who had arrived only weeks earlier. The teacher who was overseeing the dozen or so children stood up when she saw me and cheerfully encouraged the children to greet the American visitor. A little boy turned to face me, held onto his belly button, and bowed deeply until his head nearly touched the floor. A little girl ran up to me and high-fived my outstretched hand. Some other children glanced up to see who I was, and, uninterested, went right back to playing with their new toys.

As I walked back into the hallway, I was struck by the sheer difference in experiences I have had with youngsters greeting me in North Korea. Back in Pyongyang in front of Kumsusan Palace of the Sun, the little children I met bowed in sync to all visitors on command, directed by their teachers, laughed and waved on command, and smiled for pictures on command. The North Korean–born children I had just seen didn't follow orders. Without even realizing it, maybe these fortunate children who had been brought to a free, democratic country by their parents were already practicing freedom and choice before even learning the full meaning of these ideas.

Still, defectors face significant challenges adapting to South Korea socially, culturally, educationally, professionally, and financially. Many owe their brokers money before they even leave Hanawon. Trust plays a big role in the network of brokers, resettled defectors, and to-be defectors, so defectors, especially if they have family members who have already settled in South Korea, sometimes use the services provided by brokers and promise to pay them once they resettle in South Korea. Some brokers wait outside Hanawon, ready to collect the resettlement cash that the South Korean government provides to all resettling North Koreans. Others will call, harass, and even threaten new defectors to pay the broker's fee if they haven't already. For some defectors, then, graduation from the Hanawon resettlement and reeducation classes, which are supposed to facilitate their assimilation into a new society, is instead a step toward being debt-ridden in South Korea.

Many North Korean defectors also struggle academically in South Korea. With the world's thirteenth largest GDP, the entire nation prizes the education of young people for both their individual and national success, in part because South Korea lacks many natural resources and needs to invest in human capital. Education accounted for nearly 12 percent of consumer spending in 2012. On cram schools alone, parents spent the equivalent of 1.5 percent of GDP. The infamous Korean cram schools or "hagwons" that constitute a $20 billion industry were filled with students into the wee hours of the morning, so the South Korean Ministry of Education instituted a national policy for cram schools to close their doors after 10 p.m. This elicited a huge outcry from these schools and distressed mothers. Whereas North Korean authorities carry out surprise raids at night to catch people illegally watching foreign films or having unauthorized guests overnight, South Korean authorities carry out night raids to catch students to make them leave the cram schools.

The South Korean government administers the College Scholastic Aptitude Test (*Suneung* in Korean) for high school seniors once a year. The *Suneung* score will determine which college they will attend, a result that some students and families believe is the primary determinant for the students' future. Since this test is administered only once a year in November, students and their families devote all the resources they can to prepare for this fateful day. Students go on special health diets, take medicinal boosters, say extra prayers, and spend more than twelve hours a day, every day for years, studying for this test. In the months leading up to the test date, Buddhist temples and Christian churches are filled with parents—usually mothers—with a photo of their children in their school uniform, giving special prayers for their children to perform well on the test date for admission to one of the top three universities in South Korea: Seoul National University, Korea University, or Yonsei University. People refer to these three top schools as the SKY universities for short. "Reach for the SKY!" children will hear growing up. South Korea's National Youth Policy Institute and other centers that survey students found that South Korean high school students sleep, on average, just 5.5 hours every night, because they spend the remaining hours studying.

On exam day, the entire nation contributes to positive test-taking conditions for the 600,000 eighteen-year-olds by giving all other students the day off so that the schools are quiet. The stock market, public offices, and banks all open one hour later to keep the streets free of unnecessary traffic for students to get to their testing centers on time. All planes are rerouted or grounded during the afternoon's English-language listening test so students can focus on listening. The Korea Electric Power Corporation, the largest electric utility corporation, commissions four thousand electricians to be on standby in case any testing center's lights go off. Police officers take emergency calls in the morning to whisk late students to their testing locations on their police motorbikes.

North Koreans can struggle to assimilate into this competitive society. Students at Yeo-Myung School, a Seoul-based alternative private school for North Korean defector students, say, "We couldn't live in North Korea due to hunger but we cannot live in South Korea because we do not understand the society." Many fall behind in South Korean schools, drop out—or worse. North Korean defectors have a suicide rate three times that of South Korean natives, according to South Korea's Ministry of Unification data. And according to 2015 health statistics by the Organisation for Economic Co-operation and Development (OECD), South Korea consistently has the highest suicide rate of all thirty-four OECD countries, and suicide is the leading cause of death among teenagers there.

Despite all the challenges that North Koreans face while living inside North Korea, and, for some, while escaping the regime and living in a new country, they have proven themselves to be an extraordinarily resilient people. This book strives to change the perception of North Korea as a hopeless, impenetrable black box. Outsiders often think that no information enters or exits the country, but in fact its boundaries are more porous than people think, and certainly more than its autocratic leaders would like. Leaders' attempts to keep an airtight seal on its informational borders are breaking down, and they are losing their monopoly over the dissemination of information among citizens.

1 IMMORTAL GODS

Why North Korea Is Such a Durable Regime

On June 11, 2012, a flash flood hit Sinhung, a county in North Korea's South Hamgyong Province. A fourteen-year-old schoolgirl named Han Hyon-Gyong desperately tried to keep the plastic-wrapped portraits of Kim Il-Sung and Kim Jong-Il hanging in her home above the floodwaters. She drowned while trying to save the sacred images.

The North Korean state posthumously awarded Han Hyon-Gyong the Kim Jong-Il Youth Honor Award. Her parents, teacher, and Youth League leaders also received awards for her heroism. Her school was renamed after her. The country's official newspaper, *Rodong Sinmun*, praised a system that "nurtures such children."

How can a nation that cultivates and praises such acts of "heroism" exist in the twenty-first century? To understand North Korea today, it's important to consider some key moments in the country's sixty-eight-year history.

NORTH KOREA'S INCEPTION AND HISTORY

The Korean Peninsula's history starts in the Paleolithic era. In 2333 BCE, the legendary Gojoseon was established. An ancient Korean kingdom, Gojoseon was invaded by the Han dynasty of

China during the Gojoseon-Han War in 108 BCE. As a result of the war, Gojoseon was divided into many dynasties, which later became the Proto-Three Kingdoms. These kingdoms then became Silla (founded in 57 BCE), Goguryeo (founded in 37 BCE), and Baekje (founded in 18 BCE). Through a series of wars, the Goryeo dynasty unified the Three Kingdoms in 936. In 1392, the Joseon dynasty, the last Korean dynasty, was established.

In 1905, Korea became a protectorate of Japan, and in 1910, the Japan-Korea Treaty marked the annexation of the Korean empire and the beginning of the brutal colonization of the Korean people. When the Allied forces defeated the Japanese in World War II, Korea gained its independence, but in 1945, the peninsula was divided at the 38th Parallel. The Soviets took the northern part, and the United States took charge of the southern portion. On May 10, 1948, South Korea held U.N.-backed elections, and on August 15 of the same year, the Republic of Korea was established with Rhee Syngman as its president. Meanwhile, the Democratic People's Republic of Korea (North Korea) was established on September 9, 1948, with Kim Il-Sung as its leader.[1]

On June 25, 1950, North Korea invaded South Korea, sparking a three-year war. Approximately 2.5 million people died in this war, which ended in a stalemate. On July 27, 1953, the U.N. Command, the Chinese military, and the North Korean military signed an armistice agreement that enforced a complete ceasefire between military forces "until a peaceful settlement [is] achieved." Since this agreement was not a political agreement between the two governments, and since such a "peaceful settlement" has yet to be achieved, the two nations are technically still at war. The armistice agreement also established at the 38th Parallel the Demilitarized Zone (DMZ), a strip of land that is 160 miles long and 2.5 miles wide, and that serves as a buffer between North and South Korea. Despite the name, this is the most heavily militarized border in the world. During and after the Korean War, both sides planted millions of anti-personnel and anti-tank land mines to prevent the other side from infiltrating their territory. Estimates of how many land mines remain in the DMZ range between half a million to two million.

The Korean War narrative is prevalent throughout North Korea, where citizens live as if the war happened just yesterday. The political imagery, conversations, political lectures, and news create a collective social trauma that blankets the society. But the narrative that North Korea propagates is very different from the one that the rest of the world believes. In textbooks, official state media, and speeches, North Korea claims that the United States attacked the North and raped and pillaged North Koreans, and that it is because of hostile U.S. policies that the Korean Peninsula remains divided. The evil American empire is part of North Korea's foundation myth, and the "villainous United States" argument is used to justify the country's brutal internal penal code, surveillance, and monitoring system; its existential need to maintain its nuclear weapons program; and its foreign-policy decisions.

During his forty-six-year reign, Kim Il-Sung transformed North Korea into a socialist nation. By the 1960s and 1970s, the country was enjoying a relatively high standard of living. North Korea's economy outperformed its southern counterpart during this period, and so was able to inspire citizens' loyalty to Kim Il-Sung. A strong cult of personality, centered on the Supreme Leader, dominated domestic politics and daily life. *Juche*, or self-reliance, became the official state ideology in 1972, replacing Marxism-Leninism and Communism. After Kim Il-Sung died of a heart attack in 1994, he was enshrined in the North Korean constitution as the nation's Eternal President.

Heir apparent Kim Jong-Il became the second ruler of North Korea in 1994. Known as "The Dear Leader" among North Korean citizens to distinguish him from his father, "The Great Leader," Kim Jong-Il took over as North Korea suffered a tragic famine during which an estimated 800,000 to 2.5 million people perished. After his death on December 17, 2011, he was designated the "Eternal General Secretary" of the Korean Workers' Party, among other titles, in keeping with the tradition of granting "eternal" names to dead members of the Kim family.

It was assumed that Kim Jong-Il's oldest son, Kim Jong-Nam, would succeed him, but he fell out of favor when he was caught in 2001 trying to visit Disneyland in Tokyo with a fake Dominican passport and a fake Chinese name, Pang Xiong, which translates as "Fat Bear" in Mandarin Chinese. Kim Jong-Il's second son, Kim Jong-Chul, was thought to be too "feminine in character." That left Kim Jong-Un, the son of Kim Jong-Il and his consort Ko Yong-Hui, who is very similar to his father in character and demeanor and has been appointed "The Great Successor." Since North Korea's leaders are considered gods, they are assumed to live forever after their mortal deaths.

At the time of writing, Kim Jong-Un is the thirty-three-year-old Supreme Leader of North Korea—and all of the North Korean political, social, military, and cultural systems have been designed to keep him, his progeny, and the next heir in power.

JUCHE: THE OFFICIAL IDEOLOGY

The official state ideology, *juche,* is often conflated with the leadership of Kim Il-Sung. The government claims that juche is a unique North Korean application of Marxist-Leninist thought and that it pervades all areas of life—political, social, individual, economic, artistic, and literary.

The three main principles of the North Korean ideology are: (1) political and ideological independence from other nations, including China and Russia, (2) military independence and sufficient national defense, and (3) economic self-dependence and self-sufficiency.[2] It's important to note that one of the main individuals who helped craft this North Korean political philosophy, Hwang Jang-Yop, defected to South Korea in 1997. To date, the late Hwang Jang-Yop is the highest-ranking North Korean to have escaped the country; I'll describe his experience in more detail later.

To make the ideology of juche practical, the Ten Principles for the Establishment of a One-Ideology System were officially announced by Kim Jong-Il in 1974 for all North Korean citizens to memorize and live by. The ten principles are:

1. We must give our all in the struggle to unify the entire society with the revolutionary ideology of Great Leader Kim Il-Sung.
2. We must honor Great Leader comrade Kim Il-Sung with all our loyalty.
3. We must make absolute the authority of Great Leader comrade Kim Il-Sung.
4. We must make Great Leader comrade Kim Il-Sung's revolutionary ideology our faith and make his instructions our creed.
5. We must adhere strictly to the principle of unconditional obedience in carrying out the Great Leader comrade Kim Il-Sung's instructions.
6. We must strengthen the entire party's ideology and willpower and revolutionary unity, centering on Great Leader comrade Kim Il-Sung.

7. We must learn from Great Leader comrade Kim Il-Sung and adopt the Communist look, revolutionary work methods, and people-oriented work style.

8. We must value the political life we were given by Great Leader comrade Kim Il-Sung, and loyally repay his great political trust and thoughtfulness with heightened political awareness and skill.

9. We must establish strong organizational regulations so that the entire party, nation, and military move as one under the one and only leadership of Great Leader comrade Kim Il-Sung.

10. We must pass down the great achievement of the revolution by Great Leader comrade Kim Il-Sung from generation to generation, inheriting and completing it to the end.

In addition to the Ten Principles, there are sixty-five subclauses that detail how North Koreans ought to incorporate these principles to work toward a unified state under their leader. These principles are intended to regulate not only the political, physical, and social lives of every North Korean citizen, but also their psyches. The importance of instituting these principles into one's life is reinforced by weekly self-criticism and peer surveillance.

During weekly self-criticism sessions in classrooms, offices, and factories, citizens are supposed to criticize themselves and each other for how they have fallen short of living in perfect accordance with the Ten Principles, which are recited during the sessions. These confessions and criticisms start at an early age for children (about first grade). In a classroom session, for example, children take turns standing up to berate themselves for how they failed in some way the previous week, and they cannot sit down until they identify at least one other child for his or her wrongdoing. Self-criticism sessions also take place in *inminban* meetings.[3] *Inminban,* literally "people's group," are neighborhood-based mutual surveillance groups to which every citizen is assigned.

In 2013, General Kim Jong-Il's name was added throughout the Ten Principles.

SONGBUN: A SYSTEM OF SOCIAL CLASSIFICATION

Established in the 1950s, *Songbun* is the socio-political classification system that the government uses to exercise complete control over its population. Every citizen is assigned to one of three main categories according to his or her perceived political loyalty to the regime and his or her family's political background, dating back to the inception of the North Korean state. The three categories—the core class, the wavering class, and the hostile class—are themselves divided into fifty-one specific categories.

Examples of Songbun categories in the core class include:

- "Revolutionary families": descendants of "those who were sacrificed in the anti-Japanese struggle"
- "Families of Patriots": descendants of noncombatant patriots killed in the Korean War
- Families of soldiers killed in the Korean War

Examples of Songbun categories in the wavering class include:

- Defectors (and their families and descendants): those who, after liberation, betrayed the party and the regime and defected to other countries

- Political prisoners (and their families and descendants): those who "spent time in North Korean political prison camps for anti-party, anti-revolution, or anti-state activities"

Examples of Songbun categories in the hostile class include:

- Pro-Japanese and/or pro-American personnel
- Capitalists (and their families and descendants)
- Spies

Unsurprisingly, all political leaders are of the highest Songbun class, reinforcing the Korean War narrative. But many who belong to the higher Songbun classes experienced direct trauma or "made sacrifices" during the Korean War, such as losing parents or relatives. These descendants of the Korean War maintain their high Songbun status as long as they do not commit any crimes, and they grow up hearing frequently about the sacrifices made by their older relatives. Their status permits them to attend prestigious universities in Pyongyang, rise higher in the party ranks, and lead relatively comfortable lives. Deep historical links to today's social-class system keep intense anti-American sentiment alive, and breathe new life into the regime with each new generation.

One's Songbun status will determine the opportunities available in almost all areas of one's life: education, career prospects, marriageability, ability to join the Korean Workers' Party, and so on. One can always be demoted in rank, but there is little room for upward mobility based on merit. Individuals with higher Songbun status are rewarded with extensive privileges, whereas other citizens who are marked with lower status live with fewer opportunities. Not everyone is aware of his or her

Songbun classification, especially those who are of lower rank. Some of the people profiled later in this book learned of their lower status somewhat late in life, and became extremely disillusioned with the idea of working hard for their families and for the state.

The proliferation of grassroots markets across North Korea since the mid-1990s famine has given rise to new social norms that have made parts of the Songbun classification system less relevant. For example, those descendants of individuals who fought with the Japanese who have been banished to rural North Korean cities have always been marked with lower status. And because the state's public distribution system rarely reached provincial cities, especially during and after the famine, people living in these areas inevitably became entrepreneurial and created informal—not to mention illegal—grassroots markets in order to survive. Consequently some of these individuals have more cash than comrades with higher Songbun status living in Pyongyang, and are able to bribe their way in and out of sticky situations. Indeed, North Korean nouveau riche are often from lower Songbun classes that faced a choice: death by starvation during the famine, or engagement in illegal capitalistic market schemes to survive. These informal markets have injected unprecedented amounts of cash into the pockets and livelihoods of lower-status individuals, who can now create opportunities for themselves and their families to live more comfortably than they otherwise could have.

NORTH KOREAN PROPAGANDA AND FALSE HISTORY

The Propaganda and Agitation Department is the primary government agency tasked with creating and propagating throughout the country ideological campaigns and education rooted in juche. It is linked with the Organization and Guidance Department to guarantee ideological alignment and continuity with the state, as well as with the Ministry of Culture, which oversees control over cultural and artistic efforts in North Korea. The State Security Department and Ministry of Public Security control and block radio and television broadcasts entering North Korea. Official periodicals, including *Rodong Sinmum*, the state's official newspaper, receive clearance from the General Publications Guidance Bureau and Newspaper Administration Bureau before publication. These organizations are part of a larger landscape of overlapping and multilayered bureaucratic and political entities that fuel North Korea's domestic and foreign propaganda engines with the sole aim of providing a singular narrative for domestic and foreign consumption.

The government teaches people its own version of the Korean War: that the United States attacked North Korea in 1950, causing the painful separation of the two countries and the division of millions of families. When I visited North Korea's War Museum in Pyongyang in 2013, I saw English-language newspaper articles dating back to June 1950 reporting that Imperialist Americans had attacked North Korea. The wording in these articles was clearly fabricated. Three-dimensional wax exhibits showcase American soldiers with big noses and crazy blue eyes raping young Korean women and viciously spearing Korean babies, as well as doctors performing surgical experiments on terrified Korean men without anesthesia. I stood face to face with a life-sized wax model of a U.S. marine in uniform, killed by North Koreans. His corpse was being pecked by black crows. This false history and nationalist narrative—of imperialist Americans controlling and puppeteering South Koreans, ready to declare war on North Korea at any moment—is inculcated into North

Koreans' psyche in neighborhoods, schools, and workplaces, and as part of politics.

By contrast, Western history states that on the fateful morning of June 25, 1950, two years after Soviet-backed North Korea and U.S.-backed South Korea declared themselves to be separate sovereign states, North Korean troops marched into Seoul. South Koreans and U.N. troops led by Americans fought North Korean soldiers, who in turn were supported by Chinese troops, throughout a three-year war that ended in a stalemate.

Learning to hate "American bastards" begins at a young age. The Korean phrase for "American bastard" is so common that it's not perceived to be a curse—it is just the normal way that North Koreans refer to their existential enemy. Children learn how to add and subtract by counting dead American soldiers. Posters hanging in kindergarten classrooms depict happy young children attacking a helpless, bloodied American soldier with bayonets and rifles. Every high school student has military training and learns to use rifles because the country must be ready in case the "Yankee Imperialists" attack. A popular game among children is dressing up in military uniforms and attacking dummies of U.S. soldiers with their toy weapons.

Some things that young North Korean defectors tell me they were told about South Korea and the United States include:

- South Korea's intelligence services whisk people away and take their blood
- North Koreans' organs are at risk of being stolen because everyone is jealous of North Koreans' health
- Ordinary Americans randomly hit and beat people up on the streets

- Being a puppet state of the United States, South Korea is so corrupt that some South Koreans grow little horns on their heads

The Youth League, established in 1946, includes every child in North Korea, and is tasked with teaching young children the political ideology of the state. The proper way to bow to statues of the Great Leader and Dear Leader, the sacred importance of cleaning portraits, and knowledge of the utmost danger of being exposed to foreign media are all inculcated into the young minds of North Korea's children by the Youth League.

Distribution of verbal, visual, and mental state propaganda is ubiquitous. Portraits of the Great Leader and Dear Leader hang in every classroom, office, and home. Juche slogans printed on enormous banners praise the state and the leader, and hang in open fields, where passersby simply cannot avoid looking at them. The dates of the leaders' visits to a facility (such as a hospital) or institution hang on a placard above the doorframe. Every household has a state-sanctioned radio with a disabled tuner that broadcasts state propaganda throughout the day. The volume of these radios can be adjusted, but cannot be turned off entirely.

A CULT OF PERSONALITY

Tremendous resources have been devoted to crafting, polishing, and sustaining godlike images and biographical "histories" of the three Supreme Leaders and their families. Promoting a cult of personality is not a strategy unique to the North Korean regime, but among socialist societies this country has been by far the most extreme in instituting drastic measures to sustain this part of their culture.

All of the three leaders' official biographies have been massively exaggerated, from their birthplaces to their shooting abilities when they were three years old. Below are some "facts" about their leaders that North Koreans are expected to believe:

- Kim Jong-Il was born on Paektu Mountain, the highest mountain on the Korean Peninsula, with a glowing star and a double rainbow heralding his birth. The creation myth of Korea centers on this mountain, where the mythical figure Dangun Waonggeom was born in 2333 BCE and became the founder of Gojoseon, the first kingdom of Korea. Soviet records, however, indicate that Kim Jong-Il was in fact born in the Siberian village of Vyatskoye.[4]

- Official North Korean records state that Kim Jong-Il learned to walk when he was three weeks old, and talked fluently by the time he was eight weeks old. By the age of three, he was able to shoot bull's-eyes on targets with a gun. State media reported in 1994 that the first time Kim played golf, he shot a thirty-eight-under-par round on North Korea's only golf course, including eleven holes-in-one.

- The state newspaper, *Rodong Sinmun*, reported that Kim Jong-Il's suits, made of a North Korean fabric called vinylon (a blend of anthracite and limestone), became a global fashion icon. This is simply not true.

Every citizen must obey the state policies by showing sufficient reverence to images of their leaders. Anyone who exhibits a hint of suspicion at the veracity of the state's history or their leaders' biographies faces a cruel reprimand. Punishments may include prison sentences or even political prison camps. Nothing about the country is to be questioned.

There are an estimated thirty to forty thousand statues of Kim Il-Sung across the country. The most prominent of these was constructed in 1972 on Mansudae Hill in Pyongyang: this seventy-two-foot bronze statue of Kim Il-Sung has become a place of reverence for North Koreans and all foreigners who visit the nation. In 2011, Kim Jong-Il's statue was constructed to the left of his father's.

After a long flight into Pyongyang Airport with a layover in Beijing during the summer of 2013, my Harvard classmates and I were immediately taken to Mansudae Hill to pay our respects to the Great Leader and the Dear Leader. Most of us had moral qualms about bowing at a ninety-degree angle (a sign of profound respect) to two of the worst dictators in recent history. But it was tacitly understood that unless every person in our group bowed properly, the group would not be able to continue our week-long tour. Our tour guide walked us over to a beautiful North Korean woman dressed in an elaborate *han-bok* (Korean traditional dress) and asked if any of us would "voluntarily" purchase flowers from her to present to the two statues. Having just arrived in North Korea, none of us picked up on the irrelevance of the "voluntary" portion of our tour guide's statement, and we awkwardly shuffled our feet in the ninety-five-degree heat. At last, a classmate and I grudgingly offered to buy two fresh bouquets from the woman.

Our group was given strict instructions on how to interact with these statues. The students with the flowers were to walk respectfully and slowly toward the two statues, bow, place the flowers at the statues' feet, and walk back to the group. Then the next row of students was to follow suit. No laughing, smiling, or gesturing was permitted. We were told we were welcome to take photos of the statues, but we had to ensure that the entirety of the statues was captured in the photos. Our tour guide looked through some of our cameras to check whether the photos were taken properly. I did not capture Kim Il-Sung's right hand in my photo, and my tour guide bluntly commanded: "please delete."

Images and portraits of Kim Il-Sung and Kim Jong-Il are hung prominently in both private and public spaces. Every household, classroom, office, vehicle used for public transportation, and public place is required to have pictures of both Kims hanging on a wall, on which nothing else may hang. The portraits must be hung up high in a central place in the room or facility, where no one's head is higher than the portraits. There are special cloths that are distributed with the sole purpose of cleaning these portraits every few days. Since people are not permitted to draw images of their leaders, the only portraits that people are allowed to hang are those made by government-approved artists. On May 15, 2007, the Organization Bureau of the Central Party issued instructions entitled "Overall Inspections on How to Carry Out Respect for the Portraits of Great Leader and Beloved General," which sparked thorough inspections of homes and workplaces across the nation to assess people's up-keep of the portraits. Individuals who were accused of not properly exhibiting respect for the portraits—for example, if dust was found on the portrait frames or glass—would have their names recorded on a blacklist by the Party's Organization Bureau. Some would be called in and subjected to long lectures, while others spent time in detention facilities.[5]

The Mansudae Art Studio in Pyongyang is the central body tasked with producing propaganda paintings, billboards, posters, murals, and monuments revering the leaders and the Kim family. The propaganda units in local administrations, schools, military units, and other places of work are responsible for reproducing propaganda messages for their employees. Korean adults are required to wear a lapel pin above their hearts; whether the pin has one leader or two depends on their political standing. Images of the leaders found in publications, newspapers, or magazines must never be covered, folded, bent, drawn on, or misused. All unwanted publications with images of the leaders must be returned to the state, never thrown away.

When I boarded Air Koryo with my classmates, we were each given English copies of that day's *Pyongyang Times* and a glossy magazine titled *Democratic People's Republic of Korea*. Both were dated with the juche year. North Korea's calendar year starts in 1912, the year that Kim Il-Sung was born, so year 2015 is juche year 104. As passengers were flipping through these rare publications, we were given the instructions described above; we were not to fold, bend, draw on, or spill anything on the images of the leaders. If we no longer wanted the magazine or newspaper, we were to carefully return it to the flight crew.

North Korea has the world's largest mausoleum dedicated to a Communist leader. Kumsusan Palace of the Sun was built in Pyongyang in 1976 and served as Kim Il-Sung's residence until his death in 1994, when it became a mausoleum. The cost of converting this residence into a mausoleum is difficult to verify, but estimates range from $100 million to $800 million. Both Kim Il-Sung and Kim Jong-Il's bodies lie there, embalmed, in separate rooms.[6]

My classmates and I visited the mausoleum with our assigned tour guides on a Sunday (foreigners are allowed to visit only on Thursdays and Sundays). We had to check all of our belongings in a room and wait in a massive line for our turn to enter.

No photography, talking, smoking, videotaping, nor laughing is permitted. We walked through a series of long travelators in deep solemnity. Although I certainly felt no respect for the two individuals to whom we were about to supposedly pay our respects, it was hard not to be serious, because all the North Koreans around us treated their visit to this mausoleum as a holy experience.

We saw large white marble statues of the leaders and a series of images of grieving people from when Kim Il-Sung died. We filed through a powerful dust-blowing machine to ensure that when entering the sacred rooms our bodies would be free of dust. We then entered a dark, freezing-cold room (the whole mausoleum was air-conditioned in the mid-August summer heat) where the transparent crystal sarcophaguses lay. Stern North Korean men in uniform brusquely instructed us to line up in groups of four, and bow in sync at Kim Il-Sung's feet, bow again to his left, walk past his head, and then bow again in sync to his right. Next we were funneled into adjoining rooms that were filled with his personal belongings, gifts, awards, and honorary degrees that he had apparently received from all over the world. A similar process for bowing to Kim Jong-Il's encased body and viewing his belongings and accomplishments ensued.

While I was going through the motions, purely to avoid serious trouble with the North Korean authorities, I was amazed by how much veneration the North Koreans showed. I was born into a Christian family and have attended church my entire life. I've attended churches of various denominations in different countries, and have accompanied my Muslim friends to their prayer services at mosques in Middle Eastern countries. As someone who is very familiar with the important role that religion and spirituality play in many people's lives, I have never witnessed such solemnity and reverence shown for a leader or god. Spending two hours in the Kumsusan Mausoleum made me realize how deeply embedded this cult of personality has become in North Korean society.

For readers of this book who grew up in democracies, understanding how people can believe in something so seemingly irrational may be difficult. I feel the same way. Yet I can recognize that a "leap of faith" is part of other traditional belief systems as well. Generations of my family have been Christians—even when Christians were grossly persecuted in Buddhist Korea in the early 1900s—and I have been raised to believe in the Immaculate Conception and the Holy Family. Jesus Christ came as both a full man and God to the world, and died later on the cross to die for my sins. He then rose again three days later and now lives in Heaven, watching over me. I fully believe this Gospel. As a holder of two Harvard degrees, I am often questioned about how an educated person could believe in something so irrational. My life is based on values and beliefs that I derive from my Christian faith, in spite of external skepticism. Similarly, I try to understand North Koreans' belief in the Kim family as a kind of religion.

At the same time, who knows if the tears in the eyes of the men and women I saw bowing before the Great Leader were sincere, or if they were a strategic career move intended to be seen by peers and superiors? No one will ever know, unless those individuals feel they are in a sufficiently safe space to speak frankly about the authenticity of the emotions they felt while paying their respects to their leaders. North Korean defectors and North Korea observers will generally say that the older generations of

North Koreans who experienced a relatively prosperous North Korea under Kim Il-Sung's rule have sincere reverence for Kim Il-Sung, while the younger generations do not share this loyalty to Kim Jong-Il or to Kim Jong-Un. Reasons for waning loyalty among younger generations include having experienced the Great Famine, a broken public distribution system, dependence on illegal and informal street markets, and increasing exposure to foreign information and media.

When Kim Jong-Il died in 2011, red flowers called *Kimjongilia* surrounded his crystal sarcophagus. The flowers were bioengineered by Japanese botanist Kamo Mototeru to bloom every year on Kim Jong-Il's birthday, February 16. In a North Korean report published in 2005, President Kim Il-Sung was quoted as saying:

The new flower Kimjongilia is very beautiful . . . Newspapers should widely carry the fact that Kimjongilia has appeared in the world, give publicity to the flower and propagate it in bulk to disseminate it. Kimjongilia is a variety of tuberous begonia. It is a rare bright and crimson flower that represents the personality of the energetic great man as dozens of corrugated, evenly arranged petals form a big, clear and lovely flower supported by heart-shaped leaves. It is an immortal flower symbolizing the greatness of Kim Jong-Il who adds brilliance to Korea throughout the world with his Songun revolutionary leadership, and a flower of reverence, which has come into full bloom amid the desires of humankind in the age of independence. This standard is instituted to make Kimjongilia in full bloom across the earth as an immortal flower and as a celebrated flower in praise of a great man.[7]

THE NORTH KOREAN MILITARY

North Korea has the fourth largest military in the world, after China, the United States, and India. Given the government's secrecy regarding any information about its military, the number of military personnel is not known for certain, though it is estimated at 1.1 to 1.4 million.[8] The World Bank estimates that in 2013, the Korean People's Army (KPA) had 1.379 million members. To put this figure in perspective, North Korea's population is around 25 million people. By contrast, China, whose population is 1.4 billion, has 2.3 million men and women in its People's Liberation Army.[9]

In a rare televised speech on October 10, 2015, a national holiday commemorating the founding of the Korean Workers' Party in 1945, Kim Jong-Un addressed his nation. As part of his commentary on his military's power, he said, "Today our Party can proudly state that our revolutionary armed forces are capable of fighting any type of war the U.S. imperialists opt for, and have made full preparations for firmly defending the blue sky over the country and the security of the people."[10] Most people outside North Korea would strongly disagree with this comment that North Korea's military force is a formidable match for the U.S. military. The number of military personnel is not the best indicator of that military's power or effectiveness in conflict. Yet the United States, South Korea, China, and other neighbors have been careful not to underestimate the might of the North Korean forces.

Estimates of North Korea's military expenditure as a share of its GDP range from 15 percent to 35 percent. The Korea Institute for Defense Analyses (KIDA), a South Korean state-run think tank, and the U.S. State Department are two of several entities that have worked to derive this important statistic.[11] This task is particularly difficult because the military expenditure figures that North Korea officially publishes cannot be trusted, and they have not released any GDP figures for decades. What is not contested, however, is North Korea's willingness to devote far more of its GDP share toward its military than its adversaries do. By way of comparison, South Korea's military expenditure in 2014 was 2.6 percent of its GDP, China's was 2.06 percent, and the United States devoted 3.5 percent of its GDP to its military.

The KPA conscripts all eligible men into the army for ten years—the longest military conscription in the world.[12] There have been recent reports that women between seventeen and twenty years old are also required to serve until they are twenty-three years old. In August 1994, the minimum height and weight requirements for men to serve in the military were lowered to four feet, eight inches, and ninety-four pounds in order to increase the pool of men who could serve.[13]

In the mid-1990s, Kim Jong-Il implemented *Songun*, or "military first," as the driving principle for the country's domestic and foreign policies. More than before, all citizens had to devote their energy, resources, and support to their military.

A NUCLEAR NORTH KOREA

The main reason why the small and impoverished country of North Korea remains highly relevant to policymakers, especially those guiding the foreign policies of the United States and China, is its nuclear weapons program. North Korea's nuclear arsenal, and the uncertainties that shroud its capabilities and purposes, have been its primary negotiating chips in bilateral and international forums. The country's standing army and consistently aggressive behavior toward the United States, South Korea, and its neighbors certainly merit attention, but those factors pale in comparison to the possible threat posed by its nuclear program.

For the past twenty-five years, then, negotiations and agreements have been penned with the single goal of dismantling North Korea's nuclear program. Rounds of U.S.–North Korea bilateral negotiations, three-party talks, and six-party talks have by turns raised and dashed hopes for the North's denuclearization. North Korea's withdrawal from both the International Atomic Energy Agency in 1994 and the Treaty on the Non-Proliferation of Nuclear Weapons in 2003 sparked major negotiations to bring it back to the table.[14] The 1994 Agreed Framework and the September 19, 2005, Joint Statement were bilateral and multilateral initiatives that North Korea signed, only to renege on them soon thereafter.

A robust mix of negotiations, followed by strong U.N. resolutions, multilateral and unilateral sanctions, international condemnation, and isolation have not prevented North Korea from continuing to build its nuclear arsenal. In addition to numerous missile and rocket tests, North Korea has conducted four successful nuclear tests to date, in October 2006, May 2009, February 2013, and January 2016.

In March 2013, North Korea adopted the *Byungjin* policy, which translates into "progress in tandem," with the goal of developing their nuclear program and economy in parallel. Despite strident warnings from states that such a parallel development policy will only lead to increased isolation from the international community, Kim Jong-Un's administration continues its simultaneous pursuit of guns and butter. In a 2013 speech addressing the Korean Workers' Party, Kim Jong-Un said, "The United States is now most fearful of our miniaturized, reduced-weight and diversified nuclear deterrent . . . We should increase the production of precision and miniaturized nuclear weapons and the means of their delivery and ceaselessly develop nuclear weapons technology to actively develop more powerful and advanced nuclear weapons."[15]

Former top American military commander in South Korea, General Curtis M. Scaparrotti, stated in 2014 that he believed North Korea had most likely been able to miniaturize nuclear warheads to mount onto ballistic missiles. If North Korea indeed has mastered the dreaded combination of miniaturization and delivery capabilities, then the United States and its allies could change their calculations of North Korea's military threat level.[16] On January 6, 2016, North Korea conducted its fourth nuclear test, claiming that it had successfully detonated its first hydrogen bomb. While it was indeed a nuclear test, scientists and officials across the world dismissed the regime's claim that it had detonated a hydrogen bomb.

North Korea's missiles and rockets are proudly shown off at military parades in Pyongyang, and grandiose statements are made about how North Korea has the world on its knees because of its nuclear power. Nuclear weapons allow the government to create a false sense of national security and power among its citizens. In 2013, North Korea revised its constitution to declare itself as a nuclear power, though the United States and its allies have refused to accept North Korea as a nuclear state. Still, the potential threat is being taken seriously by all. Protecting America's homeland, safeguarding America's allies in East Asia, and pursuing peace in the region by denuclearizing the Korean Peninsula are all reasons to dismantle North Korea's nuclear program.

NORTH KOREA'S SECRETIVE NATURE

Few North Korea experts exist. I consider myself a North Korea watcher. Even North Koreans born and raised inside this secretive country have been cordoned off from information not only about the world outside North Korea, but also about the reality inside the country. Most North Korean citizens have not traveled far from their home towns due to domestic travel restrictions. Defectors who used to work for the government in Pyongyang have told me that they were shielded from the knowledge that extreme poverty and starvation existed in their country. When I returned from my trip to North Korea, which included spending a few days in Pyongyang, some of my North Korean defector friends asked me what their former capital city was like, since they haven't ever been there. Pyongyang crafts, packages, and distributes extremely airtight stories of North Korea, consisting of state-approved messages that align with the regime's domestic and international narrative. North Korean efforts to contest or challenge these narratives would be considered treason.

Never wanting to give other states the upper hand in policy negotiations, North Korea treats ordinary data as top national-security secrets. Information about the population, economy, leadership, decision-making, and the health of the leader are kept secret, so that other countries' intelligence bodies have to resort to estimating and extrapolating even such basic information.

Occasionally, too, some information will leak out of North Korea, and some citizen journalist will take the high risk of meeting with outsiders to share bits and pieces about life inside North Korea. *Rimjin-gang* is a small magazine published by Asia Press International in which North Korean journalists report on North Korea. Started by a Japanese and Korean editorial team, *Rimjin-gang* has been secretly operating within North Korea with journalists and reporters embedded there. The dozen reporters, including North Korean citizens and defectors, receive media, computer, and journalism training in China and take extraordinary risks to capture footage from all over the country.

Rimjin-gang's footage and reports have been reprinted and quoted by major news outlets. The group claims to have captured over one hundred hours of footage since it started to operate inside North Korea in 2007. In 2010, a North Korean reporter smuggled out a short clip of a twenty-three-year-old homeless woman in South Pyongan Province that gained international attention. The reporter, who interviewed her with a secret camera, later found out that she died of hunger in a cornfield. Her body was already in a state of decomposition when it was found and removed.[17]

Rimjin-gang, as well as grassroots efforts to smuggle information out from North Korea, continues to be powerful and noteworthy, but they offer only glimpses into life there. The scarcity of real information about the country, especially its government, has placed a premium on anything related to North Korea and led to misguided stories and false rumors. A dramatic example of a rumor that went viral within minutes in February 2012 is when Kim Jong-Un was said to have been killed in a possible coup. After a flurry of activity in media outlets and intelligence communities worldwide, it turned out that this was just a rumor on Weibo, the Chinese equivalent of Twitter, that had spun out of control. Lack of real information has also consumed tremendous resources and brainpower in academic and intelligence communities as scholars and analysts try to understand events inside the country and make predictions. Scholars have been predicting the North's collapse for over twenty years, yet the country endures.

The high demand for the low supply of information coming out of North Korea has also created a cottage industry of sensationalized stories on North Korean daily life, or what some call "a North Korean fetish." The best one can do is to pursue knowledge of this country with discipline, persistence, and a healthy dose of skepticism.

NORTH KOREA'S RECORD ON HUMAN RIGHTS

With a fabricated world history, a pseudo-religious cult of personality, and an obsession with the goal of regime survival as a "socialist paradise" for North Koreans, the North Korean regime has become one of the worst state violators of human rights in modern history. It is reasonable to claim that the North Korean government systematically violates every fundamental human right of its citizens. North Korean defectors share that the Korean term for "human rights" does not exist, and that the concept of having inalienable rights is foreign to those living in North Korea. Only after escaping from North Korea do people learn about rights and political freedom.

Since the mid-1990s, the number of North Koreans who have escaped their country to live in China and South Korea has increased. These individuals bring stories of extreme poverty, starvation, life in prison camps and other ineffably severe penal systems, and repressive experiences. The memories of North Korean defectors have been shared in books, televised interviews, and speeches.

A North Korean citizen has one freedom, which is the freedom to be born. Every event that occurs after an infant's birth is officially determined by the state. One's Songbun status will determine the life path that is deemed appropriate for that particular political standing: one's home town, school, highest grade to attend in school, career, and social opportunities. Moreover, every citizen must exhibit utmost loyalty to the state, the party, and Kim Jong-Un. Language and thoughts that stray from the official party line are punished. Even complaining about not having enough food is considered an expression of political grievance, because it is interpreted as criticism of the benevolent and generous leader. More than any other country today, North

Korea has politicized access to food as a means to control and punish its population.

There is no freedom of movement for North Koreans. To travel within the country, they must state the purpose of their desired travel to the government and obtain a travel permit. It is completely illegal for them to leave the country without the regime's permission. Border guards are given shoot-to-kill instructions for anyone suspected of trying to escape the country. A North Korean defector who mentors new defectors resettling in South Korea captures North Korea's state of rightlessness well: "North Korea is a country where people don't even have the freedom to escape."

Guilt by association is one of the most effective ways that the North Korean government has been able to control its citizens. Three generations of a criminal's family members are punished for a crime. The idea behind this policy is captured in a 1972 statement by Kim Il-Sung: "Factionalists or enemies of class, whoever they are, their seed must be eliminated through three generations."[18]

North Korea is infamous for its prisons and detention centers. There are currently five large political prison camps across the country, with an estimated 80,000–120,000 North Koreans in them. The number, location, and size of these political prison camps have changed since the 1950s. People are sentenced to these camps without trials. Most are not even told why they are being sentenced, though common accusations for sentencing include attempting to defect from North Korea, having made contact with South Koreans or religious organizations, stealing from the nation, and watching foreign materials. Upon entering a camp, one becomes a ghost of the North Korean state.

Most of the horrific stories that we see in news reports are of *kwan-li-so,* or political prison camps. There are five main types of prison and detention centers: (1) *kwan-li-so,* (2) *kyo-hwa-so,* the correctional or re-education centers, (3) *jip-kyul-so,* the collection centers for low-level perceived offenders, (4) *ro-dong-dan-ryeon-dae,* or labor training centers, and (5) *ku-ryu-jang,* which are police interrogation and detention facilities.[19]

Kang Chol-Hwan was nine years old when he and generations of his family members were taken to Yodok, a political prison camp, for the "high treason" that his grandfather had allegedly committed, about which no details were provided. He spent a decade in Yodok witnessing severe beatings, casual killings of prisoners, forced abortions, forced labor for all prisoners, brutal sexual violence against women, and public executions. His work included carrying and burying the emaciated corpses of fellow prisoners who had perished from mining and blasting accidents, or from starvation. Once he and other inmates were ordered to stone prisoners who had attempted to escape the prison. "The skin on the victims' faces eventually became undone from their skeletal bodies," he later described.[20]

Dr. Park Se-Joon was born in one of the two Hwanghae provinces. He doesn't reveal which province he's from (there is a North Hwanghae Province and a South Hwanghae Province) out of a concern for being identified by North Korean authorities. While working as a dentist and conducting illegal business on the side to supplement his paltry income, he was caught traveling to and from China. Once released from prison, he was determined to defect from North Korea. At the Chinese-Mongolian border, Chinese border guards caught him and nine other North Koreans and repatriated all of them back to the North.[21] The group included families, single people, young children, and even a pair of grandparents.

Dr. Park said his time in the political prison camp was truly nightmarish. "I was actually determined to die before going back to North Korea. I needed to kill myself and therefore tried all sorts of techniques to commit suicide before entering a North Korean prison camp. We [knew] all too well what awaited us at the prison camp. I didn't think I could bear the physical pain. I guess this is why some people defect with rat poison or razors taped to their thighs so that they can commit suicide if they're caught defecting. I tried everything, but it didn't work. Maybe it was God's will. I landed in a camp, and the time I spent in the prison camp was damn hell. The worst physical pain, humiliation, the sub-zero cold, the constant beatings—it was hell for a human being."

Dr. Park was imprisoned in Chongin, a large city in the northeastern part of North Korea infamous for cold temperatures. When it was well below freezing, he and his fellow inmates had only a single set of clothing. "During my time in camp, I [came] to understand what I had been unaware of—that this country is really evil. All I could think about during my time of 're-education' was revenge. I must kill Kim Il-Sung and Kim Jong-Il. The food was 'porridge' made of salty water and cornhusks. They made us work all the time, from morning to evening, and if you slacked off just a little bit, they beat you and made inmates beat each other. The group punishments made me want to die on the spot. With over fifty inmates in one cell, I frequently saw people die. I would wake up and [think], 'Oh, he died today.' The next day, 'That man died today.' Maybe it was worse than [the] hell described in the Bible."

Regardless of how many times I have listened to survivors of political prison camps, including Dr. Park, the experiences are so foreign to me. The physical, emotional, mental and spiritual anguish that Dr. Park described are well beyond my capacity to understand. Dr. Park continued:

I learned about Christianity when I spent some time in China. Out of sheer desperation, I tried everything to die or live. I fervently prayed to this God I learned about. I said, "Please, I'll live a good life from now on. I'm really sorry about all my past sins, whatever I did. Please let me live and get out of here. If you let me leave this prison, I'll become a pastor and [proselytize] to everyone I ever meet." But nothing happened! Then I prayed again and said, "Whatever, God. This is all a lie. I'm praying *this* much, and you're not helping me. God doesn't make such deals. I guess this life and this death are my fate." If you ask me to sum up my experience in one sentence, I would say that I was jealous of the scraggly dog, running around in the fields outside the prison bars. I was so jealous of that dog. I would have loved to have been that dog, being able to run around, eat whatever it finds, and not get hit.

Then there are the public executions. Political prison camp survivors have told me that at times they had wished they had been sentenced to death instead of prison camp, because their experiences in the camps were unfathomably grueling and painful. Individuals who have committed a grave offense are executed in large public squares. The supposedly grave crimes that warrant death include interacting with a Christian while trying to defect, making international phone calls, distributing foreign media to other North Koreans, and criticizing the government. The perceived offender, usually having been severely beaten, is blindfolded, handcuffed, and tied to a tall wooden rod. He or she also has rocks stuffed in his or her mouth to prevent the shouting of anything antagonistic toward the state. Teeth are usually extracted or broken to make space for the rocks. All the townspeople, including young schoolchildren, are required to attend these executions. The crime is read aloud by the authorities, and upon command, three soldiers each shoot three times: once at the head, once at the heart, and once at the gut.

Kim Ha-Young, a young woman from Musan born in 1993, describes the first execution that she saw when she was seven years old.

My mom and I were in the Musan market, trying to buy a few odds and ends. I don't really remember what we were buying, but I remember holding my mom's hand because the markets were always so crowded. The men who were in charge of surveillance in the Musan market wore armbands with "management" written on them. They walked quickly throughout the huge market, blowing their whistles, telling us to get out of the market, including the people working the stalls. We were all told to walk to the riverbank, where there were stakes in the ground. I held my mom's hand and walked towards a huge crowd.

People tried to hide, but these surveillance men found everyone and made them head to the river bank. There were three men: one had stolen a cow, one had stolen copper from a factory and sold it to China, and I don't remember what the third person's crime was. The three criminals were all tied up and pulled out of a car. A government official in some military uniform announced, "These people have committed this and that offense against the Democratic People's Republic of Korea blah, blah and they are all sentenced to execution by firing squad." Then three soldiers in the firing squad appeared. They tied the three men at the stakes. They shot three times. I don't remember the specifics but I remember they shot at the head, stomach, and gut. The poor guys folded forward as they were shot because their bodies [were broken]. These bodies were put in huge sacks, maybe rice sacks. I don't know where the sacks were taken. I wondered where these bodies were going.

This was back in 2000. People reacted in so many different ways. Some muttered, "They deserved to die. Why commit such stupid crimes?" Some people said it was terrible. I was seven, and didn't know what it meant to die. I was more intrigued by the gunshot sounds. They were so loud: three shots in unison—BANG! BANG! BANG! After the execution, the crowds dispersed and went back to resuming business. Marketeers went back to their stalls, and shoppers immediately went back to strolling through the market to buy what they needed. Maybe in South Korea or any other country, people may linger after seeing a firing squad, my goodness. But at my first execution, I remember that everyone scurried back to their positions. Life resumed.

Political prison camps and public executions are two extremely effective ways of controlling a population. No one, not even Kim Jong-Un's uncle Jang Song-Taek, is immune to the wrath of the state.[22] A leading figure in North Korea and a key adviser to Kim Jong-Un, Jang Song-Taek was married to Kim

Il-Sung's only daughter, Kim Kyong-Hui. But in December 2013, he was accused of counterrevolutionary activities and was executed.

In classic Communist fashion, the government has also implemented policies to atomize the society by preventing citizens from creating strong horizontal social relationships. Individuals who are aware of a political "offense" (such as defection) but do not report it to the authorities are punished almost like criminals. Groups of three or more people are forbidden to gather for long periods of time, especially late at night in someone's home. Authorities conduct random checks in residences late at night to ensure that guests are not staying over without travel permits. Student organizations or any social organizations other than the Party Alliance and party leagues are absolutely forbidden. The underlying fear is that any association—political or nonpolitical—can later spark dissent.

Dr. Park Se-Joon describes this system of peer-monitoring, guilt-by-association, and group punishment in a personalized way. "When you tell someone about a complaint about the social system, and that person turns out to be anything short of a perfectly trustworthy person, then your statement of grievance goes through a very meticulous surveillance apparatus and gets reported to the secret services. When that complaint reaches the secret services, you're punished ruthlessly. And the punishments are just really cruel. You could go to prison for years, or even be imprisoned in a political prison camp. That's the worst. What's more dangerous is that the statement could affect your whole family. It's not just about you. So you can never tell others about what you're thinking and you can't even have ideas about changing the regime because you're too scared."

In February 2014, the U.N. Commission of Inquiry published a 372-page report based on public hearings involving 80 defectors and experts, and more than 240 confidential interviews with North Korean defectors. Many victims and witnesses who had escaped North Korea preferred confidential interviews due to the fear of reprisals against family members who still live there.

Directed by Australian Justice Michael Kirby, the U.N. Commission determined that they were mandated to investigate systematic, widespread, and grave human rights violations in North Korea in at least the following areas:

- Violations of the right to food
- The full range of violations associated with prison camps
- Torture and inhuman treatment
- Arbitrary arrest and detention
- Discrimination, in particular in the systematic denial and violation of basic human rights and fundamental freedoms
- Violations of the freedom of expression
- Violations of the right to life
- Violations of the freedom of individual movement, and
- Enforced disappearances, including abductions of nationals of other states.[23]

Despite several cases of North Koreans having exaggerated their experiences as victims of a repressive state, the larger truth and scope of North Korea's egregious human-rights violations remain unassailably clear.

THE "ARDUOUS MARCH" AND GRASSROOTS MARKETIZATION

In 1994, North Korea was hit with the worst famine in its history. Additionally, the fall of the Soviet Union meant an end to North Korea's Public Distribution System's largest source of food and basic resources. As a result, for a grueling four years, North Korean citizens lived through what their government euphemistically called the "Arduous March," the 1994–1998 period that self-sufficient citizens had to power through. The rest of the world refers to this period as the "Great Famine."

During this period, the Public Distribution System barely reached beyond the capital city of Pyongyang, leaving most citizens to fend for themselves in a Communist country where private enterprises were illegal. Some of the most devoted citizens who did not live in Pyongyang were the first to die from starvation as they diligently waited for their Dear Leader to provide them with food. Illegal marketeers from this period often say that the famine weeded out the loyalists from the country, leaving only the strong-willed survivors who were willing to break the rules to survive. "It's like Darwin's natural selection, North Korea style," one defector explained.

Against the regime's will, much of the country became entrepreneurial and resorted to creating local street markets to buy and sell whatever they could to purchase food and survive. Street markets are capitalist in nature, and are technically illegal in North Korea, but during this desperate, semi-anarchic period when corpses were lining the streets, most local authorities turned a blind eye to the new phenomenon. After all, most of the goods being sold were food, clothing, and other basic necessities. North Korean propaganda poet Jang Jin-Sung writes in his memoirs about coming across the Corpse Division when he returned to his home town for a few days after working in Pyongyang for years. It was deep into the Great Famine, and he saw "a swarm of homeless people who looked to be either dead or dying . . . there were also men hovering over the bodies like flies, at times poking at the inert figures with a stick."[24] When he asked his friend why men were poking at homeless people, his friend said that due to so many dead bodies around the cities, Corpse Divisions were set up in every province (other than Pyongyang) and dispatched near the train stations. People, usually men, who signed up for the work of collecting corpses received a full day's ration of food. The men he had seen were poking the homeless to see if they were dead.

An estimated 800,000 to 2.5 million North Koreans perished during the Great Famine. This famine may have been the worst and best thing to happen to North Korea. As tragic as it was, it forced ordinary citizens to think beyond their prescribed beliefs and question how such a benevolent, generous, and abundant state was unable to provide food for its citizens. What kind of paradise was a nation where village men were paid for collecting and carting off the bodies of people who had starved to death?

The famine sparked defections in large numbers for the first time. Many risked their lives and fled to China, where they worked to make money to then take back with them to feed their families. Unverifiable estimates of North Koreans who escaped to China range from 250,000 to 400,000. During these desperate times, some women would make some money in China, wrap the money in plastic, and insert it into their vaginal cavities before returning to North Korea to help their starving families. They hid the money because if they were caught by the border guards upon returning to North Korea, they would have all their possessions confiscated. Guards caught onto this trick and made their inspections of men and women returning to North Korea more invasive.

After spending an average of five to seven years working and hiding in China, many of these defectors escaped to and settled in South Korea. Many have since invited their remaining family members in North Korea to defect to South Korea by paying for brokers to arrange for their transit from North Korea to China, and then to other transit countries (for example, Mongolia or Southeast Asian nations). The family members then seek political asylum at a South Korean embassy before making their way to South Korea itself.

The famine also produced many *kotjebis,* or North Korean homeless children who would roam the streets to beg for food and pickpocket. The term *kotjebi* literally means "swallow" and is used to describe North Korean children because of their constant search for food and shelter. A country that prides itself on having no homeless or disabled people (the government exiled all disabled citizens to outlying cities), North Korea rounded up and housed the *kotjebis* in children's detention centers, which were effectively rundown apartments with no food or resources. Rather than starving to death in these centers, *kotjebis* would outrun authorities to survive on their own. Despite the large number of these kids roaming around, the state continues to forbid any mention of them in any North Korean publication or other media.

Though the famine is officially over, the majority of the population does not have secure access to food. According to a 2012 World Food Programme report, only 16 percent of households have regular access to food. Due to chronic food shortages over generations, North Korea has a stunted population in which North Korean children are on average two to three inches shorter than their South Korean counterparts.

The makeshift street markets that sprang up across the country during the Great Famine became more sophisticated afterward.

North Korea's Communist older cousin China has become the primary provider for foreign goods, which are changing the landscape of North Korea today. Marketeers have developed illicit business relationships with Chinese traders, who provide goods manufactured in China and other countries in return for cash. Once a resource for food and other goods needed for survival, North Korean street markets have evolved to become citizens' primary lifeline for sustenance, goods, and information. Some have thousands of stalls. American economists who study the North Korean economy estimate that, on average, 70 to 80 percent of a North Korean's income is from informal markets. A certain amount of private-market activity since the Great Famine has been decriminalized and even normalized. In some cities, sellers give local authorities market-stall taxes in order to participate.

Because of the national scale of private marketization that supports most citizens' livelihoods, some North Korean watchers and scholars argue that North Korea is no longer a Communist nation. "You name it, and you'll find it in any North Korean market," says Ha-Young, a twenty-two-year-old woman from Musan, a city in North Hamgyong Province, in the northeast of the country. Born in 1993, she grew up helping in her mother's wholesale second-hand clothing business, and does not recall ever having received any food or school uniform from the state. The basic market principle of supply and demand reigns in North Korean street markets today. It's a de facto capitalist society.

TIGHT CONTROLS OVER THE NEWS AND OTHER MEDIA

The Reporters Without Borders 2013–2014 World Press Freedom Index ranked North Korea 178th out of 179 countries, only above Eritrea, for its press freedom. Citizens are allowed to consume only state-controlled media. Indeed, the political leadership in Pyongyang has maintained airtight control over the type of information that is circulated, with a view toward controlling the minds and behavior of its citizens.

All North Korean news and media, as mouthpieces of the government, go through several rounds of internal censorship before being published. North Korean state media reports on domestic news that is favorable to the party and the state. Page 116 of the English translation of Kim Jong-Il's book *Guidance for Journalists* encourages—in other words, *commands*—journalists and newspaper editors "to carry articles in which they unfailingly hold the president in high esteem, adore him and praise him as the great revolutionary leader." There isn't even a pretense of neutrality or objectivity in state media's coverage of the leader. There is also obviously no reporting of government graft and corruption, social inequality and injustice, economic hardship, famine, starvation, orphans, crimes, accidents, or any other social problem. Grand stories of the leader, and exaggerated stories that "prove" North Korea's superiority as a nation, fill the newspapers instead. The government never reports on the tens of thousands of American college students who raise awareness about human rights violations in North Korea, but they repeatedly show video footage of race riots and violence and narrate how the United States is a corrupt, racist, imperialist nation.

The official newspapers in North Korea are *Rodong Sinmun* (Labor daily newspaper), which has the broadest distribution; *Joson Inmingun* (Korea People's Army newspaper), *Minju Choson* (Democratic Korea) and *Rodonga Sinmun* (Workers' newspaper). For television and radio, there are the Korean Central Broadcasting Station, Korean Central TV, Mansudae TV, and Voice of Korea. There are also two news websites for foreign consumption—the Korean Central News Agency (KCNA) and the Uriminzokkiri (which means "our nation")—as well as other official North Korean websites and profiles, including a YouTube channel.

As mentioned earlier, radios in homes and offices dialed into the nation's single radio station cannot be turned off; only the volume can be controlled. Radios and television sets are pre-tuned to receive only the government frequencies and channels and are sealed with official labels to prevent individuals from tampering with the equipment, in case they want to try accessing other channels.[25] In most cases, radios have their tuners torn out of them before they can be used in individual homes, to prevent any creative tampering. Some North Korean observers don't call these radios, but rather speakers. There are huge red banners with Communist quotes in fields, schools, buildings, and streets. Signs hang above doorways through which the Dear Leaders have walked, stating the name, date of the event, and words of undying gratitude for their visit.

With the exception of a few hundred elites (some estimate a few thousand elites), North Koreans do not have access to the internet. Rather, the intranet, called *kwang-myong,* exists for the use of North Korean citizens in schools, public libraries, and offices. Trusted officials are tasked to scour the internet for materials that they deem "safe" and useful for the people, such as select scientific articles and health-related information. Much of *kwang-myong* comprises content that North Koreans have created, including a North Korean shopping site. There are several other intranets, with some high officials and agencies having their own.

Surprisingly, North Korea has over 3 million cell phone subscribers today.[26] Orascom, an Egyptian telecommunications company, launched a 75/25 joint venture with a North Korean telecommunications company called Koryolink, and began its commercial services across North Korea in late 2008. Priced between $400 and $700 each, cell phones on the Koryolink network can make only domestic calls and are subject to frequent wiretapping and surveillance. Ordinary North Korean cell phones cannot make international phone calls. To put into context, this is in a society where marketeers making between $10 and $50 a month are considered able to afford to feed their families. As of late 2015, Cairo-based Orascom has hit financial problems in trying to retrieve its profits from this venture and has lost control of its 75 percent portion of Koryolink.

Prior to Orascom's provision of a cell phone network, in late 2002, the Thai firm Loxley Pacific and the (North) Korea Post and Telecommunications Corporation had jointly launched a 2G GSM commercial mobile service.[27] (Before that, mobile communications had been available strictly for military and senior party officials.) But this venture was abruptly stopped after an enormous train explosion occurred in Ryongchon, a city bordering the Yellow River, on Thursday, April 22, 2004. According to the *New York Times* and other Western and South Korean media, this explosion flattened 1,850 homes, damaged 6,000 more, and even knocked down a five-story building, a school, and a dozen government buildings. It wreaked so much havoc that North Korea uncharacteristically reached out to international organizations, including the International Red Cross, and made solemn appeals for aid to Moscow, London, and Geneva, breaking with past practices of either denying or dismissing such events. What was surprising to most is that only hours prior to the explosion, Kim Jong-Il's train had passed through the same station at Ryongchon. What the North Korean government described as merely a careless accident is in fact widely believed to have been an assassination attempt on the leader, triggered by remote-controlled wireless headsets. A national ban on cell phones followed soon after the event and the government confiscated these devices.

By 2012, within four years of Orascom's launch, the company had achieved remarkable growth, with more than 3 million subscribers, although this number is not without controversy. Since the authorities do not allow people to own more than one cell phone, former Pyongyang residents have said that it had become increasingly common to register under family members' names or fake names. Koryolink has incrementally rolled out more diverse services, including text messaging, video calling, and cameras. People are able to access on their phones select sites on the state intranet along with train times, weather, some prices of currencies, and the state newspaper *Rodong Sinmun;* they can also receive text messages from the party about their leaders' activities. There is even an online shopping site on the state's intranet, although I do not know how the delivery of goods works. Police often stop cell phone users on the street and ask to check the phones for any sensitive content. Officers are permitted to confiscate phones and determine any punishment on the spot. Data transfers are monitored especially tightly.

Domestic users have their own network, whereas foreign visitors are on a separate network. Calls between North Korean citizens and foreigners cannot be made on the Koryolink network. There is also a separate 3G network for senior users, or what a former Koryolink senior technical director calls "VIPs."

For over a decade, illegal phones have been smuggled into North Korea for use near the border, where the phones can catch the Chinese cellular network. Chinese-manufactured frequency detectors have been used by the North Korean authorities to detect these international phone calls, and a few years ago, North Korean authorities installed German-produced radio wave detectors because they are able to cover a wider range of activity, within an approximately five-hundred-meter radius. These devices track down phone calls longer than five minutes. Residents have become savvy to this: to avoid detection, they make a brief call, relocate, and then continue their conversation in their new location.

INFORMATION-RELATED CRIMES

One of the most heinous "crimes" that a North Korean can commit is to consume foreign media or interact with any foreign influences not sanctioned by the state. Under North Korean law, "listening to unauthorized foreign broadcasts and possessing dissident publications are considered 'crimes against the state' that carry serious punishments, including hard labor, prison sentences, and the death penalty." In 2013, the government reportedly executed eighty people across seven cities in one day, mainly for distributing illegal media inside North Korea.[28] At the time of writing, I learned of three people who were privately executed in Ryanggang Province in August 2015 for watching South Korean films on Bluetooth-enabled smartphones. In Ryanggang Province, a Bluetooth-enabled smartphone could be purchased for 2,500–3,000 Chinese renminbi ($392–$470), whereas a flip phone could be purchased for 800–1,200 Chinese renminbi ($125–$188).[29]

These people are punished because the regime knows the precariousness of a system in which people are given a false reality. South Korea did *not* spark the Korean civil war in 1950, Kim Il-Sung and Kim Jong-Il are *not* immortal, North Korea is *not* paradise on Earth, the United States is *not* seeking to start a war with North Korea, and there is absolutely *no* reason why 25 million North Koreans have to be living in the longest-lasting Communist experiment under an authoritarian dictatorship.

In order to maintain the purity of juche thought, the regime utilizes sophisticated technologies and equally sophisticated human networks to block foreign information and media from entering the country. North Korean defectors have said that witnessing their neighbors and friends silently disappear made them believe that Kim Il-Sung (and later, Kim Jong-Il and Kim Jong-Un) could read their minds. Therefore, they tried everything to prevent themselves from even *thinking* subversive, anti-regime thoughts.

The government even monopolizes the information distributed for foreign consumption. The state reveals only the information that it wants the world to see; it has a website, www.uriminzokkiri.com, that presents Korean-language content from official news sources in North Korea, as well as a Twitter feed, Facebook page, Flickr account, and Google+ account. The YouTube channel has clips of their news as well as documentaries the regime produces in order to condemn vocal North Korean defectors who speak out about their difficult experiences living in their North Korean home towns. Recently, the North Korean government has also made documentaries to counter outside reporting by political prison camp survivors and female defectors who had experienced and witnessed brutal sexual violence while in North Korea.

The sheer inhumanity of the North Korean regime is unquestionably chilling. No sweeping quantitative descriptions—including death tolls, the percentage of the population that is starving, the pennies that the average North Korean citizen makes per month, the number of people in prison camps, the number of failed defections—can fully capture the haunting experience of individuals trying to survive under this repressive regime.

2 CRACKS IN THE SYSTEM

An Information Revolution

All humans have a basic desire, a basic fabric that [they] share, I believe. It doesn't matter if someone lives in a socialist system or a free market system. That is, if we are told to not do something, [we] will tend to want to do it; there is more curiosity for things we are told not to see or listen to. All it is is just basic human nature.

— Ji Seong-Ho, who defected from North Korea in 2006

As the Great Famine hit North Korea in the mid-1990s, the small markets that the government had once barely tolerated as a way for its population to survive became too big to shut down. As the markets became more sophisticated and began to offer nonessential goods based on North Korean people's demand, foreign media and information started to flood the marketplace. In spite of severe punishments for consuming foreign media, people were clandestinely selling and buying VHS tapes and DVDs of South Korean TV dramas, films, and pop music, among other goods. Recognizing that "imperial poison" was infiltrating their country, the state launched nationwide crackdowns on both distributors and individual consumers of this material.

One of the people whom the state recruited to conduct surveillance and inspections was Kim Heung-Kwang. Born in 1960 in a northeastern city called Hamhung, Kim Heung-Kwang dedicated his life to serving the state. He studied operating systems, network theory, and hardware technology at Kim Chaek University in Pyongyang, one of the most prestigious universities in North Korea. For nineteen years, Kim taught computer science courses at Hamhung Computer College and Communist College, from which some of his students would go on to join the infamous Bureau 121, North Korea's cyber warfare units. He stands at about five foot eight or so, and has a strong build for a Korean man in his mid-fifties. In his favorite blue suit he wears often, his professorial tendencies and academic upbringing are obvious.

In addition to his work as a professor, Kim was recruited to work for a government bureau that tasked him and his colleagues with seizing contraband with foreign content from fellow citizens and analyzing it, reporting data crimes, and punishing the offenders accordingly. The goal behind such work was to create better detection tools to prevent further illegal information from infiltrating the country.

"We tried to monitor the inflow of movies and digital content from overseas into North Korea. My colleagues and I would search houses for anything that would disrupt North Korean life, criticize the Kim family, or otherwise reveal aspects of life in a democracy. From 1997 to 2003, we took reports of what happens in households, investigated any suspicious leads, and wrote reports to send to the police." Kim was very matter of fact about his work. He believed in the dignity and importance of his duties:

Information started trickling in around 1995. Before then, North Korea maintained a relatively stable public distribution system and strictly prevented internal migration. People were fixed to their assigned factories and work assignments. But with the famine driving people into more and more desperate circumstances, illegal markets and trade sprang up. With these illegal trade networks, "CD running" businesses were created. North Korean people got their hands on CDs and cassettes— back then, VHS tapes were common—loaded with Chinese, Korean, and American films. They would bring them into cities, sell them, and use the money to support their families. People didn't need much money to get started. [They would] just get ripped-off copies for cheap from China, mark up the prices, and make a profit. As the demand grew, the market for these naturally developed and became more sophisticated.

HOUSEHOLD INSPECTIONS

All households have to register their electronic media equipment with the local authorities. Such equipment included audiotape players, DVD and CD players, computers, and radios. For years, Kim and his colleagues asked local police departments for the list of registered households with media equipment. They would then knock on the doors of those households and demand to see what was inside their electronic devices. After pressing the eject button, he and his colleagues would sometimes find illegal content, such as American TV series. If so, they would arrest members of the household and seize the DVDs to send to their superiors in Pyongyang.

People quickly caught on to the tactics of comrades working for what was essentially Kim Jong-Il's thought police: once they heard pounding on their door, they would quickly eject and hide foreign media. So Kim and his colleagues learned to circumvent this trick by shutting off the electricity in an entire apartment building before going to a few households in the building and asking for their electronic devices. The officials would then turn the electricity back on in order to press the eject button on these machines. This way, there were very few opportunities for the households to hide the illegal media.

Jeong Gwang-Seong, a young man from Hoeryong, explained,

When the electricity comes on, everyone does it [watches foreign films]. My home had a front door, which we locked. Luckily, this bought us time when inspectors came. But some homes don't have front doors. The electricity would be on for thirty, sometimes forty minutes, just short of an hour. The authorities gave you just enough time to almost finish watching something. Just short of an hour, the electricity would be turned off in my entire village. You can't take out your [DVD] from your digital DVD player because the eject button won't work without electricity. Since there's a blackout, people know the inspectors are coming. So they wait at home. They wait, dreading. And then bam! The inspectors arrive. They go door to door, and sometimes bring screwdrivers with them to unscrew the DVD players in the homes. They'll take the [DVD] away to the station to play it on their own machines to check the content. They don't ask you to follow them just yet. If it's a foreign film, then you're done. Bribes go a long way though. We were never caught, but my older cousin was. This was after I defected. He went to prison.

Contrary to what some North Koreans believe about their Dear Leader's ability to read their minds and keep his eye on everything they do, he can't. Nor can his internal security apparatus keep its eyes and ears on every citizen. Therefore, the regime has created a brilliant system of internal security and social norms to keep everyone in line. By cementing interconnected social networks, and incentivizing snitching, they often prevent minds and behavior from straying. The powerfully frightening combination of cult of personality and terrorizing punishment is what has made North Korea so effective at controlling its people and surviving as a nation. Yet the brutal policies of this Communist country are not matched by its ability to provide for all its citizens. This has allowed cracks to emerge in the regime's foundations, cracks that are evident in part by the information that does seep in, despite its control mechanisms.

WILLING TO RISK IT ALL, BUT WHY?

If citizens find out through illicit means that there is a free world outside North Korea in which they could be active participants, they could perhaps become disloyal to the regime, and commit "treacherous acts," such as circulating outside information among their social networks inside North Korea, defecting from the country and telling the world about the secrets of North Korea, or maintaining communication channels with their friends and family inside North Korea and therefore increasing the number of people who know more about the world outside their own reality. If a sufficient number of people become disillusioned with the regime, especially those who have political sway inside the country, then the possibility of organized resistance does not seem far off. Resistance is in fact far from possible inside North Korea, where the regime will pummel any modicum of resistance until it disappears. But this scenario has taken place repeatedly throughout the history of brutal regimes.

So if the regime fears an informed citizen more than any other domestic threat and consequently punishes a citizen for consuming foreign media, why do North Korean citizens go to such lengths and risk their lives to seek forbidden information and media, such as South Korean dramas, radio programs, American literature, Hollywood movies, political news, and romance novels?

Curiosity is a universal trait that has been both a blessing and a curse throughout human history. The insatiable yearning to learn new things, to discover new parts of our world, to learn how other people live, is a universal hunger, even if it comes at a high cost. In addition to an innate curiosity about the unknown, the forbidden nature of foreign media makes it ever more enticing. Think about all the things that you have searched for on the internet with excitement, and how you have waited impatiently for pages filled with new facts and images to load. Think back to rushing to the bookstore or library to read and watch the newest books and movies when they were released. Why do we watch the news? Why do we ask questions? Humans are curious, and North Koreans are no different. They just pay a much higher price for the information that they access.

Some younger defectors simplified the calculus for me, and shared that they were just bored with the state media.

A DMZ SOLDIER'S CURIOSITY

On a recent trip to the DMZ from the DPRK's side, amid the North Korean and South Korean flags straddling the 38th Parallel and dozens of tourists, I cautiously struck up a conversation with a North Korean military officer in his mid-fifties. At first, he scowled and demanded that I, a Korean-speaking American, stand far from him. Yet I kept near him, pretending that I had no wiggle room among the dozens of fellow tourists who were also at the DMZ.

After his military colleagues cleared the area, the officer casually covered his mouth with a folder, looked away from me, and in a low voice started asking me questions about my life in America. After all, he couldn't have his colleagues seeing him be so friendly with a foreigner, much less an ethnic Korean. He asked me what life was like in America, what my parents did, and how I had learned to speak Korean in America. For ten minutes, we stood by each other in a crowd while looking opposite directions, carrying on our clandestine conversation in Korean while having both of our mouths covered. After telling me that he wholeheartedly wishes that the two Koreas will reunify so that all Korean people, *hanminjok,* can live together in peace, he asked me: "Do I look like your father?"

I didn't really know what he was asking, and when I asked him to repeat his question, he said: "Well, I know that we're *hanminjok,* but I'm curious if I look like a Korean man in the United States. Am I as tall as him? Same face?"

At this point, I held back my tears, and made some joke about how much more handsome the military officer was than my father, even though the man was significantly shorter, thinner, and more weathered-looking than my father. I was standing in front of the flesh and blood result of a divided country, seventy years later, in human form. My father could have easily been born in North Korea. But he was born thirty-five miles south of the DMZ, and his fate could not have been more different than that of the man I was facing.

A rush of military officers headed our way, abruptly ending our guarded conversation. The officer shoved me out of the way and barked at me not to stand so close. I tried to wave goodbye, but he ignored me. He may have acted like that because he was in the company of his colleagues. When it was time for my group to get back on the bus, I caught his eye and winked. Without smiling, he winked back.

Even he, a trusted soldier, expressed curiosity about the world outside his own. Curiosity simply cannot be quelled.

DR. PARK SE-JOON, DISILLUSIONED AND ANGRY

Before having spent time in a political prison camp, Dr. Park Se-Joon had led a relatively privileged life. Born in the 1970s when North Korea's economy was at its peak, he belonged to a politically privileged family because his father was a senior officer in the North Korean intelligence services. He received an elite education, went on to medical school after graduating from high school, and specialized in dentistry.

"I was a real Communist, and was so committed to defend[ing] and protect[ing] North Korea's juche ideology. I was incredibly loyal to the North Korean system, believed in the juche ideology, and genuinely believed Kim Il-Sung and Kim Jong-Il to be gods. I truly loved Kim Il-Sung with all my heart. My parents, my brother, and I were all members of the Korean Workers' Party, and everyone in my family followed an elite career track. I had no reason to oppose the North Korean regime since I reaped the benefits of the system. I was living in Pyongyang, and lived and breathed what I thought was true socialist paradise."

Dr. Park has salt-and-pepper hair and a full, genuine smile that belies the complicated history he has lived through. Now in his forties, he still wears a backpack and holds onto both straps right below his shoulders, as an obedient student would.

Since North Korea restricts all travel, including domestic travel, Dr. Park wasn't able to move freely across cities or provinces, though he lived comfortably in Pyongyang. He was assigned to a hospital where he had to work on patients, but he didn't have sufficient equipment, tools, medicine, or painkillers to treat them. The patients brought empty beer bottles from home for Dr. Park to fill with hospital-made saline solution. Needles were always reused until they were so rusty that they wouldn't properly puncture the human skin. Syringes were sterilized with lukewarm salt water. Blood-soaked cotton balls were washed and dried for future use. Dr. Park would write down the names of medications that patients would need, and send them off, hoping that they would have the money to buy them from street markets. Stocked pharmacies were a mere fantasy for both doctors and patients alike. The few bottles of medication that he was given were officially reserved for true dental emergencies, but he would sell them on the black market to supplement his income.

He tells me: "I was trained as a doctor in North Korea, but feel immense guilt to this day because I was unable to save lives in the very profession that is defined by saving lives." He added:

> I heard rumors of people dying around the country, but thought this was nonsense. No one around me [in Pyongyang] was dying, so I didn't believe it. One day sometime in 1995, I was traveling on a train outside Pyongyang and was utterly confused by what I saw. When my colleagues and I got off the train at some station, *kotjebis* [homeless children] flocked toward us, asking for food. These tiny children in ragged clothes with nearly black faces because they hadn't bathed for so long had one hand over the other, both hands facing upward, begging us for food. I later learned that these were orphans from broken families whose parents [had] died from the famine. These *kotjebis* were scattered throughout the city

as far I could see. It was my first time seeing such a thing. I thought to myself, "What the hell is going on? How could this be?" That was the first time that I thought something was wrong.

After returning to Pyongyang, Dr. Park fell into a deep, existential dilemma. How could the streets of his country be full of homeless children begging for a scrap of rice cake? Was it worse in more remote parts of the country? Seeing the reality beyond Pyongyang propelled him into a state of doubt, which opened up his mind to listening to foreign radio.

Around the time of the Arduous March, ration deliveries slowed, and eventually came to a halt, even for him. When he occasionally visited his older hospital colleagues, they were struggling far more. Dr. Park had still been living at home with his parents and together they were able to scrape by, but his colleagues who had families of their own had no food. These loyal party members refrained from doing anything illegal, like participating in side businesses, and made watery porridge out of wilted vegetables, a handful of rice, and salt. Their children constantly had diarrhea.

He describes what happened next:

The future for doctors, even privileged doctors, looked very dim and unclear. I decided that being supremely loyal wasn't for me, simply out of survival. So I started a private side business of selling Chinese goods inside North Korea. I developed Chinese contacts who provided the goods that were cheaper and [of] better quality than the North Korean equivalents. I learned through looking, touching, and using Chinese products that China was significantly more developed than my own country. So I grew very curious about the outside world. In 1999, I had the opportunity to go to China with a Chinese salesman and continued to jump the border for business purposes by bribing border guards. The first, most shocking thing I saw in China was a market in a tiny, rural town. It was filled with poor people, but they weren't that thin. And this market had everything! Rice, oil, bananas, meat—anyone could just buy and eat these. It was cheap. Even ordinary *farmers* could buy and eat anything. I realized that something was very wrong. Through this process, I started comparing myself to other people. "Why do people in my country have to starve so much? These little *kotjebis* who live at train stations have nothing to eat, so they roam around, begging, stealing, and getting frostbite in the winter. Then I cross the border into China and it's a *totally different* world. There's food everywhere. People even throw food *away*!"

Like many other defectors, Dr. Park Se-Joon was shocked by how people from lower social strata like "ordinary farmers" had full access to food. People from lower Songbun in North Korea do not have reliable access to plentiful food, which is reserved for people of higher political status—a status determined by their ancestral roots dating back to the inception of the North Korean state.

GWANG-SEONG, MORE CURIOUS THAN AFRAID

"When I was younger, we would have to leave during class to watch [public executions]."

Jeong Gwang-Seong was born in Hoeryong in North Hamgyong Province, and grew up dreaming of becoming a police officer. The masculine qualities of the uniform, the austere equipment that hung from an officer's belt, and the respect that residents showed to officers appealed to Gwang-Seong. When he turned nine, his parents shared with him his family background and why they lived in Hoeryong, one of the northeastern towns of North Korea, cut off from Pyongyang's good graces, and home mostly to families who have fallen out of the state's favor. His grandfather had been born in Pyongyang and had been a chief prosecutor in the 1960s. Right after being married, he found out about his brother's past as part of an anti–Kim Il-Sung faction when Kim Il-Sung was consolidating his power. When this background was revealed, entire generations of the family were exiled to Hoeryong. The grandfather lost his position, the grand-uncle died in prison, and Gwang-Seong was already marked for life even before his birth.

When Gwang-Seong learned of his poor Songbun status, his dreams of becoming an elegant, authoritative police officer were dashed. He said, "Once your family is stuck with that sort of stigma, even if it's from way back in the 1950s and 1960s, the family cannot advance. Not your sons, not your grandsons. I was part of such a family." His father bought shoes at wholesale prices in Chongjin and sold them at a markup in Hoeryong. There was no point in working hard, studying, doing homework, or impressing his teachers. Even if he were to get top grades, his teachers would know that academic merit would not lead to his getting a good job. At an age when children around the world daydream of what they want to be when they grow up, Gwang-Seong knew well of the glass ceiling—rather, steel ceiling—that he would eventually hit. Life became monotonous for him. "People like me would wake up, go to school so that we [wouldn't] get in trouble, sit there, go through the motions, go to self-criticism sessions, come back home, sit around, eat if there was food, sleep, repeat. There [was] no need to think. I wasn't even allowed to think. Boys like me would then get married, have kids, get old, die, and turn to dust. That was it."

After each school day, he and his classmates would walk over to the homes of students who did not attend school that day to drag those students back to school to face verbal criticism or harsher punishment from teachers. If the presence of a few students did not put sufficient pressure on the absent students to go to school, then more students would show up to apply more pressure. Students on this reporting duty would complain to their truant classmate, "Come on! Hurry up already and come with us to see Teacher. It's already dark outside and I want to go home!" This peer-pressure-based reporting mechanism was initially used to ensure student attendance, but was later repurposed to locate and investigate missing students if they defected from North Korea, as defections rose significantly in the late 1990s.

Gwang-Seong was sometimes the missing student whose classmates would then come searching for him after a long day at school—a day that was often filled with fieldwork and cleaning duties. "I knew how annoying it was to go searching for missing classmates, but sometimes I just didn't care to attend school. What the hell was the point? I knew it would piss off classmates because searching and bringing me back to school would cut into their evening playtime, but I didn't care."

Even though life was monotonous, he doesn't have particularly bad memories from his time in North Korea. "There is this really famous fruit called *baeksalgu*, which only grows in the cold regions. *Noona*, when the Koreas reunify, I'll take you to my home town and you'll have to try this fruit." Gwang-Seong and I have developed a sibling-like relationship over time. Since he first met me, he's been calling me *Noona*, a Korean word that means "older sister" and is used by males, blood-related or not, to refer to an older female. It usually connotes endearment, affection, and warmth.

"*Baeksalgu* grows only in cold regions, and boy, Hoeryong is really cold. The city was upgraded a bit because Kim Il-Sung's wife, Kim Jong-Suk, was born there, so there's a historical exhibit, a preserved cottage where she used to live, things like that. I played a lot. In the summer, I went swimming with friends in the stream, and in the winter, we'd find things to sit on and go sledding. It snows so much, and the students, especially the boys, had to shovel snow. Shovel snow at school, at home, the roads, things like that. It was really fun, and I had a great time with my friends." In describing people in his home town, Gwang-Seong's face lights up to match his answer: "People in Hoeryong? They're so *soft*. So naive, so unadulterated."

During one of his routine visits to a close classmate's house, his friend lowered his voice and asked, "Do you want to watch a movie? It's a foreign movie." Gwang-Seong recalls being nervous and hesitant, knowing the punishment they could face if caught watching it. "Everyone knows that watching foreign media is dangerous. Even little kids know it."

In 2000, Gwang-Seong watched his first foreign movie with his classmate. They were both eleven years old. His friend closed all the windows and shut the curtains, inserted the movie *Blue* into his DVD player, turned down the volume to almost mute, and then asked Gwang-Seong to shut the front door behind him and press his ear against the closed front door from outside to check if he could hear the movie. They were taking the obvious precautions to prevent any suspicious, meddlesome, or indiscreet neighbors from telling their inminban leader or even the local authorities that something suspicious was happening in Gwang-Seong's friend's household.

He felt a combination of fright, curiosity, danger, and excitement while watching *Blue*. "It was scary, but amazing. The South Korea I had learned about as a child—a place where people were poor, starving, and near naked—was so different from the South Korea I saw in the film. I [had] learned that South Koreans make up lies to seduce people and abduct them. I [had] learned that they kidnap foreigners and take their blood. Really weird things. There were nice cars on the street, and so much traffic! So many cars. People were so well off, and the Seoul-ites' way of speaking Korean was so interesting, so elegant. It had a romantic appeal to it. When I came home, I couldn't stop thinking about it. I wanted to watch it again and again. I later went to that friend's place again and asked him to watch the same film again."

He later asked his father to buy a DVD player, which he did. As long as the foreign films Gwang-Seong bought or borrowed from friends weren't politically inappropriate, his parents were fine with him watching them. He also watched *My Boss, My Hero*, a South Korean gangster comedy. Gwang-Seong and his friends imitated the thuggish curse words among themselves in their homes and cracked themselves up. They couldn't do it outside, or else they'd reveal to others that they were watching films. *Autumn in My Heart* and *Winter Sonata* were other dramas he watched, and *Into the Storm* and *All In* were South Korean TV shows that he especially enjoyed. *All In* is a South Korean drama series starring Lee Byung-Hun and the beautiful Song-Hye Kyo about a man's rise in the competitive world of gambling. The episodes are set in Jeju Island and Las Vegas.[1]

"To me," Gwang-Seong said, "Jeju Island was just so beautiful. Jeju Island and Vegas were sheer freedom. When I think of Vegas, I think freedom. Just freedom. I had a vague wish to go there. The beautiful imagery didn't convince me to defect by any means. But I just thought, 'wow.'"

Gwang-Seong was hooked. In North Korea, he explained, the social networks in which people exchanged films with friends were larger than the actual market of films for sale. Friends watched films together, then borrowed from other networks and circulated the films among other groups of friends.

As part of a political class that "wasn't even allowed to think or ask questions," Gwang-Seong started to question his reality, little by little. Movies were movies, and he knew that plot lines and characters were dramatized, but they couldn't all be false. He started thinking about why there was such a wide discrepancy between what North Korea taught him and what he saw in foreign movies and shows. Why did North Korean authorities claim that South Koreans were desperately poor when they were obviously rich? The kids his age in the films wore such nice, elegant clothing, and seemed so happy to hang out together in school. "I get that movies [can] be exaggerated," he explained. "But still. The houses were so big, and kids got to go on family vacations with their parents. The traveling element was so enviable. I couldn't go anywhere outside Hoeryong and I never thought anything of it before. My thinking changed little by little."

Yet Gwang-Seong, along with almost everyone else I spoke with, continued to experience tremendous cognitive dissonance between his belief in what the state taught him and what he was learning about the outside world through foreign media. "Of course I still hung on to some of North Korea's education because that's what I learned continuously. If you're told a lie is true over and over again, especially in your formative years, you'll believe it, even if it's a delusion. Call it whatever you want—idolization, brainwashing—anything. That's how I grew up. But while watching these videos, I don't think I had the time to think about how our country was wrong. I was too absorbed in the world of films."

South Korean interviewers who interrogate all North Koreans seeking to settle in South Korea have been asking questions about their exposure to foreign media while they were inside North Korea, and about the impact that such materials had on them. Several of the researchers and interviewers who have been doing this work since the early 2000s have shared that almost all defectors coming into South Korea have seen foreign films while in North Korea. A common answer to the question "What did you feel when watching foreign films?" was that the defectors liked the storylines about family, romance, and action. Seeing how people lived in other places was enticing, and they liked that the films were not overtly political.

Some people, especially young people, may develop an envy of the things they're seeing on the screen. But such envy of smoother skin, elegant South Korean speech, and brightly lit streets at night rarely translates into actionable desire to defect. Chores around the house, school, work, and the daily grind quickly replace the wishful thinking and envy that the foreign movies sparked once the films are turned off. Others are able to mentally relegate foreign films into a taboo hobby category, and convince themselves through sheer willpower that the film's value is solely entertainment. A professor made an analogy to Catholics. "North Koreans enjoy a 'worldly life' by watching things they shouldn't. And then they attend self-criticism sessions to clean their slate. Some Christians and Catholics, I'm sure, watch 'red videos' and then may go to confession to seek forgiveness for seeking worldly pleasures." (This grandfatherly professor was referring to pornography when he said "red videos"; he just couldn't bring himself to say the term.)

Gwang-Seong witnessed three public executions when he was young. "They used to drag us out of classrooms and gather all of us around the big marketplace in Hoeryong in Manghyang-dong, a high traffic area, and make us watch. I heard that the executions in Hoeryong are at a different place now. Only one execution that I attended was for distributing foreign media and movies. This was around the time when the popularity for foreign videos had gotten out of control and they wanted to make an example out of somebody."

His facial expression did not change at all when he was describing these executions. He was engaged in our conversation, but the topic of someone being publicly murdered for circulating movies did not seem to be particularly novel to him.

"What effect did an execution by a firing squad have on the neighbors? Did they stop watching?" I asked. He answered: "Of course the activities quieted down for a while, not because the execution scared people from permanently watching foreign movies, but because people were waiting for cues on when the authorities would loosen up. I would start playing films again, with the volume almost off, and increase it little by little. I sure as hell was not going to stop watching movies!"

I was surprised at both the resoluteness and nonchalance of his response to witnessing the physical consequences of someone watching films. Of course the poor soul who was killed that day was probably a scapegoat and was used to instill fear into the residents of Gwang-Seong's village in Hoeryong. But even execution was not a sufficient deterrent for Gwang-Seong and his peers.

A COUNTRY WHERE MONEY CAN BUY OR SOLVE ANYTHING

Even in North Korea, having lots of money could make you like you're in heaven. Even the police treat you in a special way.

—Ji Seong-Ho, who defected from North Korea in 2006

There was this crazy, wealthy, meddlesome, jealous woman in my neighborhood who was envious of every woman who had items she didn't have. One day, she pushed her way into another person's home to demand how the owner obtained fine goods in her home. This escalated to an explosive fight—you know how Koreans are, with their uncontrollable anger once they pass a threshold—and the jealous crazy woman whacked the owner over the head with a wooden laundry stick. The owner died! The crazy lady paid off the right people with the right amounts of money. She spent six months in a local jail, as a formality, nothing serious. The last I heard, she is back in her home, still meddling and butting into everyone's business. She's off the hook, even for killing an innocent neighbor. In North Korea these days, or at least the part where I'm from, you can even get away with murder if you have money.

—Kim Ha-Young, who defected from
North Korea in 2008

The increasing prevalence of black markets and illegal trade across the country gave rise to a bribe culture. "You could fix any problem, buy anything, or figure out any sticky situation in

North Korea with money," North Korean defectors often say. The desperate country is experiencing cracks in its Communist system: people are turning to illegal black markets and capitalistic practices to survive. It is understood that dependence on the state is for the elite classes and for the hopeful souls from the Kim Il-Sung era who still cling to the memory of North Korea's glory days in the 1970s.

According to American academics at the Peterson Institute for International Economics, based in Washington, D.C., almost half of North Korean families rely on variations of private trading—mainly street markets—to survive. As mentioned earlier, some state that 70 to 80 percent of adult individuals earn part or all of their income by engaging in market activities.

There have been cases where the local police tried to shut down these markets because they're illegal, private, capitalistic ventures, but people argued and bribed their way out of being shut down. Otherwise, how else would these people survive? The local police well know just how difficult it is for people to eke out a living, especially outside the big cities.

A WEAKENING HOUSEHOLD PATRIARCHY

Despite North Korea's socialist values, the country still adheres to a patriarchal system whereby the father and husband are expected to be the breadwinners and decision makers of the household. Yet increasing numbers of housewives are working in the street markets because their husbands who work in the moribund state factory system often do not get paid sufficiently. Worse, if the factories don't have work, the men have to pay their factories or state company for the "privilege" of not working. A North Korean woman who describes herself as "the average North Korean woman of today" explains that she earns between 2,500–3,000 won a day, or approximately fifty cents, at black market rates. This is double what her husband would earn in a whole month, if his company were actually paying him. Bear in mind that a kilogram of rice on the street markets costs about 5,000 to 7,000 won.

Female defectors explain that making more money than their husbands allowed them to "speak louder" in the household, which is a significant social development in a society where domestic violence is estimated to occur in more households than not. The wives are becoming the ones making money, feeding the families, and consequently making the significant household decisions. Some wives go as far to giggle and call their husbands "puppies" or "pets" because they have to be cared for and fed without contributing meaningfully to the household.

In addition to challenging the patriarchy, black markets have encouraged people to depend increasingly on capitalistic practices and consequently doubt one of the fundamental pillars of their Communist state. Witnessing the regime's increasing inability to provide for individual households has encouraged more doubts overall about the regime. This broadening trend in North Korean domestic society is another crack in the system observed by defectors and outsiders.

HA-YOUNG, A CHILD OF THE MARKETS

On a humid day, I made my way to Seoul Station to help a North Korean defector youth service group called UNISEED. The group is part of a growing phenomenon among young North Korean defectors in their teens and twenties who volunteer to serve underprivileged South Koreans as a way of showing other South Koreans that defectors are not a social burden, but rather are contributing, responsible citizens of their new country. One of their service projects is preparing and distributing North Korean–style food to homeless men and women at the busy Seoul train station every third Saturday of the month. Two dozen North Korean defectors, mostly college students, raise small amounts of money to purchase ingredients and cook in a borrowed kitchen starting at 9:00 on those Saturday mornings. White rice, soup, kimchi, and a few side dishes are carefully packaged in disposable plastic bento-box-like cases, and several hundred of these are distributed along with spoons, chopsticks, and napkins.

When I observed these well-dressed young North Korean defectors, they were standing in an assembly line to greet, distribute food, and chat with homeless men and women (mostly men came to take food) for over two hours. With the exception of some questioning by the Seoul Station authorities for not obtaining a permit for this activity, the food distribution went seamlessly. As the group walked over to a cafe afterward to unwind, debrief, and have iced coffee and ice cream cones, some volunteers peeled off to walk around the station and pick up the trash that had been left behind from these meals. Volunteers scooped up kimchi that had been dumped onto the ground and picked up dozens of plastic food cases, wooden chopsticks, and even soju bottles (UNISEED didn't distribute soju, but some people had apparently acquired some of this alcoholic beverage to pair with their meals).

As I sipped my iced coffee and listened to the group talk about their experience and plan for the future, which even included an "MT," I was in awe of these young peers' resilience. "MT" is short for "membership training," a term that describes a social retreat, usually for one night and two days, for members in campus student groups across South Korea. The purpose of these social retreats is to foster friendship among members through activities including outdoor events, games, cooking, eating, and drinking. I was impressed because although many of the students do not have family in South Korea or elsewhere, and have only recently endured the harrowing process of defecting and the testing process of resettling and assimilating, they were volunteering to serve others in their newfound country.

On an emotional high note, I was one of the last persons to leave the cafe. Most had dinner plans or other social engagements, so they bolted once the official debriefing meeting had adjourned. A boy claimed he had to leave early because he had a "special meeting," and his buddies blew his cover by announcing to the rest of the group that it was actually for a date with his special female friend, which triggered a series of "Ooh!" and funny, teasing comments like "*He* has game?"

As I gathered my things to leave, a young woman stepped in the doorway to stop me. About my height with a very petite frame, she had fair skin, light makeup that included black eyeliner, and auburn-colored hair and eyebrows. She asked me, "Are you from America?"

"Yes."

"My name is Ha-Young. I came from Musan, North Korea, years ago and I'd like to tell you my story. It's underwhelming, and undramatic. But it will balance the more dramatic stories of other defectors out there. It's my story, and it's only reflective of my experience in Musan. I'm not speaking on behalf of the entire country. Can you make time to listen?"

A few days later, we met up at a trendy study cafe near her university. With jazz-ified American pop songs playing in the background, we stepped into a walled-off private room inside the study cafe so that no one else could hear her. "I still gotta be careful. Don't want people to make suspicious of me and think I'm a Commie," she explained to me. "My story takes place in the city of

Musan, in North Hamgyong Province in North Korea, from 1993 to 2008. Everything I say is about this period, and in this location." Ha-Young emphasized this throughout several of our conversations because she thought it was distasteful, inaccurate, and self-promoting for other defectors to speak about their experiences as if they were representative of those of all North Koreans.

Ha-Young was born in 1993. Her father was a driver for a famous mine for steel production in Musan, where he loaded and transported steel. He didn't make any money in his official job as a driver, so he used to pocket a little diesel oil from the car he drove. Since imported diesel oil was very expensive, he was able to make some extra cash to support his household by selling small amounts of the diesel oil he stole. Even so, Ha-Young's mother was the one who made most of their income. The couple had quite different Songbun statuses. In fact, Ha-Young's maternal grandmother vehemently opposed the couple's marriage, for the mother's side had very high social standing, with the grandfather having met Kim Il-Sung and Kim Jong-Il, whereas Ha-Young's father's sister had defected to South Korea, which had marked his whole family. Ha-Young's mother had insisted on marrying the man she loved, but Ha-Young's grandmother did not prepare a dowry—any money, furniture, or a home—which was considered very shameful for the newly wedded couple. Having nothing, the young couple rented a small room, which was where Ha-Young was born.

Ha-Young was born one year before Kim Il-Sung died and the Great Famine hit. She remembers being wrapped in a Korean *podaegi* (baby wrap) attached to her mother's back while her mother walked around train stations to sell pieces of bread and drinks.[2] Her mother saved the pocket change she made, which ultimately allowed her to start her business. When Ha-Young was growing up, her father and his friends were on the liberal side, to Ha-Young's mother's dismay. They dealt in expensive antique goods from China, and learned about China and money matters through their business travels to China.

Eventually, her mother herself ran a wholesale business for second-hand Chinese clothing, which she sold to North Korean marketeers who would then sell the clothing to individual customers. It was strictly profit-driven. She would buy 500 kilograms (1,100 pounds) of clothes at a time and pay off everyone she had to along the way so that she could transport the clothing from the Chinese-North Korean border by car or train. Once the clothing was home, Ha-Young would help her mother categorize the pieces as "good," "average," or "bad," and price them accordingly. There were women who then would sell several pieces of clothing at a time in their small stores, which carried no more than a hundred pieces. Bigger sellers would approach Ha-Young's mother and buy clothing by the kilo. The more expensive, high-quality pieces were sold to sellers in bigger cities like Pyongyang, Chongjin, and Hamhung.

"If the clothes were of bad quality, [with] holes in them, they would go for about $1. If they were average, they sold for about $5. Some women bought 30, 40, 50 pieces at once. Once my mom sold some high quality clothes, she would break even and everything else was pure profit. If my mom made 50 percent profit, that was a bad season. If she made 100–200 percent profit, that was a good season."

The way Ha-Young described her mother's technically illegal business made me momentarily forget that she was describing life back in North Korea, a country that's known to be socialist. Ha-Young was describing a business with economic terms that worked exactly like a typical wholesale clothing business in South Korea or the United States.

"We were able to afford anything and buy anything to wear and eat. We certainly were not part of the elite. Just the upper middle class. We had refrigerators, washing machines, a TV, a fan, a rice cooker, everything. Our dinner table looked like an upper middle class dinner table: we had the basics: rice, kimchi, soup, and side dishes. But we also had different types of kimchi—cabbage kimchi, radish kimchi, and other pickles. I hung out with the popular girls at school and ignored other people who didn't have as much money as us, or didn't dress as well. That's how I lived. Pretty ordinary, problem-free, and not dramatic."

But her family couldn't be too flashy with their belongings and wealth, or they'd draw suspicion about the sheer scale of their illegal business. Everyone did it and the government tolerated it to a certain degree, but her mother was operating on a whole different scale. Most of her friends farmed to help their families make ends meet. "The really poor kids chopped trees to sell wood in the markets and buy rice with the cash they made on a daily basis. There were also the *kotjebis,* the wandering street kids who would beg for food. They were everywhere! They would steal from people as they were eating. As they grew thicker skin, they got tougher and became thugs and robbers."

Ha-Young snatched the croissant in my hand that I was eating with my coffee and said, "like that. Someone would be walking with food in their hand, and a *kotjebi* would steal it from their hand, and quickly swallow it while running away. People would chase after them, super pissed. It was funny at the time, watching hysterically angry adults run after raggedy kids, but really sad to think about it now."

"Honestly though, the weak or weak-willed people had all starved to death in the Arduous March. The famine filtered out most of the loyal citizens, except for the elites in Pyongyang, of course. They were always taken care of. Most of the North Koreans who survived that period and are still around are very tough. Nowadays, people don't really starve to the degree that they did in the 1990s."

There were patrol forces across Musan and between cities to prevent people from running businesses like the one Ha-Young's mother had undertaken. But the patrol forces had to make a living, too, so bribes went a long way. Since her family was consistently profitable for the police, there was a patrol officer dedicated to protecting Ha-Young's mother in case she got into any trouble. The mother would hand over money, or some clothes for the men to give to their wives. The complicit officers ended up working harder to protect her as time passed because if they were caught helping her, they would be punished, too. It was a symbiotic relationship that strengthened with time and risk. "We were lucky and pretty happy. My mom never got into legal trouble, and never had to go to prison."

It still shocks me that not going to prison was the metric that this young woman used to measure her luck.

CHOI JUNG-HOON: A DANGEROUS GAMBLE

Imagine a stereotypical North Korean military man in the news. That's what Choi Jung-Hoon looks like. Everything about him—his looks, his language, his speech, his passion for his work—is fiercely disciplined and focused, fiery, brusque, almost militant. His gaze is cutting. We first chatted in the radio broadcast room in Seoul (which is also Kim Seong-Min's radio station and work space), where the windows are covered and several armed security personnel rotate every twelve hours to provide security for him. We quickly moved our conversation to a different office, however, because smoking is not allowed in the radio room, and a half hour into our conversation, Choi had to have a smoke. He offered me one. I don't smoke, but don't mind if others smoke around me, especially if it eases conversation around difficult, sensitive memories.

Choi Jung-Hoon was born into a politically loyal family in Hyesan, a big border city in Ryanggang Province. His father always told him and his siblings that "if Kim Il-Sung dies, then you die. You must give up your love, your life for your country." The familial atmosphere was militaristic and disciplined. "I sincerely, sincerely believed that Kim Il-Sung was the greatest ruler in the world," he told me.

He finished his schooling in Ryanggang Province and later worked in internal security, monitoring students at his university. In 1994, he was transferred to Kim Il-Sung Technical University, where he studied for another three years, and was then sent back to Ryanggang Province to oversee 120 soldiers. In 2005, he joined the Sang Man construction company. Despite his favored standing, he struggled to make ends meet. After the chaos that followed the Great Famine in the mid-1990s, he noticed that low-class marketeers were skirting policies to make money by running small businesses, and that powerful people at the top were exploiting profiteers by pocketing kickbacks. Desperately poor and hungry people were everywhere. "There was a newfound freedom where people could break the law to make money to survive," he explained.

One fateful day, a contact in China called him about a job opportunity. A daughter of a man who had been kidnapped by North Koreans was offering $10,000 for Choi to find her father. "My eyes flipped around when I heard that number. In 2006, if you had that much money, your entire family could live off of that amount for the rest of your life."

The whole setup was illegal, and particularly dangerous for a trusted party member like himself. Interacting with a foreigner, connecting her with a North Korean, and then taking money for this service were all illegal acts. But money trumped political allegiance, and Choi set out to find this man. His wife thought he was insane. After all, the only information he had to help him identify this man was his name with three Korean syllables: Choi Uk-Il.

The man had been kidnapped more than thirty years earlier, on August 18, 1975, when a South Korean fishing boat, with thirty-three people on board, had been taken by the North Koreans. Although North Korea never admitted to taking the boat, everyone assumed this was the case. Family members of the abducted fishermen had begged the South Korean government for decades to find their fathers, their older brothers, their husbands.

The woman who approached Choi's contact was the daughter of that boat's manager. She was ten years old when her father and his fishing boat had been kidnapped, and she had vowed that she would find her father before she died. Here she was at age forty, then, offering $10,000 to a man she didn't know to find her father, who had to be somewhere in North Korea. Choi Jung-Hoon set out to search the country, using his political connections to move across city and provincial borders and discreetly finding leads along the way. After two months of traveling through broken public infrastructure and traffic systems, Choi Jung-Hoon found himself in a village in North Hamgyong Province. His proper and very Confucian upbringing had naturally led him to purchase two kilograms of rice and some meat as a gesture of goodwill.

The old, wrinkled man lived and looked like a beggar. He was haggard and gaunt, and had eyes devoid of life. He had been an innocent, young South Korean citizen who had left to go fishing and ended up living his pitiful life against his will. Choi Jung-Hoon explained to him what he was doing in this elderly man's home. The elderly man looked to his wife, seeking permission to meet his daughter from his previous life. After Choi Uk-Il was kidnapped, he had remarried a North Korean widow who allegedly had been tasked with monitoring him and writing weekly reports on him. They had two children from this marriage.

The North Korean wife gave her blessing for Choi Uk-Il to see his daughter briefly in South Korea, so the men prepared to take off. "Spousal relationships aren't robotic. Even if she had been tasked to monitor her husband, things change. They had children and they were growing old together," Choi Jung-Hoon explained to me.

Before they set off to meet the daughter, the two men agreed that the elderly man would be brought back to his North Korean home afterward. Briefly connecting divided families was bad enough, but facilitating the defection of a South Korean abductee would mean severe punishment for Choi Jung-Hoon and his family. The elderly man also wanted to return to North Korea because he had a wife and children there.

The men bribed a twenty-four-year-old border guard to let them pass into China by crossing the Amnok River, assuring the guard that the two would return to North Korea. Over the next six days, they made their way across the North Korean–Chinese border and used cell phones to coordinate their travel toward Yanji, a Chinese town near the border where he was to meet his family member. But the woman waiting for the elderly Choi Uk-Il in a safe house in Yanji was not his daughter whom he had been separated from thirty years earlier. Instead it was his first wife, Jong-Ja Yang, the South Korean woman whom he had married as a young man, and with whom he had had four children. He hadn't seen her since the day he had been abducted by the North Korean government, more than thirty years earlier.

Instantly, the two recognized each other's faces, embraced in desperation, and sobbed and sobbed, hysterically. They pinched and poked each other's faces, wondering if they were dreaming.

Choi Jung-Hoon clucked his tongue and told me, "I didn't even know these people, but I cried too. The sounds these elders were making were not human cries. They sounded like beasts. They sounded so deeply, momentously, desperately sad. I didn't know that I was capable to feel such emotion. I had no idea humans were able to cry for that long. They just kept on sobbing."

In that moment of empathy, Choi Jung-Hoon realized he had been living a lie. He felt betrayed by his government, because it was the government he had so loyally served that had kept this faultless husband and wife apart all these years. His passionately patriotic heart turned wholly against his government. He spat on the ground, cursed the Kim regime, and damned them for deceiving him and his countrymen all this time. At the same time, he also was fully aware of group punishment, especially for government officials like himself. His child and his wife were at home, waiting for his return, and if he did not return, or was caught committing these crimes, they would all be punished. He knew that he had to cross back into North Korea, as did the elder Choi Uk-Il.

As Choi Jung-Hoon tried to pry him out of the arms of his first wife, his first love, the elderly Choi Uk-Il changed his mind. He broke his word and decided to defect. Late at night, he snuck out of the safe house with his South Korean wife without Choi Jung-Hoon knowing and sought refuge at the South Korean embassy in China. While there, he told them everything about the abducted boat from three decades earlier and that he had crossed into

China with the help of "a Mr. Choi Jung-Hoon," among other escorts and brokers. This sensational story immediately caught the attention of the Seoul Broadcasting System and Korean Broadcasting System, as well as many major news outlets around the world. Kim Jong-Il, too, quickly learned the news and ordered that everyone implicated in this case be killed immediately.

The twenty-four-year-old border guard named Kim Yong-Il who had let the two men cross into China was killed. Choi Jung-Hoon called his wife, who hysterically ordered him to not return to the house because there were four policemen with guns pointed at the house. She pleaded with him to defect to China. In fact, he had no choice but to defect. The only other alternative was to return to his home, be arrested by the authorities, and face horrendous consequences. He desperately told his wife he needed to see her and his young son before defecting. Leaving their home town, comfortable life, and two-story house behind, and without any money, any contacts for defection brokers, or any idea of an escape route, the wife and son also defected with armed North Korean authorities on their heels.

KIM HEUNG-KWANG, FORMER ENFORCER

After working for so long to prevent foreign information from entering his country, Kim Heung-Kwang was curious about the foreign content that the border guards and customs officials kept seizing at the border and in the black markets. This curiosity led to a life-altering experience of breaking the rules. In the late 1990s, when its economy was in its most desperate state, North Korea asked other countries to sell it their trash by the ton, so that North Korea could use it for recycling.[3] According to Kim Heung-Kwang, between 1998 and 1999, France and Germany sold waste to North Korea for approximately three hundred dollars a ton.

"Students and people on break from their factories would cut open the plastics and separate them. Parts of them were melted and reused. Other waste was just burnt. But in this process, people found other things in the rubbish, including tapes and reels. There were CDs and cassettes. Children [would] play catch with the CDs and pull out the seemingly never-ending reels from the tapes. They had no idea what these were. But the professionals knew exactly what these 'toys' found in the rubbish were."

He gestured, pretending to clean an invisible tape with an invisible cloth dipped in alcohol, and said, "Using alcohol, someone would clean the bits off and put the relevant bits back into a cassette, trying to salvage this foreign imported good." That "foreign imported good," of course, referred to banged-up cassette tapes that had been pulled out from mountains of trash imported from another country—giving new meaning to the phrase "one man's trash is another man's treasure."

Kim Heung-Kwang snuck a few of these cassettes into his pocket when he was sure no one was looking, and watched some "really fun stuff, really unimaginable stuff. Seventy percent of the materials I watched were about families and about romances. I used to think back then, 'Europeans must not do any work. All they must do is just play.' It was the first time in history, probably, that North Koreans watched TV shows and videos from another country."

There is no way to track or verify if Kim Heung-Kwang and his colleagues were actually the first North Koreans to watch foreign media. But their experience definitely occurred around the time when *Hallyu*, or the "Korean Wave," was sweeping across Asia, including North Korea. The Korean Wave refers to the striking increase in interest in South Korean popular culture that began in the late 1990s with Korean dramas and music. South

Korean exports related to pop culture generated more than $5 billion in revenue in 2013 alone.

Kim Heung-Kwang in particular knew the severity of the ramped-up charges that unlucky people faced when they were caught watching or listening to foreign content. "Of course I knew that if I were caught, especially given my job, I'd face grand punishment. But you know, despite all that, a curiosity, a desire for the new and an opposition to things being hidden, is inherent in people and [they] will pursue it to the end. It's in people's DNA. Anyone, including North Koreans, wants to watch what [they]'re told not to watch. If you watch one episode, you want to watch two. If you watched two, you want to watch three. If you're young or an intellectual, even if you can't eat and have to skip a meal, you'd rather spend the money to get your hands on this stuff to watch."

He could not stop at films; in 1996 he started to listen to radio programs. South Korean researchers who have interviewed thousands of North Korean defectors state that secret listeners of radio programs in North Korea already have more critical distance from the regime than people who start off watching films. This was the case for Kim Heung-Kwang. "I listened mostly at night. I still remember the programs. From 9 to 10, KBS had their program *Hanminjok;* 10 to 11 p.m. was Voice of America, and from 11 to 12 a.m. was Radio Free Asia. Sometimes, I would fall asleep with the headphones in my ears because if the connection was constantly weak and made buzz[ing] sounds, I would mentally tune out and doze off. On Saturday nights, I would listen to these radio programs for three hours without sleeping."

"At night?"

Kim Heung-Kwang picked up on what I was alluding to. "Of course, my wife would ask, 'What are you doing?' and I would tell her, 'Ah, I'm just learning English through headphones.' I would have to pacify her because who knows? What if she felt insecure about her husband—me—listening to foreign programs? If our relationship ever became rocky, I'd automatically be in danger because she would have sensitive information about me. I didn't want to be threatened, and I also didn't want to make her feel vulnerable."

It was better that way, just keeping it to himself for his safety and for his wife's security. It got me thinking about the issues that spouses keep from each other in the United States and elsewhere. Questionable sources of additional income, unscrupulous ways a spouse is spending money, the way business is going, or maybe an extramarital affair. But for Kim, listening to foreign radio programs was considered so sensitive that it too was kept secret even from the person with whom he shared his bed.

Like most other North Korean listeners of foreign radio programs, the effects these programs had on Kim Heung-Kwang were nonlinear. It is never as simple as listening to a radio program and immediately being turned off from the regime. From the people I interviewed, it seems that the effect of foreign media is more like a mental tug-of-war between pro-regime beliefs on one end, and disbelief and skepticism on the other. People would enter a fantasy world by watching foreign media, and despite the questions that would swirl in their minds, when the film or program ended they would return to real life.

"At first, you think this [what you hear on the radio programs] is all a lie. The South Koreans are good at lying and are trying to change our minds. It's just a psychological plot," explains Kim Heung-Kwang. Yet "you keep listening because it's so . . . different from anything you've been exposed to. But one day you think, 'that sounds right,' and you nod along with the radio announcer's words, as if she's sitting next to you. You turn the tuner to find another South Korean program to see if there's anything else that's worth exploring. You may hear someone bashing the North Korean leader. It's too harsh, so you get pissed that someone outside the country is denigrating your mother country and then think all this foreign media is a hoax. After cooling down for a few days, you secretly turn the radio back on and hear something more reasonable and interesting. Through this back and forth process, your mind opens up without you even realizing it at first."

The cognitive dissonance that ensues breeds internal conflict, particularly among people who work for the government, and even more so among people who are part of the surveillance apparatus or monitoring bodies.

Kim thinks that six months of listening, questioning, and thinking critically about what one listens to is all that's required for one to come to the realization that the North Korean government is based on lies. Initially, the mental gymnastics have to be an individual process because a person does not know whom it is "safe" to talk to about these ideas, which are mutually exclusive to the regime's "truths": "Not even my wife. It doesn't have anything to do with *her* or that she's particularly not trustworthy. It's just how the regime trains people to view others. What if she genuinely did not like what I said or questioned about the regime based on what I heard and tells the authorities? That's it. But I did tell my friends about what I was listening to. Not too many times, though. I encouraged them to listen to radio and we discussed it."

Even though asking my next question threatened to bring up feelings of guilt and hypocrisy, I had to ask. "During the seven years you monitored people's homes to check and punish people for consuming foreign media, how were you able to listen to radio? How were you able to commit the same 'crime' that you were punishing others for?"

"I turned a blind eye to a lot of people because I understood their circumstance," he replied. I recall his telling me of various ways he would be gruff, making various threats to people he caught in possession of films, precisely to avert the impression that he was breaking the rules himself by not doing his job. Being lenient on crime could end up jeopardizing his own safety, after all. After putting on a tough show, though, he would let them off, making them promise to never, ever do it again. But when monitoring households with his colleagues, he would have no choice but to arrest or punish perpetrators.

His job led to his having an extremely sharp eye for behavior that may have been affected by foreign influences. "I'm no fashionista, but women, especially young women, were wearing their hair and makeup a little differently. I would catch people referring to the United States as just 'America' and not 'bastard invaders' or some other colorful [phrase]. People also called South Korea *Ah-re Dong-nae* (which translates to the "neighborhood below us" or "southern neighborhood"), which has warm and friendly connotations. People started getting bold, especially during and after the worst of the famine, and made economic complaints to local, low-level bureaucrats. People were too smart and savvy to criticize the government. But they would make critical observations in the third person: 'Why is it so cold? Why is there no food?' I noticed many people dying around me."[4]

Listening to radio sparked a domino effect in his mind: he wanted to seek other forms of information. "I liked videos because they were visually entertaining, but they t[ook] time [to watch]. They require[d] an external machine, you ha[d] to sit with [them], and especially if you were dealing with VHS tapes, then you were constantly worried that you [wouldn't] have sufficient time to evade detection. Radio was good because you could put one earphone in, fall asleep with it, and listen to a variety of programs."

In the early 2000s, the South Korean government donated to the North two hundred computers, two of which were given to Kim's university. Realizing that the hard disk drives had been reformatted, he tried to recover some files. One of the drives had been erased completely, but Kim was able to recover on the second computer a plethora of photos, digital books, movies, short videos, and other media. Of the books, he particularly remembers reading one about blood types and personalities, a biography of Andrew Carnegie, and another about "the Four Strong Men of the Middle East." The book about the dictators of the Middle East made a particularly strong impression on him. It described the price that the citizens of countries ruled by Hussein, al-Assad, Gaddafi, and Khomeini had to pay for these dictators' obsession with regime survival. He also learned that these "bad guys," as he described them to me, were all close with Kim Il-Sung, his leader. Reading this book and looking through the other files that he had recovered from this donated computer helped push his mind away from the regime.

"It was a happy, happy thing. I found gold. I had something interesting to read, to study, to think about—something others did not have. I became a professional when guessing people's blood types. (In Korea, people tend to associate personality traits with blood types.) When someone would be shocked by how accurate I was about guessing someone's blood type, or how much I knew, I couldn't say I got it from a book."

He became enamored of, and obsessed with, what he was watching. "The fear of punishment eventually [waned]." One of the films he watched was the South Korean television drama *Sandglass*. He was utterly hooked. This television series, one of the highest-rated South Korean dramas in history, captures the dynamic relationship among three friends living through the politically and socially tumultuous 1970s and 1980s, when South Korea was ruled by a military dictatorship. And there is a love story between a man and woman, not a story about a citizen's undying love for her country, which would have been the narrative had it been a North Korean film. The young protagonists in the series participated in pro-democracy demonstrations against their South Korean military dictatorship, even though speaking out against the government broke South Korea's censorship laws. The series includes a gruesome reenactment of the Gwangju Uprising, the nine-day rebellion among citizens of the southeast South Korean city of Gwangju after South Korean President Chun Doo-Hwan's administration sent in paramilitary troops to silence university students participating in peaceful protests, thereby killing hundreds of innocent civilians.

Kim was shocked after watching these scenes of students and civilians protesting their government to demand change, scenes of people criticizing their government, and scenes of young people expressing their romantic love for one another. He had to share this newfound imagery and content with someone else, so he carefully loaned them to his colleagues in his office, along with a film about the Korean War and an American film called *House on the Road*. Unfortunately, one of his colleagues was detained by the authorities when he was caught distributing copies of the films. After extensive interrogations he gave up Kim's name as the source of the DVD copies.

Cold sweat instantly covered Kim's entire body when he heard that his superiors knew that he had watched something illegal and was passing it around to his colleagues. Through smiles and laughter, the laughter of disbelief that accompanies retelling of a tragic phenomenon only decades later, Kim shook his head, jabbed his right index finger in the air, and told me, "I made him *promise* not to tell anyone my name if he got caught! Ah, well."

"For a week, I went to jail, and was interrogated in the dark and tortured. I thought I wouldn't be able to leave." As a husband and father, Kim had to quickly make a plan for his family to leave the country and reach safety. The risk of being caught while defecting meant slow torture, public execution, or instant death by a border guard's bullet, yet Kim knew that the crime he had committed was too serious—he had to leave. Not only had he consumed foreign media, but he had also exploited his trusted position of authority to make it happen. His life and the lives of his beloved wife and daughter were on the line, and he had to defect as quickly as possible.

Kim was sentenced to a reeducation labor camp where he had to work for a year on finishing various farming projects. He was banned from lecturing, and was warned that he would be expelled from the Communist Party for any further mistakes. Every day he spent tilling the land increased his hatred for it. He grew to despise the regime that lied to him and his compatriots. So, rather than becoming re-educated on how to be a more loyal citizen before reentering North Korean society, Kim spent that year planning his escape.

"This is what one CD does. How embarrassing, how *humiliating* it was to go from a professor to a farmer. I couldn't even lift my head while working, because I was so embarrassed. I knew that even if I were to have my sins forgiven by the government, I would be forever stained. This reputation would follow me forever, that I did something wrong, was corrupted by the public, and was untrustworthy. The pain was not so much physical as it was mental," he said.

In a twisted way, a form of equality exists among North Koreans. Everyone is equally subject to the regime's wrath.

3 "OLD SCHOOL" MEDIA

From Trader Gossip to Freedom Balloons

After talking about the newest ways to send information into North Korea with several of his colleagues, Kim Heung-Kwang, three other North Korean defectors—two in their late fifties, with graduate degrees, and a young woman my age named Eun-Ji who is studying English in Seoul—and I went to have dinner to wind down.[1] The balmy July afternoon in Seoul quickly turned to an evening with torrential rain, and the five of us ran under brightly colored umbrellas to a generic "American restaurant." "An American needs to have American food!" they told me.

"This restaurant has no concept," Eun-Ji whispered to me as we walked side by side along the dinner buffet line. Eun-Ji has assimilated very well into South Korean culture. Rail thin, about five feet, seven inches tall, with milky skin and light-brown hair styled in a blunt bob, she sported a short blue A-line skirt and a white silky top that showed off her tiny shoulders. "It's not American, Korean, or even fusion. But I hope you like it. The desserts look pretty, don't they?" Keeping her voice low, she casually looked around to see if Kim Heung-Kwang, who was treating us to dinner, was within earshot. We did not want to offend our host.

After we had all sat down, I asked the three older defectors how they had learned unofficial news and information when living inside North Korea. Kim Heung-Kwang said, "Probably word of mouth. Rumors spread like wildfire in North Korea. Bad news certainly spreads faster than good news. If I heard something, I'd check with a few trusted friends to see if they [had] heard it, too. If so, I thought of it as true." The others nodded.

"For example," Mrs. Lee chimed in, "when we were in college, I heard that to contribute to the country's war effort, we should all have our appendices taken out. So I had my appendix taken out." I sat there, stunned, but not wanting to overreact and possibly embarrass anyone at the table. So many questions swirled in my head. Did certified doctors conduct the appendectomies? How did this make sense? Which *war*?

Mr. Soo and Kim Heung-Kwang both chuckled. "Me, too," both added. Kim Heung-Kwang said, "Guys got together and egged each other on. If you didn't get your appendix taken out for the war effort, you were seen as a wuss."

Listening to the three defectors reminisce about this in a light-hearted manner was so strange, yet so telling. I picked up on the rationale behind these preemptive appendectomies performed by doctors or middle-aged women who learned how to take an appendix out without getting medical degrees. If war broke out between the two Koreas, and all the doctors and nurses had to treat North Korean soldiers, who would treat patients who had appendicitis? No one. It was therefore considered wise to have one's appendix taken out preemptively.

"So—why appendicitis? Also, were you even in pain before you got it out? Did you actually need the operation?" I asked incredulously. "There was nothing wrong with our appendixes when we got them taken out. It was just a trend that people

[said] was for the good of our nation. I don't know," Mr. Soo said. Mr. Soo and Kim Heung-Kwang are close friends. Mr. Soo is soft-spoken yet speaks rapidly. He wears round spectacles, often dresses in a light gray suit with a blue shirt, and has a modest demeanor. "I guess someone just started to say it, and it just became the thing to do. I got mine taken out in my early twenties. Of course there were no anesthetics."

"Of course not. Anesthetics for appendectomies? Oh, come on. No way." Mrs. Lee shook her head. Kim Heung-Kwang smiled when he saw my jaw drop. "Your friends did it, so you did it."

Eun-Ji, who is almost thirty years younger than the three defectors at the table, said, "A little appendectomy is no big deal. My appendix ruptured when I was thirteen. I was visiting my uncle in the countryside for a few days and I didn't feel too good. Realizing what it was, he called his friend whose nickname was the 'neighborhood surgeon' and [he] came over with his tools. At this point, I had downed a few pills because [of] the abdominal pain . . . [My] mind was blurry, and I overheard my uncle saying to his friend, 'You bastard, you should've at least sharpened your scalpels before coming here!' "

In the 2013 Intermedia Report "A Quiet Opening: North Koreans in a Changing Media Environment," the researchers wrote, "Consistent with expectations in any tightly controlled media environment, word-of-mouth sources—people sharing with those they trust—are the most common sources of information for the majority of North Koreans."[2] The conversation I had with North Korean defectors about preemptive appendectomies underscored Intermedia's point about the power of word-of-mouth sources, even over foreign media sources. Word of mouth was and still is the most trusted and widely used source of information for

North Koreans, regardless of whether the information is correct, safe, or sound.

Information is smuggled in via the black markets, along with South Korean beauty products, American chick flicks, English dictionaries, Hollywood movies, candy, European perfumes, calculators, flip phones, and DVD players, among many, many other items. Markets that initially formed to allow people to acquire basic necessities have been transformed into trading places for foreign media and general informational access to the world outside North Korea. Increasingly sophisticated black markets with richer variety of foreign media have, in turn, allowed for more illicit information to flow into North Korea, providing, for example, home addresses of long-lost family in China, and giving people an even grimmer understanding of their circumstances.

Not all information is intentionally subversive. Through informal foreign trade with Chinese traders along the border and increasingly more in inland areas, North Koreans are learning about economic conditions, commodity prices, and even the weather from Chinese traders. This awareness, in turn, has pushed North Koreans to become more critical thinkers and realize that their government has been presenting them with false "facts."

NEHEMIAH PARK: A DETERMINED ENTREPRENEUR

Nehemiah is a survivor. As a mutual South Korean friend once said about him, "If you drop Nehemiah on an island, or even on Mars, with no money, no contacts, and no food, he'll figure it out and thrive." Nehemiah is also an entrepreneur with an extraordinary range of "business" experience spanning both legal and illegal activities across North Korea and China. To protect his mother, who still lives in North Korea, Nehemiah calls himself various English names from the Bible. At about five feet, eight inches, he's muscular, with deep smile lines that frame his big eyes. With his Seoul speech, easygoing sense of humor, and strong build, he blends in well in South Korea, where people place extreme importance on conformity.

But Nehemiah's successful social and educational assimilation into his new country was not easy. His muscular build came from delivering big furniture, bussing tables at restaurants frequented by condescending young customers, and working odd jobs, including for massive construction projects, that were generally relegated to able-bodied men without much education in South Korea, and that paid him below minimum wage. He knows Seoul's streets, roads, and bridges so well—so much so that he often suggests alternative routes for cab drivers—because he used to haul furniture on his motorbike, zipping across the city, always late for his next delivery.

Nehemiah was born in 1981 in Musan, a northeastern city in North Korea. "Before I escaped, Musan's food supply had already ceased for five to seven years, so the markets quickly replaced them. The mountains were barren because people stripped the trees for personal energy use. We always heard bombs growing up. People would go to the mountains to farm the little they could, or sell things on the markets. This was the norm." The "bombs" Nehemiah refers to were actually explosions from the Musan mines.

Since the age of six, Nehemiah had crossed the border to visit a relative in China once every year or so, always bribing and promising the border guard that he'd be back. His father was also involved in private business, and Nehemiah had learned the value of becoming close with local police "and those types of people" by bribing them to get his way. Nehemiah bribed his way across numerous city and provincial checkpoints to visit Pyongyang three times. This is quite remarkable, given how far Musan is from Pyongyang. In addition, he traveled to Haeju, Sariwon, Chulsan, Sungchun, Yeongchun, and Gosan. Other defectors who come from nonpolitical families are astonished to learn that Nehemiah traveled to seven North Korean cities. Most ordinary citizens never leave their home town due to state restrictions.

Always curious, Nehemiah got his hands on copies of *The Count of Monte Cristo, Robinson Crusoe,* and *Pinocchio,* and dreamed of traveling the world and supporting his family by becoming a successful businessman. He remembers first having accessed foreign information at the age of fourteen. Similar to Kim Heung-Kwang, who found tapes in trash sent over from France and Germany, Nehemiah snuck out at night to scrounge through the bins of plastic waste. "I looked for anything useful, anything interesting. I picked out nude magazines, recording tapes, and plastic baskets with my friends. I saw nude magazines for the first time in my life. So shocking! The audiotapes, cassettes, and recording tapes were all broken, so I reconnected them with tape or glue, put them in audio players, and listened to rock music for the first time. Only having listened to calm North Korean music, [the] loud music scared me. I turned it off immediately and threw the tapes away because I [had an overwhelming] fear of being arrested. My family and my teachers always taught me that if I came into contact without permission [with materials that weren't] North Korea related, I would be arrested. This was common sense," he said.

The idea of serving and possibly dying in the military was despicable, so he dropped out of high school. It was possible to drop out of school during this period because the system of monitoring students was crumbling. No one came looking for him, so, thinking he was safe, he found work in the Musan markets.

During this time, there was one large market and one small market. The big market had about four hundred sellers with many more buyers walking through the rows of goods and services. He practically lived there because he was a seller in one of the stalls. "Out in the open, you would see food and drugs. Rice, vegetables, fruits, medicinal Chinese drugs, second-hand clothing from China, industrial products, electronics. Even ice cream. You name it, you'[d] find it on the North Korean market."

By virtue of being immersed in the markets, he heard and learned much about commerce, money, supply and demand, and the world outside his country. He said, "When you're doing business, hearing foreign information is easy. When I sold agricultural pine mushrooms, regular customers and business partners were all Chinese. I heard about how Chinese people live, and since the Chinese broadcasted South Korean television, I heard about South Korea as well."

None of the Chinese traders shared information with him out of goodwill or charity, but rather as part of handling business. Nehemiah's interest was always, "How do I make more money?" The questions he had while working and trading with Chinese people to sell goods in his market stall were always related to increasing profit. Big political questions about micro and macro economic matters didn't interest him. For example, he was intrigued by trends for and against certain goods. Did certain foods have seasonality? What kind of products did Chinese traders want from North Koreans? Information on currency exchange rates was always helpful, too, since U.S. dollars and Chinese renminbi were exchanged in addition to the North Korean currency.[3] The history, status, and future of capitalism and socialism outside North Korea were not of interest to him. He needed only that outside information which would improve his business and his cash flow.

Information about Chinese traders' demand for North Korean goods was always in high demand. "For example, if our Chinese counterparts needed gold, word would spread like wildfire. People's eyes became huge and antennae would become extra sensitive to find[ing] gold. Why? Because the Chinese would give us hard cash for it. If China want[ed] to buy pine tree flowers, all the pine trees on the mountains would disappear. If they wanted pine mushrooms, then all the North Korean pine mushrooms would disappear. If Chinese traders wanted North Korean antiques, especially those of arguable Chinese origin, then all the antiques would disappear. Anyone who heard what the Chinese wanted would go to heaven, hell, and then back to find those goods to earn cash."

Information about international aid coming into North Korea was especially sensitive because aid had a direct effect on food items in the market. If the U.N. or the World Food Programme provided food, the price of food products in the street markets would go down, so owners of food businesses had to quickly sell their perishable goods to make money. "They would find out this kind of information instantly. I don't know how. North Koreans are super smart."

PARK SANG-HAK AND FREEDOM BALLOONS

Park Sang-Hak, born in 1968, was assigned to a prestigious job in the government's propaganda office in Pyongyang after college, because of his social status. His father, a senior official in the Korean Workers' Party, had been responsible for smuggling computer technology from other countries into North Korea. Like all North Koreans, regardless of his standing, Park conducted self-judgment sessions, and went through the motions as a loyal citizen of the state and a member of the party. In 1999, Park's elderly father surprisingly decided the family should defect. Decades of serving his government and turning a blind eye to policies that he believed were morally reprehensible had finally compelled Park's father to shift loyalties, and he became just as committed to defecting from his country as he had been to serving it. Park Sang-Hak thought the idea was insane, and resisted, but his father insisted that the family could not contribute to the survival of such a heinous regime, much less live within it, any longer. Through a broker, Park's father sent a message to his family in Pyongyang to flee to China. After arriving in South Korea, Park and his family learned that Park's uncle had been beaten to death as retribution for the Park family's defection, and that his cousins had become beggars.

Park Sang-Hak renounced all former political allegiances and became a fervent activist for human rights in North Korea. He founded Fighters for a Free North Korea, and as part of his organization's work based out of Seoul, he sends twelve-foot-high helium-and-nitrogen-filled balloons that carry pro-democracy and human rights literature; transistor radios; USB flash drives loaded with movies, literature, and other foreign content; as well as about 200,000 thin, waterproof plastic films that have freedom messages printed on one side, and images of the Dear Leaders on the other. A small portion of these leaflets have U.S. dollar bills stapled to them. Some of these balloons even contain packaged sweets. The balloons float north and eventually land somewhere in North Korea.

The dollar bill is a simple yet effective incentive for civilians to look for these leaflets fluttering down on them from the sky. Park told me he has heard rumors of husbands telling their wives to go out and look for these subversive leaflets because there is money attached to them, money that could help them buy foodstuffs from the black markets. The images of the Kim dynasty protect the North Koreans who pick up the literature, because a bigger crime than picking up a freedom message off of the floor is to cover, fold, wrinkle, or—God forbid—throw away an image of any of the country's leaders, past or present. So even if a North Korean is caught with this little leaflet, both the civilian and the police are caught in a catch-22.

To date, Park claims to have sent approximately two million freedom messages into North Korea. It is obviously impossible to track how many of North Korea's 25 million inhabitants have read these messages, but many defectors have shared that they have seen or heard of them. These messages so infuriate the North Korean government that they have threatened to bomb South Korea for every balloon that enters their territory. But interstate bomb threats and personal threats such as Pyongyang's promise to "physically eliminate the kind of human scum that commits such treason" have not stopped Park.[4] In 2011, North Korea took another step: it sent a spy into South Korea to assassinate "Enemy Zero" with a poison needle. Although the South Korean intelligence service caught the assassin just in time, Park's life is always at risk. He remains among North Korea's top ten targets for defector assassination, and as of October 2014, soldiers at the DMZ were still exchanging gunfire over leaflets being flown in from South Korea. Aware of the extreme political sensitivities around his form of information campaigning, Park continues to launch the balloons because he believes that the truth of the political reality in North Korea will, over time, erode the commitment of the regime's believers.

South Korean nongovernmental organizations (NGOs) are not reinventing the wheel when flying balloons with leaflets into North Korea. During the Korean War, the United States, coordinating with South Korea, dropped leaflets that encouraged Chinese soldiers to stop fighting and urged North Korean soldiers to defect. After active hostilities had ended, the South Korean government continued for decades to send via air massive amounts of freedom messages along with goods including toothbrushes and pens. The North Koreans retaliated in kind, sending aloft balloons filled with their own propaganda to reach the South Koreans.

In the 1960s and 1970s, South Korean children living close to the DMZ would go *"bbira* hunting,"* competing with each other, even during the frigid winter months, over who could collect the highest number of leaflets sent by the North Koreans. Children would then race to local police stations to hand in the leaflets they found; the police would collect the leaflets, pat them on the heads, and reward them with pretty pencils, which were scarce back then. The fanciest pencils had colorful designs on them and pink erasers affixed to the ends. *Bbira* is Korean slang for a propaganda leaflet. Though the origins of this term are disputed, one guess is that *bbira* is from the English word "bill" (short for "handbill"). During World War II, American military personnel handed out propaganda handbills to Japanese civilians, who called them *hira*, or "piece." Perhaps the combination of "bill" and *hira* led to *bbira*.

LISTENING IN: THE IMPORTANCE OF RADIOS

North Korea's regime employs elaborate systems to jam radio waves streaming in, and criminalizes individuals who are caught listening. Yet defectors have shared that they and their friends would clandestinely listen to foreign radio programs that were able to circumvent the country's jamming systems. Examples of radio programs that broadcast into North Korea include Voice of America, Radio Free Asia, Radio Free Chosun, North Korea Reform Radio, and Free North Korea Radio (FNKR).

Voice of America is a radio news service, funded by the U.S. government, that was started in 1942 in order to target listeners in both war-torn countries and closed societies. Guided by the VOA Charter, signed in 1976 by President Gerald Ford, it has evolved into a multimedia news broadcasting service that addresses the international community at large. Also based in Washington, D.C., is Radio Free Asia, a private nonprofit corporation whose mission is to "provide accurate and timely news and information to Asian countries whose governments prohibit access to a free press."

North Korea Reform Radio, directed by Kim Seung-Chul, a former North Korean civil engineer, broadcasts daily into North Korea in order to "encourage the development of independent public opinion inside the country." Radio Free Chosun and Open Radio for North Korea—both shortwave radio stations targeting North Korea—recently joined forces along with Daily NK and OTV to create a consortium called Unification Media Group. And Voice of Freedom, which is run by the South Korean military, is a radio program that plays on FM radio in Seoul and on shortwave radio, which can reach North Korean listeners.

Finding a radio is its own problem. People who live near China can buy Chinese radios. Others can contact local "underground radio makers" who will manually construct simple radios from wood and disparate components from disassembled Chinese electronics. But there are difficulties with handmade radios. First, without the digitally projected numbers or any visual aid on the radio, it's hard to tune it to catch outside frequencies—defectors say that delicate hand and wrist skills are necessary to use these handmade radios successfully. A second difficulty pertains to

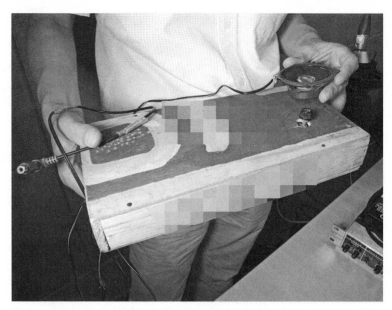

A homemade radio by a North Korean defector that was used inside North Korea. The radio was smuggled out by defectors; this photo was taken in Seoul.
Illustrations copyright © 2016 by Jae Hyeok Ahn

Inside of a North Korean homemade radio
Illustrations copyright © 2016 by Jae Hyeok Ahn

extending the internal radio antenna to catch a strong signal. Since many of these have short internal antennas, North Koreans are required to wire the antenna to an external signal amplifier, which, once connected, can catch signals coming from all across Asia. The third challenge with using homemade radios in North Korea has to do with the low volume. But defectors certainly manage, and listen quietly in their homes, usually between 11:00 p.m. and 1:00 a.m.

DR. PARK SE-JOON'S AWAKENING

Once a North Korean–trained dentist, Park Se-Joon shared with me a Korean allegorical tale about a frog in a well. Throughout the frog's life, it looks up at a round sky. But one day, the frog leaves the well, and realizes that the sky isn't round—it's wide and limitless. He told me this story to describe how, like that frog, he had lived with physical and mental constraints enforced by the government—that is, until he learned the truth about North Korea, and like the freed frog, now saw the world as being expansive and hopeful, like a boundless blue sky.

At home, Park Se-Joon's family owned a Sanyo tape recorder for listening to North Korean music.[5] Park knew that he could listen to media more freely if he wanted to, since his father was a senior officer in the secret services and his home wasn't subject to frequent inspections. After witnessing the poor *kotjebis* and thinking it through, he locked his bedroom door, went under his bedcovers, plugged in headphones, held the earphones up to only one ear so that he could keep the other ear free to listen in case his parents called for him, and entered a whole new world. South Korea's and China's miraculous economic growth and the domestic events occurring in the United States were "all going straight into the brain."

He learned that ordinary people in South Korea had cars. He became aware of the concept of traffic, which otherwise, based on what he saw in North Korea, seemed improbable. And "air conditioning" seemed too good to be true. Protests, he learned, were a legal way to air grievances in other places. People were able to travel abroad without permission from the government. Was it all false propaganda? He couldn't discuss this material with anyone, because that would immediately reveal that he was accessing foreign information. When he heard the same things from different radio programs, he started to trust what he was hearing more and more, although he yearned to verify it.

Like many other secret listeners of foreign radio programs, Park did not set out with any personal political agenda. He listened in order to learn more about his own country, and about the outside world. What exactly was going on in North Korea? He hadn't realized that so many people were dying during the Arduous March.

"I listened to KBS the most, then MBC. The news, the talk shows, music were all interesting. The current affairs were always fun to listen to. The radio is addict[ive]. This is how it works. Let's say you listen to it for the first time and you hear something really shocking. For example, South Koreans only need a passport to travel abroad, and almost anyone can get one. You can go anywhere you want, and work anywhere you want, in South Korea. I kept asking myself whether this could be true, [and] I became more curious to listen to more. Very, very curious. You listen to more sources, more programs, and start trusting [them]. It's like watching a really good TV show in South Korea. In the first episode you're introduced to the characters and you start guessing the plot, but you have to watch the second, third, fourth episode to learn more. You're so curious about the ending, and you stay up all night watching, even if you know there are consequences like being tired in school or at work."

KIM SEONG-MIN: UNRAVELING OF A MILITARY PROPAGANDA WRITER

As the youngest of six and the only son of a professor at Kim Il-Sung University (the "Harvard" of North Korea, according to North Korean defectors), Kim Seong-Min was born in what he describes as the "boonies" of Jagang Province.[6] At the age of two, he followed his family back to Pyongyang, where he attended the People's elementary school and junior high school with other children of elites in the nation's capital. At age seventeen, he joined the People's Army. During his ten years of service, his superiors noticed his talent for writing and ordered him to be a writer for the military. To meet the requirements for his position, he had to receive an additional three years of education at Kim Hyoung-Jik University. Afterward, he was commissioned as an artistic propaganda writer in an artillery unit.

Eventually, Kim was promoted to colonel in the People's Army. "There are a lot of colonels in the North Korean army. I mean, the army is twice the size of the South Korean army, so in essence, it's not such a high position. It's not an elite position. You hear some defectors who call themselves part of the former North Korean elite. That's bull——." He stopped himself, and slowly smiled. He pointed to the audio recorder that was recording this particular conversation between him and me. "I forgot this was being recorded . . . But you know what I mean." Taking a puff from his cigarette, he looked out at what I guess is a window, and said as he exhaled smoke, "we were all slaves to the regime. My happiness was being loyal to the Party. I truly, truly believed in the regime."

All of the windows in his office in Seoul were covered in black curtains. Several armed police officers assigned by the South Korean government served as his twenty-four-hour personal security detail. Most of the high-profile defectors who have had attempts on their lives by North Korean assassins have armed security details assigned to them. North Korea's defector assassination target list, published from time to time, is not a bluff; spies are commissioned and sent into South Korea to take the targets out. Such spies usually are further compelled by collateral held by the North Korean government, usually children or other family members who are released if the spies' mission is successful.

Information warfare is not a new phenomenon. During the Korean War, the U.S. government engaged in extensive psychological operations against North Korea with the goal of convincing North Korean soldiers to defect to South Korea. After the war ended in a stalemate, South Korea resumed the use of psychological warfare, often in the form of loudspeakers at the border, and, as described earlier, the dropping of airborne leaflets—in this case targeting military populations in the North.

Kim Seong-Min's unit was among the many military units tasked with collecting and disposing of these leaflets before civilians could see them. During one particular stretch, he "pitched tents to prepare for the drills. Every morning, the leaflets from South Korea would rain down from the sky, [and] we all had to collect [them] by spiking them [with] a long thin metal rod. Only after we finished collecting every leaflet in sight would the officers allow us to eat our meals. We were forbidden to look at the content of the leaflets. Since the other privates [were] close to [me], picking up all these damn leaflets and monitoring each other, I couldn't read them too easily."

"Were you curious?" I asked.

"Of course I was! I was eighteen years old. The first leaflet that I was able to sneak into my pocket was a photo of a former North Korean People's Army sergeant with an absolutely stunning South Korean woman. They looked like young lovers. They were leaning against an elephant and looked so elegant. I thought to myself, "wow, a former North Korean sergeant . . . this guy. Is South Korea a place where such beautiful women live?"

"Mr. Kim, *that's* the first thought you had?"

"Of course! These thoughts naturally flooded my eighteen-year-old mind at the time. Just from a single photo. The other side of the leaflet was a calendar. Not too interesting. I ended up carrying that leaflet around in my pocket for a while. The young South Korean woman was so beautiful. I ended up throwing it away."

The second leaflet he remembers looking at was one depicting Kim Il-Sung and Kim Jong-Un carrying a gourd with rice. "I remember getting furious, thinking, 'These South Korean bastards. Even if it's propaganda, how dare they defame our leaders like this? I got so hot in the head, I was so angry." A different leaflet had a group photo of Kim Jong-Il as a small child, and stated that his birthplace was Khabarovsk in the former Soviet Union, and not Paektu Mountain, as North Korea states it is.

Another leaflet he recalls had a picture of a multitude of South Koreans with bright yellow umbrellas in Yeouido Square, Seoul's main business district, where the National Assembly Building is located. The picture was taken on the Buddha's birthday. "That hue of yellow was so bright! In North Korea, a raincoat or poncho is so valuable. But everyone in that photo had a bright yellow umbrella. That picture was particularly memorable."

Propaganda leaflets were only part of what the South Korean government packed into the balloons sent over into North Korean territory. Snacks, pens, lighters, and even small radios fell out of these balloons. "My soldiers under my command would turn in any radios they found, because radios could quickly become a political issue. The other stuff—pens, lighters, etc., we just erased the markings like brand names, and used them." Given his high rank in the communications unit, he was subject to less scrutiny than those below him. As an officer, he used a separate room in a separate building designated for his writing. He would go into this room and listen frequently to South Korean radio broadcast programs, using the radios that rained down from the sky.

"What radio programming did you like?"

"I liked everything, but especially those about literature. There was a broadcast announcer named Kang In-Deok who used to speak about graft and corruption in the Worker's Party. His opening commentary was: 'Hello dear members of the Party, this is Kang In-Deok.' His voice came out so clearly. Also, defectors would come speak about their programs. I listened to a lot of religious broadcasting as well. Not just Christian stuff. Other religions, too. And news segments all the time. Basically, all the programming was great. As a writer for the North Korean military, the literature-related programming was particularly interesting to me. The broadcasts about corruption slowly helped peel my eyes open to the reality I was living in."

Kim Seong-Min mentioned something many other defectors had shared as well. "The voices of the defectors were the ones I paid special attention to. The other voices (the South Korean native speakers) were a little suspicious. I didn't know them. Defectors, though, they're born in my country. We could know and sense in our hearts whether they were lying, or mumbling their way through broadcasts, or if they were telling the truth. I could tell that these defectors were speaking the truth from their hearts. It was so natural. I could feel it. A *huge* take-away from listening to these radio broadcasts was learning that defectors are not killed. In North Korea, we are told that North Koreans who defect to South Korea are killed, but [by] listening to defectors over these secret radio programs, I realized South Koreans do not kill them. And they're doing well enough to speak on radio programs."

As an officer, he listened to the radio and heard Frank Sinatra's *My Way,* a song he still cherishes to this day. "So elegant," he reminisces. He first learned of *My Way* when he was in college. A male classmate who played the acoustic guitar really well played *Secret,* and *My Way.* "I remember once saying to him, wow, how do you know how to play these songs so well? Where are these songs from?' The classmate replied, 'These songs are hit songs played by Joseonjok [ethnic Koreans in China] in China.'"

But of course, Kim Seong-Min didn't spend all his time in the military secretly listening to radio broadcasts in a private, isolated room. While he was still in the service, he would be visited from time to time by a fellow soldier with relatives in China. The legality of the soldier's visits is unclear. He'd sneak in a magazine or two along with rice cakes "wrapped in paper of a quality I had never seen in North Korea. In North Korea, you can't find this quality of paper. We'd be sent to find paper like this to write special letters on the birthdays of Kim Il-Sung and Kim Jong-Il. I know it seems like a very minute detail, but this made a really big impression on me. The paper that the rice cakes were wrapped in was very special, very beautiful. I thanked my colleague for the rice cakes, sent him away pretending to be busy eating the gifted rice cakes. Once I knew he was gone, I unfolded the papers that the cakes were wrapped in."

Kim Seong-Min did not realize that this moment sparked the unraveling of his security in North Korea. The papers were the last six pages of *Chosun Monthly* magazine, and they happened to have information about helping families find each other. Millions of Korean families had been separated during the Korean War, and remained so after the DMZ was established. North Koreans were unable to leave their country, so family reunions were a very common aspiration. Given the huge demand for information to connect families, countless businesses—many of them shady or outright illegitimate—promised to connect families or at least find information about long-lost family members for huge fees.

Kim Seong-Min's mother had passed away when he was fourteen years old; his father had died only two years later. All five of his older sisters had married by the time he joined the army, so he didn't have anyone to see him off. He remembered his father always telling him to find his uncles because otherwise he would never meet his cousins. His father's words came back to him when he saw the pages of *Chosun Monthly*. Kim Seong-Min wrote the magazine a letter stating that he had two uncles in South Korea, and gave their names, as well as the information that one was probably a Christian pastor. He sealed the letter, gave it to the colleague with relatives in China, and asked him to deliver it to his relatives so they could mail the letter to South Korea and bring back any reply if it came.

Nonchalantly, he told me: "It was nothing, really, just a simple request to help find my uncle."

The *Chosun Monthly* actually wrote back, stating that it knew men with the same names who also had relatives in the North, but they were not the same people for whom he was looking. Disheartened, Kim Seong-Min thought that he and his late father had incorrect information about his uncles. Or perhaps the men just didn't want to be in touch with their relatives in the

Communist North and actually *were* his uncles. Maybe they were just lying. So Kim Seong-Min wrote another letter to *Chosun Monthly,* this time with much more detailed information, listing his late grandmother's name and other relatives' names and occupations. Maybe if these men who simply "happened to have the same names" were reminded of the mutual relatives they had, they would be willing to help. The magazine wrote back with a similar response, that the men they knew were not his uncles. Racking his brain, Kim Seong-Min wrote a third letter, this time asking the magazine to help him find his uncles. The magazine staff replied that they would help.

What Kim Seong-Min didn't know was that his letters were also going through the North Korean Security Ministry. In North Korea at that time, Seong-Min explained to me, "90% of letter envelopes were made by the person mailing the letter. What you would do is take a piece of paper, fold it into an envelope, and use cooked rice to create a seal. What I later found out was that the Security Ministry would hold these envelopes over a steam pot, which would loosen the hardened rice, and the envelopes would pop right open. They would read the letters, reseal them, and have them delivered to me, without issue. I only found out about all this much later, by talking to someone who was part of that unit."

"During this time, the soldiers paved the roads in North Korea. So I would sing songs and cheer up my soldiers as they did this backbreaking work. One day, while I was out trying to [lift] my soldiers' mood, I received a notice saying that my unit wanted me back immediately. I knew right away that they wanted to arrest me."

In October 1995, he escaped to China. A Korean-American pastor named Kim Dong-Shik introduced him to a broker in

China, who was subsequently arrested by the Chinese security forces, resulting in Kim Seong-Min's capture in Darien, China, and repatriation to North Korea.[7] He was extradited to Pyongyang for a series of investigations to "accurately" determine the reason for his crossing. Did hunger or politics inspire his escape? In 1995, many border residents crossed into China due to hunger, and although they were brutally punished, many were released because the authorities deemed that hunger was the main factor and that they planned to return to North Korea (as many did of their own volition, to return to their families). In the case of a high-ranking officer from Pyongyang, however, such relative leniency surely would not be granted, because being in China obviously meant that permanent defection was the intent. The train ride from the detention facility where Kim Seong-Min was held in Onsong (the northern tip of North Hamgyong Province) to Pyongyang took several days back then. Just to provide a sense of distance, according to Google Maps the drive between these two cities should take about 10.5 to 12 hours, depending on the route taken.

Before telling me the specifics of his dramatic escape, Kim Seong-Min pulled out a cigarette and said, "I'm sorry, but I gotta smoke one when I talk about this. You mind?"

He then proceeded to share the story with me. "Given my background, my job, rank, and occupation, my punishment would be execution. I didn't even know that. I found out much later that I was to be executed by firing squad. All the soldiers were supposed to gather and watch the execution. Not knowing any of this, I sat on the train, tied up in transit. There was no escape. There were two armed soldiers sitting in front of me, with their rifles. Another armed soldier next to me. I couldn't fight my way out. By the second day, I sensed the guards were getting tired. Before reaching Pyongyang, we had to pass through a place called Shin Sung Chun. It was the third night, and I remember all these girls got on the train. I could tell they were office girls commuting to and from work. For three days straight, I [had] thought about and planned my escape. Look at my hands—they're a bit small, right?"

"[Before starting my journey by train, I had been] caught in Darien, China, and was there for about forty days. Usually, people are processed quicker before being dragged back to North Korea, but there was no interpreter. [I] spent another nine days at a detention facility in Tumen and throughout these few weeks, I caught some disease where lice sucked the blood from every crevice of my body. My small-ish hands were all puffy from the lice, so they forced the shackle cuffs over my cotton winter prison clothes around my wrists. It's hard to explain, but these shackles were like a saw, and the officers locked the shackles on the last tooth of the saw. If you moved, or tried to pull them apart, the shackles would close up and get tighter, preventing you [from] attempt[ing] to pull them apart or squeez[ing] your way out . . . For three days on that train, surrounded by these guys with rifles, I made sure not to move, and maintained the shackles in the same position as when I was first tied up.

"Trains don't have light due to electricity shortages, so at night, the trains are pitch black. Another thing to note is, no one cleaned that train, so you could only imagine how absolutely disgusting the bathroom was, especially the floors, after three days. I asked to go to the bathroom, and noticed that no one followed me into the bathroom. North Korean train window frames, at least back then, were made of wood instead of steel like South Korean or Chinese trains. Knowing that this was my only chance, I broke the window, jumped out of the speeding train, and kept moving forward. I hid in the mountains and made my way back to China, where I hid for three years. I arrived in South Korea in 1999 through an uncle and a fake passport. I went through about ten months of investigations by South Korean intelligence because of my complicated background and occupation."

After the intelligence agency of his new country had finished its extensive and grueling investigations, Kim Seong-Min was released into a free, capitalistic society, where he attended Yonsei University and received a master's degree. Simultaneously, he worked for the Korean Broadcasting Station (KBS) as a radio-show writer, after which a man named Hwang Jang-Yop reached out to invite him to join an association for North Korean defectors in South Korea. He is now pursuing a doctorate at Myongji University in South Korea.

"This man I didn't know was reaching out, telling me to go here and there, and giving me these orders. I had no idea who he was. He then wrote me a few letters to convince me to join his organization, saying that he knew my father." It turns out that Hwang Jang-Yop is the man largely credited for crafting North Korea's official ideology of juche, and is the highest-ranking North Korean defector to date. Hwang was so close to the ruling family that he tutored Kim Jong-Il when he was young. He also served three terms as chair of the Supreme People's Assembly and eventually rose to chief secretary of the Central Committee. For years, he watched the ideology that he had established degenerate into a tool used to maintain a cult of personality, at the cost of citizens.

While in Beijing on his way back from Tokyo, Hwang Jang-Yop and Kim Deok-Hong (a former head of a North Korean trading firm in China) left the North Korean Embassy compound after telling their colleagues they were going shopping. Rather than going to the mall, they walked into the South Korean embassy in Beijing and sought asylum. North Korea initially accused South Korea of abducting Hwang Jang-Yop in Beijing, shocked by the sudden defection of such a high-ranking official. In a huge blow to Pyongyang, Hwang Jang-Yop wrote a public letter to prove that he had defected voluntarily—a letter that included the line "At a time when workers and farmers are starving, how could we consider people sane who loudly say they have built an ideal society for them?"

After his defection, Hwang Jang-Yop lived in an undisclosed location in South Korea under police protection. For the thirteen years he lived in South Korea, he said and wrote extensive, cutting criticisms about his former government. To no one's surprise, the North Korean government called him a traitor and "human scum." They also repeatedly threatened him publicly with statements such as "You must not forget that traitors have always been slaughtered by knives," and warned that he would "not be safe anywhere." Hwang Jang-Yop countered by telling the Japanese newspaper *Asahi Shimbun*, "They call me a traitor, but the real traitor is Kim Jong-Il who let his people starve and die."

Hwang Jang-Yop received several death threats, and was under constant threat of assassination. In 2004, a package containing a portrait of Hwang, with red paint splashed on it and a butcher knife piercing the forehead, was delivered to the North Korean Defectors Association, the organization for which he was an honorary chairman. An example of a failed attempt included two North Korean agents who posed as defectors and were on a mission to assassinate Hwang by "slitting the betrayer's throat . . . because he was a thorn in the eye of the North." The two agents, both army majors who were attached to North Korea's General Bureau of Surveillance, were caught by South Korean security officials only months before Hwang Jang-Yop's natural death on October 10, 2010. Upon their capture they said that they had been prepared to commit suicide after they had accomplished their mission of killing Hwang.

It was this Hwang Jang-Yop who asked Kim Seong-Min to join his organization. Kim Seong-Min first worked as the secretary general for Hwang's North Korean defectors association and then as director, for a total of four years, before moving on to start his own radio broadcast, which was the first by a North Korean defector to be broadcast into North Korea. One of several impetuses for starting Free North Korea Radio was the use of honorific monikers for Kim Jong-Il in KBS's broadcasts into North Korea; Kim Seong-Min thought that this was "not the way radio stations should be referring to Kim Jong-Il if they were trying to subvert the listeners." This was around the time that South Korea's loudspeaker broadcasts at the border targeting North Korean listeners were stopped. As Kim Seong-Min put it, "We realized it would be, and should be, up to us North Korean defectors to start broadcasts into North Korea."

Kim Seong-Min began his station with internet broadcasting, but just a year and a half later turned to shortwave broadcasting. "There wasn't much to it; just produce and record the radio broadcasts, give them to private companies that operate the shortwave antennas . . . and after twelve years of this work, here we are."

When I asked him how he selects, creates, and curates content to broadcast, he answered,

> This [may] sound very arrogant, but I listened to the broadcasts while in North Korea, and I was a writer for the military. I don't think there is anyone else with my background. So for

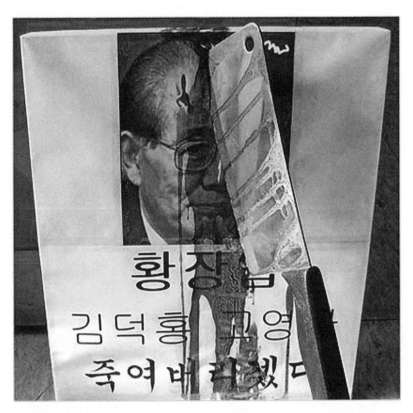

This was inside the death threat package sent to the North Korean Defectors Association by the North Korean government. The portrait is of Hwang Jang-Yop, the highest ranking North Korean to have defected from North Korea.

all the programming from the beginning to end, I wrote everything. Now that I've done this for twelve years, I have a lot of materials that I can use for the shows. Since I listen to radio so much, I know what is needed, what the people in North Korea would like to listen to. In the past, defector leaders met up every three months to discuss the content of radio programming. We don't meet up much nowadays, but back then, we talked about specific musical genres that might be popular up there, and other good material. But what we thought was particularly important was programming that talked about the corruption of the Kim regime. This was important to broadcast.

Free North Korea Radio ran into serious accusations and problems, including those caused by a former colleague who allegedly ran up false charges under Kim Seong-Min's name and so got the station into trouble with the U.S. State Department, which provided large portions of its funding. Another point of contention was certain programming they ran.[8]

Hwang explained:

Two years ago, before the UN opened an office in Seoul, we produced a program titled *We Warn the Dictatorship* where we featured defectors speak[ing] about their experiences and anger about mistreatment in North Korea. For example, we had a defector who was beaten by the *Bowibu* [North Korea's internal intelligence unit] and spoke about his experience on the program.[9] Another defector spoke of her time in a labor reform prison camp and how she lived like an animal. She said on the program: "The reason why I defected to South Korea and am living here is so that I can work hard, save money, buy a gun, and shoot the perpetrators, the prison officials who treated me like an animal." There was clearly a lot of pent-up anger and rage among some defectors. The State Department heard this content and labeled it terrorist programming, saying that it was worse than Al Qaeda's broadcasts, and that they had to stop such extreme language on the radio program. Otherwise, they'd cut funding. So we stopped this particular program. But we received six calls from North Korea, demanding to know why the segment stopped. We played and stopped other programming, without receiving any complaints from our listeners. But our North Korean listeners really were interested in defectors' experiences while in the North.

Another segment that FNKR ran back in the day when they had more funding—and so could afford to broadcast five hours a day—helped listeners search for family members and relatives. The year before, a defector had come to Kim's office to ask if he could say a few special words and phrases over the air. The defector explained that he had promised his family in North Korea that after he had left, he would get on the program that they listened to and say these special phrases to signal to them that he had arrived safely. Kim agreed to let him read his special letter on the program for a month to ensure that his family could have a chance to tune in and hear their signal phrases.

A more inclusive segment encourages supporters' engagement through the program *Letters from America*. Anyone can e-mail in a letter expressing his or her hopes and dreams for the North Korean people, which is a powerful way to change the image that North Korean people have of Americans or foreigners in general. These letters are read, translated, and broadcast into North Korea.

Weather forecasts are also popular segments broadcast by FNKR and some other radio stations. According to the South Korean intelligence service that interviews every defector who arrives in South Korea, defectors—especially those who worked on fishing boats, or were involved in market activities—mention that they enjoy listening to weather reports. Accurate weather forecasts helped people improve their daily lives.

Kim Seong-Min proved to set a strong example for other de-fectors who set up their own radio stations. There is a small yet growing number of defector-led radio programs that broadcast into North Korea, and Kim Seong-Min says that each station plays its own role. "Our role at FNKR is to directly target soldiers in North Korea with our content. Since I was a former officer and we also share office space with the North Korea People's Liberation Front's members, who were all former soldiers in the north, it only makes sense to do so.[10] They have a program called *People's Army,*

Kim Seong-Min showing me letters that he has received from North Koreans who listen to his program. Some sent him letters while they were in China; others contacted him after they had arrived in South Korea.

Twenty-Four Hours, which is a program directed at soldiers broadcast by defectors who were former soldiers, asking questions such as 'your youth that you are sacrificing and dedicating—Who is their service for?' There isn't a special method here—just former soldiers from North Korea, talking to the soldiers in North Korea. We tell them at the end of every program: 'Today's your last chance—take your rifle, leave your post, and run away from North Korea.' That is what we deliver in our message to soldiers. Of course we get criticism for this tactic and message. But I know we're sending in information that is pertinent and relevant to soldiers."

He wonders if a lot of his FNKR listeners are officers like he once was. People in the North can't express what is on their mind. "I know this. I was an officer too. Any free time they had, I'm sure they [were] listening to these types of broadcasts at home. All officers have radios. Internally, this type of fact would not be revealed. But I think that these officers are listening to outside radio programs in secret and with great interest."

Kim Seong-Min recognizes that the demand for video content, not so much radio, is rising, particularly among young people. When he visited the Dandong region in China most recently, he saw that Joseonjok businesspeople were selling TVs to North Koreans. Not just any TVs, but small HD TVs with solar power. The ones he saw sold for about $150. He explained: "$150 is a lot of money. Obviously, the North Koreans buying these were those involved in business and trade at the border. These businessmen became rich by selling these small TVs just to North Koreans. Selling solar power units with TVs to people who don't have access to uninterrupted electricity is one hell of a clever idea."

But he chooses to pick his battles, and will press on with radio for the foreseeable future. At a policy conference in Washington, D.C., he showed attendees a shortwave radio that had been sent in through various organizations' efforts. Such a radio cost $4.40 to purchase in South Korea. If such radios were purchased whole-sale in China, the unit price would be $1.32. Kim Seong-Min then showed a hand crank radio, of which he sent 10,000 into North Korea with the help of an American missionary group. Such radios were rechargeable by winding a handle attached to them to recharge their batteries; no external batteries or electric-ity were needed. He asked a rhetorical question, "What if we sent in five million of these [hand crank] radios? The minds of the North Korean population [would] flip."

Lastly, he showed a Chinese smartphone filled with photos and videos, which his contacts had smuggled out of North Korea. He held the phone next to my ear so I wouldn't miss a note. One video in particular was a home video of a small family singing. The youngest child's voice was the strongest, piercing through the adults' singing voices. Listening to the bright singing voices with clear North Korean accents, playing on a Chinese smart-phone, emphasized the fact that North Korean people are so close to us—geographically, and technologically in some cases. Yet they remain a universe away.

CHOI JUNG-HOON'S VISION: "DEMOCRACY WITHOUT WAR"

After hiding in China for nine months, Choi Jung-Hoon, along with his wife and son, safely made their way to South Korea with the help of good Samaritans. Over the next two years, he managed to arrange for his parents and two brothers to escape to South Korea, while one brother remained in North Korea.

Choi Jung-Hoon questioned why he had been so blindly loyal to a government that not only lied to him throughout his life, but also wanted to execute him and his family for helping an

Examples of radios used inside North Korea
Kim Seong-Min, director of Free North Korea Radio

old abductee reunite with his long-lost wife. After mulling over his past life in North Korea, Choi Jung-Hoon decided to help his fellow countrymen come to the same realization that he had. Outside information was North Korea's Achilles' heel, so he started a broadcasting service. The North Korean government learned of this and arrested Choi Jung-Hoon's youngest brother, his only remaining sibling inside North Korea. On December 31, 2011, the authorities publicly executed the youngest Choi brother by firing squad.

"You see," said Choi Jung-Hoon, his face wrinkled with pain, anger, heartbreak, and guilt, "that brother was eleven years younger than I am. He feared me more than he did my father because I was so strict with him. I cared for him as dearly as I did for my child. I wanted him to grow up properly, with sufficient discipline towards the state, so I was extremely tough with him. When I lost him, I felt like I was losing a part of myself. That young man did nothing wrong[; it was] just that his older brother got involved with projects that the North Korean regime despised."

He continued:

Executing someone on December 31 is sheer evil. Everyone looks forward to New Year's Day, even prisoners, because people will eat a tad better that day, even if [they]'re eating someone else's scraps. I'm sure that my little brother had no idea that he was going to be killed, much less killed on the day where everyone has a little temporary reprieve from their suffering. But to kill him before that!

There's a cultural tradition in North Korea. If a younger sibling dies before an older one, there is no funeral service because the younger person did not fulfill his filial duty towards the older person. So we didn't have a service for him. But he appeared in my dreams sometime in 2013. He told me that it was too cold. When someone is executed, that prisoner doesn't wear anything warm, just the bottom thin layer. December is when it's absolutely the damn coldest in North Korea. So we had a memorial service for him on his birthday. We said we're truly sorry. We pleaded for him to wait for us in a warm place, and [promised] that we [would] come for him soon.

What tortures my soul is that my brother didn't know why he was executed. As he waits for all of us in Heaven, I wonder how much he'll resent me!

Driven by rage, and deep guilt, Choi Jung-Hoon continues this radio service. Having lived in North Korea for thirty-seven years, he knew that he had to change minds by sending in outside information. "Food aid is not important because it doesn't get to people. Unless you go and deliver the rice in person, cook [it], feed [North Koreans] with your own hand, and then watch [them] swallow the food, you have no guarantees that it goes to [them]. 'Help[ing] poor North Koreans' is ultimately helping and perpetuating Kim's regime. During the famine, even the soldiers ate gruel. When South Korea sent in rice during their Sunshine policy era, the government erased all the U.N. logos and numbers and handed out some of it as though it was their own provision. And even that didn't go to most people."

"We must let people know about the outside world. The strategy here is information. This is how we get democracy without war. People risking their lives for the Kim regime are doing so because they don't know any better. Outside information is key. It's not an immediate magic bullet, but it's a crucial step because it sparks the process of distrusting the government and that distrust becomes resentment, which can evolve into practical action and changes in one's behavior."

He's now the broadcasting director of Free North Korea Radio, the station that Kim Seong-Min founded and directs. Additionally, Choi is the commander of the North Korean People's Liberation Front (NKPLF), an organization of former North Korean soldiers and military officials that works to send information into North Korea to ultimately bring down the North Korean regime. At public events, NKPLF members dress in their organization's uniforms, [which] look similar to those uniforms that North Korean Special Forces wear. Paired with sunglasses to hide their faces, NKPLF members add a sense of militancy to events that they attend and support. Details of their work will not be revealed here in order not to compromise their sensitive work, but it's reasonable to state that members try their best to apply pressure on the regime's weak points.

For Choi Jung-Hoon, his work means more than simply introducing freedom to his former countrymen. It's about seeking redemption for his defection.

UNIFICATION MEDIA GROUP AND LEE KWANG-BAEK

North Korean propaganda into South Korea was so effective during the 1980s that the regime was able to cultivate a pro–North Korean Marxist revolutionary movement among college students in parts of South Korea. Lee Kwang-Baek is an example of someone who fervently believed in North Korea's ideology and participated in various programs striving to push South Korean society to adopt North Korean–style socialism. While studying law at Wonkwang University in South Korea, this South Korean native "worked hard for the socialist movement to thrive in South Korea. [He] believed a socialist society like North Korea where everyone was equal, a society run by workers and farmers, was superior than what we had in the South."

It's hard to believe that this eloquent, genteel man with a modest stature and an easy smile was a die-hard activist committed to a socialist revolution in South Korea. During a recent conversation I had with him, he had a small notepad to jot down any long questions I had for him.

"I was in what we called an R.O. back then. A revolutionary organization. There were a lot of R.O.s in South Korea back then. I was also in a secret R.O. as the education team leader. The education team's job was to gather books and movies, and listen to North Korean radio broadcasts, and distribute this content to fellow students. When we acquired a copy of a North Korean book about their political system or aspiration, we made tons of copies of it and distributed them to different colleges. We transcribed North Korean radio programs, published them in books, and distributed them as education[al] materials. I listened to radio broadcasts intended for South Koreans on a radio this big . . ." He gestured with his arms and hands to show me that the radio was about one foot by one foot.

One of the programs he listened to, called *The Voice of National Salvation*, involved North Koreans who pretended to be South Koreans and said on the radio: "Dear listeners, how are you? We are secretly broadcasting from the Seoul, the capital city of South Korea. We are underground socialists in South Korea striving to achieve socialism in this country." This covert operation by the North Korean government aimed to cultivate a socialist movement in South Korea by strengthening the will of actual activists who were looking for allies.

"I was so committed to the socialist cause," Lee Kwang-Baek said. "I wanted nothing more than for South Korea to emulate North Korean society."

I asked him what changed his mind, and what pushed him to run a media station that pushes information into North Korea. Essentially, what made him switch sides? He replied:

The Berlin Wall fell. Then the Soviet Union dissolved. Communist countries around the world collapsed. The great famine hit North Korea in the mid-1990s, whe[n] two to three million people died from starvation. This was about my fourth or fifth year in college. I saw that the principles and ideologies to which I dedicated my youth were invalidated by reality. Realizing that socialism was not the progressive movement that I thought it was, I thought about what direction humanity should [take]. I continued to ruminate on these metaphysical questions and just wondered. So many people were starving, didn't have access to medicine and treatment, were dying from wars. I looked to far countries in the Middle East, Southeast Asia, and Africa to see where I could contribute. Not speaking any of their languages, what value could I add? My mind made its way back to North Korea, the country that I truly believed was the ideal society. Here were 25 million people, really close by, who needed democracy and improved human rights and needed to escape from violence. This led me to start my activism in North Korean human rights and democracy.

During some of the darkest days of the famine, he collected small donations—ten, twenty, and thirty dollars each—from friends and bought rice to send to North Korea. Then, as media began reporting decreasing rates of North Korean deaths from starvation, Lee Kwang-Baek turned to political issues of freedom and violence. He switched from sending rice to raising awareness about the ruthless and relentless violence that North Koreans faced. He ran a series of campaigns called "Know the Real North Korea," organized photo exhibits and talks by defectors, and wrote articles and books. Realizing that raising awareness about North Korea's egregious human-rights violations wasn't getting a peep from the government and was probably not improving a single life of a citizen inside the country, Lee Kwang-Baek changed tactics again.

Without changing North Korean society, the issue of human rights couldn't be addressed, "so we went to China and met up with defectors who were secretly crossing into China, and worked on training them as democracy activists. We thought they could lead the way to chang[ing] North Korea society. But there was no foreseeable end to this. We could only meet so many North Koreans. A few dozen every year at most. At this rate, how could we make a dent in this country? That's when we turned to radio broadcasts." It was mostly a matter of scale.

Lee Kwang-Baek got involved in radio broadcasts with other activists, including Kwon Eun-Kyung and Kim Sung-Joon (also South Korean natives). On December 10, 2005, International Human Rights Day, Open Radio for North Korea broadcast its first program into North Korea. What started out as thirty-minute daily broadcasts expanded to three-hour daily programs. Over the years, their organization continually introduced new materials, sought feedback from defectors, incorporated criticisms of their programs, and made some mistakes along the way, all with the goal of fine-tuning the broadcast's content to deliver the most relevant, appealing, and powerful information to their listeners in North Korea.

Lee Kwang-Baek, who had wholeheartedly listened to *The Voice of National Salvation* broadcast years earlier, learned that it was a propaganda hoax by the North Korean government. Despite feeling deceived, he thought it was a clever idea and turned it on its head to broadcast to Pyongyang a program in which speakers pretended to be secret democracy activists in North Korea. Beginning their programming with "We are Chosun [North Korean term for Korean] soldiers for democracy in Pyongyang," they would bitterly criticize the Kim regime with vehement language. They pretended to be North Korean activists in Pyongyang with the hope of encouraging actual underground democracy activists and energizing them to find allies in

Pyongyang and other parts of the country. The broadcast started off targeting fighters and activists, rather than ordinary citizens, to inform them that such an underground dissident group existed. "So how was that received? Well?" I asked.

Lee Kwang-Baek smiled. "We later asked some defectors to listen to these programs. They all laughed! They said this wasn't the North Korean dialect. To them, it sounded like someone who had defected ten years ago and was weaning off the North Korean dialect, or a Korean-Chinese person or a South Korean poorly imitating the dialect. It was funny to them. It definitely did not sound like a North Korean broadcast to them. Embarrassed, we realized that our mimicking the North Korean accent would only distract the listeners from the content."

Around the same time that such content was received, the National Endowment for Democracy asked the radio station for more journalism because they did not want to use American funds to support broadcasts of underground anti-establishment propaganda. They wanted more news. As his colleagues told me, "We fought with them. We wanted to broadcast our way, but the donor has the decision-making power. So we changed the direction of our station." As they explained:

It was a big improvement to have actual defectors speak in their own language for our radio station. North Korean listeners move on quickly after listening once. They don't have time to dilly-dally since it's a dangerous activity. They can understand almost everything over radio broadcast if it's in the North Korean dialect, but can only understand half the content if it's in the South Korean dialect. It's like a foreign language. The inflections are different, and there are way more words with Chinese characters in the South Korean dialect. Defectors are also much better at writing scripts that North Koreans will easily understand in terms of vocabulary and narrative. So we had South Koreans working on content to explain democracy, liberty, and North Korean defectors who initially did not know much about this [but] helped to package it in a way that was [more] understandable. South Koreans and North Korean defectors were collaborating on broadcasts!

Rather than making criticisms of the Kim regime the first priority of the station, Lee Kwang-Baek and his colleagues decided to include a much wider range of information in their broadcasts, because their station was one of the very few alternate channels that North Koreans could access, albeit secretly. Those working at the station believe that it is ultimately the choice of North Koreans to accept or not accept changes in their eventual fate. Of their daily three hours of broadcasting, then, one hour is always news. International news about the two Koreas, the United States, China, and so on is coupled with commentary and discussions about it. The second hour comprises educational content on democracy and human rights. Since North Koreans don't know the phrase "human rights," much less its meaning, the station focuses on creative content. An interesting way that they continue to share content about human rights and democracy is to discuss countries that have transitioned from starvation and oppression to reform and freedom. China and Vietnam are often discussed. They explain that just like China and Vietnam, North Korea can also break away from starvation and dictatorship. "The subject of human rights and democracy is not always that interesting, especially to young people, so we try to write radio dramas with plots and lessons with substance that's delivered in a catchy way."

The third hour contains content dedicated to music and cultural enrichment. Since North Koreans have an extremely limited selection of media, which defectors describe as terribly boring, the station plays different types of music. "Trot" music is particularly popular among older listeners. Created during Japan's colonial rule over Korea, "trot"—derived from "fox-trot"— is influenced by *enka,* a popular Japanese musical genre which uses the American foxtrot rhythm. During and after the Korean War, songs about sacrifice, loss, and tragedies were popular. Trot's popularity peaked in the late 1980s, after which it was replaced by other musical styles including R&B, hip hop, and dance music. A popular song, found on YouTube, is "Heartbreak on Mi-Ah-Ri Hill" by Lee Hae-Yun. Mi-Ah-Ri Hill was the site of a battle between North and South Korean troops during the war, where many families were separated as refugees were taken to the North by retreating North Korean soldiers.

K-pop is just as popular in North Korea as it is in other countries around the world. Soundtracks from Korean dramas that are internationally known for being utterly addictive are also played during this hour. Interviews with North Korean defectors about how they're settling in South Korea—interviews that include the good, the bad, and the ugly—are played during this time as well.

Focus groups with North Korean defectors, whose opinions are considered a loose proxy for those of listeners inside the country, help to inform the radio station's content. Materials about North Korean domestic politics, history, and the less-than-perfect biographies of the Kim family have been particularly appealing to those groups.

One of these biographies, *Taedong River Royal Family,* written by Han-Yong Yi, a nephew of Kim Jong-Il's mistress, was extremely popular. The author, who had had access to the inner circles of the regime, wrote about his own extremely luxurious life in North Korea, and why he nevertheless defected to South Korea. This memoir was made into a radio series and was broadcast.[11] Defectors would typically spend a sleepless night or two devouring the book. When Lee Kwang-Baek and his colleagues asked the readers why it was so fascinating, the response was that there is no real human information about Kim Jong-Il available in North Korea, and this book describes his daily life and habits in excruciating detail. Everyone knows that he was their Dear Leader, the most revered leader in the entire world, and they see his images everywhere. But they know nothing about his daily life. For instance, many North Koreans believed the idea that Kim Jong-Il got only "jjokjam and juegibap," as the saying goes in the North. "Jjokjam" is slang for "little sleep" and refers to the leader's supposedly amazing work ethic that allows him to get hardly any sleep. Consequently he got ten to thirty minutes of sleep here and there, totaling an hour or two a day, at most. "Juegibap" refers to the idea that the leader eats only small balls of rice, mixed with vegetables, which represents a humble meal in North Korea. This would be the case, or so the story goes, because the leader lived like the poorest workers and farmers, and he sympathized with the socialist revolutionaries of his country. When people read or heard the audiobook of *Taedong River Royal Family* and learned that their Dear Leader was not getting "jjokjam and juegibap" but was enjoying millions of dollars' worth of gifts for his birthday, and living amid unspeakable luxuries, they were overwhelmed by a sense of shock and betrayal. "Is this true? Is this really how the General lives? What about us?" the listeners would think and ask. North Koreans were also shocked when they found out that Kim Jong-Il, their conservative social-ist leader, had multiple wives.

As time passed, and North Korean residents had more access to outside information and became savvier, listeners became less obsessed with learning about the private lives of their leaders and more interested in the lives of North Korean defectors managing to survive in South Korea. Many people in the North believe that defectors will be deceived, or will be killed by South Koreans. But once they hear how defectors are faring—in their own words—they are intrigued. For instance, *Aquariums of Pyongyang*, a memoir written by North Korean political-prison-camp survivor Kang Chol-Hwan and adapted into a radio series with thirty or more episodes, aired on their radio station, and was well received.

The younger audience, however—people in their teens and twenties—doesn't have much interest even in the lives of defectors. "For them, it just needs to be fun. South Korean dramas, K-pop, things like this. Good stories. It's a little different," Lee Kwang-Baek explains.

Although conducting a statistically significant survey among North Korean residents is impossible, various surveys conducted by American think tanks, South Korean–based radio stations, and others suggest that between 8 and 15 percent of North Koreans illegally listen to foreign radio.[12] When delving into who the listeners are, the first take-away is that it's particularly difficult for the lowest social class to listen. They are the people who are struggling the most to survive on a daily basis, and they don't have the resources, mental or otherwise, for extraneous activities, especially risky ones, since they don't have the means to bribe the authorities if caught. Most listeners, then, are above this lowest class: wealthy marketeers who can bribe authorities to turn a blind eye, high-ranking officials in the military and government, as well as the children of these officials, who are less subject to frequent monitoring.

In addition to the radio station's listeners in North Korea, there are those who listen over the internet by accessing the station's website. Running basic analytics, the station managers can rank visits to their website's radio content by country: they know, then, that the country with the most visitors to their site is South Korea, and that the one that ranks second is China. Because ordinary Han Chinese people who speak Mandarin can't understand the Korean broadcast, they can only guess that listeners from a Chinese IP address are either Korean-Chinese people who speak and understand Korean or North Korean defectors hiding in China and listening. And then there are the website visitors from countries in Africa that have North Korean embassies. Countries that have North Korean diplomatic offices have high numbers of visits, and analytics show that they stay on the site for long periods, sometimes as long as an hour at a time. They can only guess that these viewers and listeners are personnel working at the North Korean embassies.

Outside information may inspire new hairstyles, clothing preferences, and speech patterns among close friends, but Lee Kwang-Baek stays focused on its power to foster distrust in the North Korean government among listeners. He told me, "I'm someone who has been working consistently for societal change for over twenty years and what I learned was that [it] does not take place through just one method. Multiple factors need to operate simultaneously. So for North Korea, something needs to occur both within and outside [the country]. Outside information alone will not create breakthrough changes in the country, but it is absolutely necessary for North Koreans to change their thinking as a prerequisite to any positive change in the future.

"For example," Lee Kwang-Baek said, "there were incidents like the *Cheonan* sinking and the *Yeonpyeong* Island shelling. At first, the North Korean government claimed that it wasn't their doing. But as news seeped in from outside about how the North Korean ship blew up the ship *Cheonan,* and about which North Korean unit bombed *Yeonpyeong* Island, and the number of people who died on the island, the word quickly spread. People share these news stories with friends at the street market or over drinks and say 'I heard this happened,' through stealthy, hushed voices. Through stuff like this, distrust of the government is formed. In a way, it's a form of minor resistance. They're not actively fighting, but they don't trust them. It's a growing phenomenon."

For a place like North Korea, protests on public streets may be nearly impossible to hope for in the near future. But resistance movements begin not in the streets, but in individual minds. Turning their backs against the government is a crucial first step. And outside radio is certainly inspiring them to do so.

One might also hope that listening to foreign radio broadcasts will inspire North Koreans to defect. But this is relatively rare. Most defectors do first acquire outside knowledge through radio or another channel of information, but it takes time and a variety of experiences to change their minds on certain fundamental issues, including their level of trust in the government. Lee Kwang-Baek did meet one person who defected explicitly because of his radio program, however. Radio broadcasts, unlike media that require content-carrying hardware like DVDs or USBs, do not limit access to North Koreans who live farther from the border. His radio station runs on shortwave, and the single frequency covers the entire world, though the quality isn't too strong and the radio signal is sensitive to geography, weather, and jamming.

As mentioned earlier, weather reports are popular, especially among fishermen who work in South Hwanghae Province. They say that foreign weather reports are much more accurate than the North Korean versions. Lee Kwang-Baek described one particular fisherman's experience: "At the end of every broadcast, we share the name of our broadcast, Open Radio for North Korea, say it's out of South Korea, and share our contact information, including our phone number. In a particular case, there was a fisherman who had listened to a foreign radio report when he went out fishing and slowly started to listen to other programs. He had zero political intent; the content was just fun. He spent months going through different radio programs and would take his radio out to sea, even if he wasn't fishing, in order to listen."

This fisherman slowly came to realize that he was no longer able to live in his country, and made up his mind to defect. But the weak signal, coupled with extensive North Korean jamming, made it hard for the man to accurately catch every digit of Open Radio for North Korea's phone number. On a certain day he was able to make out a zero and a one, but that was it because of the jamming. The next day, he made out a four, but then couldn't hear anything else. In this manner, he struggled for many weeks and listened a few more times to confirm the number. He gave a copy to his daughter, memorized it for himself, defected to China, and called the radio station from China to ask for help. Open Radio for North Korea connected this man to a broker in China who helped him defect to South Korea. After finishing his interrogations with the South Korean intelligence service and then spending a few months in Hanawon, the fisherman made his way to Open Radio for North Korea to meet the people whose voices he had been listening to for months on end.

Kim Sung-Joong, one of the associates who has been relentlessly committed to radio broadcasting into North Korea, emphasized the importance of inviting North Koreans onto their programs and including their stories. "It's important to present to the listeners how life is, not just the nice parts of South Korea."

Lee Kwang-Baek is currently the standing representative of the Unification Media Group (UMG), a new consortium of four defector-led media groups that broadcast and/or send information into North Korea. The four groups include Radio Free Chosun and Open Radio for North Korea, two shortwave radio stations targeting North Korea; Daily NK, an internet periodical reporting on all aspects of North Korea; and OTV, an NGO-based internet television channel. They have a joint goal of reaching one million North Korean adults within the next five years in order to spark organic changes from within the country. Of course, the group has elicited condemnation from the North Korean government, which has called it an "anti-Republic clown show of provocation" and criticized UMG on its propaganda website Uriminzokkiri, saying that "the manipulative existence of UMG is part of a scheme to expand psychological warfare in North Korea and is yet another provocation that cannot be forgiven."

After my last conversation with the associates at the Unification Media Group, I was invited back to be interviewed for a program that broadcasts into North Korea every Wednesday, targeting young listeners. The specific program hosts young guests from all over—the United States, South Korea, North

Korean defectors—to talk about their personal goals and dreams. The vision of this program is to inspire hope, dreams, and strength among North Korean youth and to help them think past their Songbun classification. At the beginning of every program, the radio program host reads the opening lines in Korean:

If you cultivate a chicken egg, a chick will hatch. If you cultivate a duck egg, a duckling will hatch. American President Lincoln had a dream to free slaves, and eventually emancipated slaves in his country. Similarly the dreams that ordinary human beings cultivate can become reality. For the North Korean young people who are listening to this program, what kind of dreams do you hold dear in your heart? Now is our weekly time dedicated to deliver[ing] stories of young people who have passionately followed their dreams and made them into reality.

The young female announcer and I had a casual conversation about where I was from, what I did in my free time, how I had learned to speak Korean as an American-born Korean person, and how I had become interested in North Korea. As I spoke into a microphone for this recording, I wondered what the listeners of this program must be thinking. Was I too light-hearted? Too serious? Did I sound too naive? Too optimistic?

The interview went on for a bit too long, so the announcer and her team decided to split the interview into two sessions and broadcast them into North Korea on two Wednesdays. She told me later that there wasn't the need for the content to be too packaged, especially the interviews. A casual conversational tone and a sense of authenticity would do.

JI SEONG-HO: PORTRAIT OF A SURVIVOR

When people first meet Ji Seong-Ho, they are drawn in by his soft-spoken, humble demeanor and his admirable work ethic as a law student at Dongguk University in Seoul and as director of an NGO. Later they learn that his big eyes and tendency to smile easily belie an unimaginably painful past. His resilience, humility, and perseverance are all the more awe-inspiring if one knows of the obstacles he had to overcome to do the work that he does today.

In 1982, Ji Seong-Ho was born in Hoeryong City in North Hamgyong Province, and lived near the Hakpo coal mine. Hakpo is where citizens with extremely poor social standing live and die. He was the oldest of three siblings, and had a loving mother and a father who was a party member. Yet despite his father's party membership, his family was constantly hungry. In middle school, he began noticing empty chairs in his classroom and realized that his classmates' absence was not due to laziness, but rather to their malnourishment or death. In his city, deep in the mountains, the Dear Leader's food distributions were only a myth. Neighbors who tried to survive by eating tree bark and grass passed away. His own grandmother perished due to starvation. But even as his classmates and their families were clearly dying, Ji Seong-Ho's teachers were teaching students that they were living in a socialist paradise. He recalls Kim Jong-Il's consistent message to the nation that "food would soon be made available like water coming down a waterfall."

At the far end of Ji Seong-Ho's home town was the political prison camp, Camp 22.[13] Everyone knew that political prisoners in Camp 22 were forced to mine thousands of tons of coal. A train loaded with coal regularly went back and forth between the prison camp and a power plant, and Ji Seong-Ho identified an opportunity. He could scavenge, steal, and sell scraps of coal to buy food for his family. His mother, his twelve-year-old little sister, and he would time the perfect moment to jump and grab onto a freight train as it sped up, and then sneak aboard.

Soldiers guarding these coal-filled trains sometimes caught Ji Seong-Ho and others stealing coal, and would beat them until a few bones broke. Yet the difficult task of carrying forty-five-kilogram coal sacks on his four-feet, two-inch frame was worth these sporadic beatings because it was the only way to provide for his family in such desperate times, when news of dead neighbors elicited merely a few tongue clucks as a sign of obligatory mourning.

The freezing cold morning of March 7, 1996, started in a rather typical way for thirteen-year-old Ji Seong-Ho: he ran up to a moving train and pulled himself aboard it as it left the prison camp and headed toward the power plant. But on that fateful morning he felt dizzy, since he hadn't eaten for several days. Although he had planned to jump off the train as it entered the next station, he lost consciousness. He woke up after an unknown period of time and saw that the train had passed over his left leg, which was hanging from his body a couple inches below his hip by a thin tendon. Reflexively grabbing at his split leg, only then did he notice that the train had also sliced off three fingers on his left hand. With every exhalation pushed a puff of cold air through his lips, and squirts of blood from his leg and hand exiting his flesh. Frantically scared, but also weak, he cried out for his parents and for his younger sister.

Hoeryong is infamous for having the lowest temperatures across North Korea. The freezing temperature that fateful March morning made Ji Seong-Ho's devastating injuries all the more painful. His younger sister found him in his pool of blood, and given how small she was, all she could do to console him was to take off her neck scarf to wrap around him. The freezing temperature and fear enveloped these two siblings, sitting in the train tracks, both covered in blood.

He doesn't remember how, but several men arrived to carry him to a local hospital. Ji Seong-Ho's description of the hospital he was taken to is very similar to the descriptions of hospitals offered by many North Koreans—including North Korean doctors whom I have befriended. The stripped buildings have some of the makings of a hospital—beds, sinks, operation tables—but there is no electricity, no clean water, no medicine, and no painkillers. Despite the state he was in, the hospital had no blood for transfusions or painkillers to numb the excruciating pain he was experiencing.

Blunt surgical tools were laid out on a steel table next to Ji Seong-Ho. To this day, Ji Seong-Ho remembers the sound of the surgical saw cutting through his leg bone to amputate most of his left leg. Each tooth of the saw that bit into his leg sent vibrations throughout his little body. The surgeon simply did not have the resources to save and attach the leg back onto Ji Seong-Ho's body. The surgeon then took a small scalpel to trim the jagged edges of his freshly amputated bone while slapping Ji Seong-Ho's cheek to keep him awake. The surgeon knew that if Ji Seong-Ho slipped out of consciousness, he probably would never wake up. Ji Seong-Ho alternated between screaming and near passing out. Hearing her young son's desperate cries caused his mother, who was waiting outside the operating room, to faint.

Four and a half hours later, this horrific procedure was over, and Ji Seong-Ho was discharged from the hospital without any antibiotics or anesthetics. Since his family did not have any money to purchase medicine, he and his mother simply went back home. Ji Seong-Ho explained to me that "every moment after the accident was harder than death to try to cope, to survive, and deal with the pain after this surgery." Every night, he whispered to anyone who would hear him, "Please kill me. Please kill me. Please kill me," and would slowly fall asleep as the sun rose.

This was in the middle of the famine, during which Hoeryong had been completely cut off from the state's distribution network. His younger siblings toiled to bring something, anything, back for the family to eat. The little brother scrounged in trashcans at makeshift street markets all day to collect scraps of noodles. He would then come home, wash them, boil them, and put these scraps of recycled noodles into Ji Seong-Ho's mouth. I met Ji Seong-Ho's younger brother in Seoul recently. He is just as soft-spoken and kind as his older brother. We all ordered iced Americanos at a tiny cafe in Seoul on a hot July afternoon as Ji Seong-Ho shared his story about this chilling episode of his life, much of which took place during freezing weather.

To help Ji Seong-Ho recover from his injuries, his younger brother and sister gave him all the food scraps that they found in trash bins and dumps while they ate weeds and grass. Ji Seong-Ho still blames himself for their stunted growth, and is eternally sorry not just for their height, but for all the sacrifices that their small statures represent.

With summer months came warm weather, which caused the flesh around his amputations to turn gangrenous, and pieces of his leg bones to pierce through his inflamed, infected skin. There was still no medication, but this young boy's sheer willpower, coupled with his family's relentless desire to help him recuperate, finally led to his pain subsiding. Ji Seong-Ho says that it took 240 days after the accident before the pain became somewhat bearable.

Now a "cripple," as he describes, he knew he was *really* not going anywhere in North Korean society. Until the accident, he thought that watching neighbors and his grandmother waste away were all just part of the natural order of things, that these unfortunate events were just part of the struggle that his nation had to overcome. And in his mind, he sincerely believed that the suffering was "because of the American bastards, those imperialists who were forcibly keeping the two Koreas apart. This is why we are living like this."

Given the extreme discrimination against persons with any disability, those with even a hint of intellectual or physical disability were purged from Pyongyang decades ago. People with disabilities now are forced to live in rural areas, out of sight from the core population and foreigners. The stigma attached to disability has become so normalized in North Korean culture—then and now—that Ji Seong-Ho's suicidal thoughts returned. Intense guilt overshadowed his young mind as he watched his family toil not just for themselves but also for him. They also barked back at neighbors who would make careless and offensive comments about Ji Seong-Ho. To contribute to his family's well-being, he wanted to visit China to make some money to bring back to his family.

With his wooden crutches that his father made for him, he crossed into China illegally in search of food. His intention was not to defect. Yet during his month in China, when he managed to acquire a few kilograms of rice to bring back to his family, he noticed that dogs there ate better than his desperate family.

Until Ji Seong-Ho crossed into China, he had believed the state's narrative. He was convinced that while people were starving to death in his town and across the rest of the country, the Dear Leader was also suffering like they were. With this faith, he and others had tried to push through the difficult times and look forward to better days. But while in China he encountered people who spoke out about Kim Jong-Il and cursed him, criticizing him as a "worthless leader" who was starving his people. These words were jarring, shocking to his ears. Ji Seong-Ho had never heard anyone ever openly criticize the leader. Since he was in China illegally, he knew not to confront any of these irreverent Chinese locals. He simply asked someone, "What makes people want to criticize [Kim Jong-Il]?" A man who recognized Ji Seong-Ho as a North Korean but didn't care to report him bluntly responded, "How can someone who is suffering with the rest of his comrades, and supposedly eating only rice balls, be so fat? If the Leader was actually starving, he should be as gaunt [as] you and others I see like you, begging for food around here. Look at the officials who follow him around. They're bigger than you, too."

Ji Seong-Ho left that conversation thinking to himself, "Ah, well maybe the Dear Leader is ill. Maybe he has some sickness that causes him to not eat and swell up in weight, like how a starving baby's belly swells up. He's not deceiving us. He's our Dear Leader." But the more conversations he had, the more his mental grip on North Korea's "truths" loosened. As he passed the time in China, he also turned the knobs on the radio out of boredom and heard North Korean radio programs, which were familiar to him and made him feel almost at home in this foreign and wealthier country. But then he came across South Korean programs. Such a foreign concept! He continued listening to these programs, free of punishment, while in China.

A specific question he remembers a South Korean broadcaster asking was: "Do you know how much money a North Korean laborer earns in one month?" She answered her own question, which was a dollar. Upon listening to her answer, he had no concept of what one dollar was or meant. But after spending some time in China, and watching countless transactions take place around him, he realized that one dollar represented a very small amount. Comparisons took shape in his head: he got a sense of how much a Chinese person, a South Korean person, and a North Korean person would earn in a month.

Surprised that a South Korean person made more money than a North Korean, he continued to listen to South Korean radio programs. In North Korea, South Korea is described as a place where people are hungry, almost naked, and poor. But in China, a place that Ji Seong-Ho instantly recognized to be wealthier than North Korea, he noted that Chinese people were looking to South Korea for trends, products, and style. Chinese people were even buying South Korean toothbrushes because they were considered to be higher quality than Chinese-manufactured toothbrushes. *Hallyu,* or the South Korean wave, was permeating Chinese culture. "So," he tells me, "you have North Koreans who went to China to eat and survive, but you have Chinese people who go to South Korea to make money. This fact alone showed a huge gap between North Korea and China and between China and South Korea. Even from afar, South Koreans dressed better, had better skin, more stylish clothes, better hair. In so many areas, South Koreans were just so much better than Chinese. So, this left me thinking, South Korea is way better off than North Korea. This shocked me, and got me to question the basics of my education in North Korea."

Through some connections, he met some Korean missionaries in China who offered to take Ji Seong-Ho to South Korea. People in a church told him that if he went to South Korea, he'd be given a prosthetic leg and arm. "This was my biggest dream!" he told me with excitement. But his filial desire to be with his family trumped his corporeal desire to walk again, so he declined the offer.

A few people Ji Seong-Ho befriended in China, who had pity on a man with a handless arm that was tied to a wooden crutch by string, tried to convince him not to return to North Korea. How was he going to save himself and his family back in Hoeryong? "Save yourself!" he was advised. Dismissing their appeals, Seong-Ho gathered several kilograms of rice, candy, and sweet cookies and crossed the border back into North Korea.

On his way back to North Korea, North Korean border guards spotted him and followed him to his home, where they arrested him and hauled him to a police station. Ji Seong-Ho remembers their words to this day: "A worthless cripple like you is embarrassing our nation and our Dear Leader! How dare you illegally cross to China to beg for food? You're defaming and damaging the dignity of our Dear Leader! Someone like you needs to silently die, out of sight." A man missing a leg and hand who had illegally crossed an international border to find food to help his family in a starved nation was being doubly condemned for being a national embarrassment due to his disability. This was almost as painful as the completely unconstrained torture he received. The soldiers called it a "special punishment" that they reserved for disabled people, which was a series of more painful beatings and tortures than those that able-bodied border crossers received. Furthermore, they confiscated his crutches and the precious kilograms of rice that he had obtained, which were the reason he had snuck into China in the first place.

He wondered to himself during his beatings, "Is *this* the homeland I came back to?" Before seeing China and learning what the rest of the world was like, he had always assumed that he or his fellow citizens deserved whatever punishments they received. It was simply the natural order of life. But after becoming more aware of the world, he realized that "the North Korean government ha[d] been lying to us the whole time that they would give us food to eat, and [that it] continued to lie as a few million people wasted to death, and as several hundred thousand people fled to China. Amidst their faults, it was *I* who was blamed for the circumstances I was in."

Being punished for breaking a domestic law of crossing into China was bad enough, but that was somewhat justified in his mind; it was a law, no matter how twisted. But being punished for a disability, something he had nothing to do with, but that was the result of desperate acts that the state's inability to provide for his family had led him to, was the last straw of injustice. "It was a mistake for me to return to North Korea. I would have lived more as a human being if I were a servant in a foreign country, rather than a citizen of my own country," he told me. "I was living in a system where injustice and misfortune are skewed as justice, where the conscience is fooled, and where even educators have to resort to lying."

Eventually, he made his way back to his family's home and slipped back into the way of life in his neighborhood. Around 2003, he started watching movies on DVDs. His family's house didn't have a media player, so he would go to his friends' houses to watch them together. DVD players from China cost only about two to three hundred Chinese renminbi.

"We'd lock the main door, lock the door [of the room], pull the curtains, turn the volume down really low where we could barely hear the movie, and watch things in secret. It was frightening, but also more fun. I watched a lot of South Korean movies with great interest. I don't remember the titles, but remember watching dramas and movies. I watched American movies, a few

Chinese movies, and some Russian movies. The ones that would cause the most trouble were South Korean films. I couldn't believe everything I saw, but there seemed to be credibility to most of [it]. I could see the changes in the outside world. Emotionally speaking, the movies were spot-on. Human desires were beautifully expressed. It was a slow addition. I was falling into it slowly. Inserting yourself into the plot, putting yourself in the movie or the show. [People] would start styling their hair like [the actors] on South Korean shows or movies. If friends were drinking, they would say lines from South Korean movies [to] each other." Secretly watching movies became so prevalent in his home town that if someone was not watching shows, or didn't know the names of characters in a show, that person would be considered behind the times.

Transplanting himself into different worlds through film was only part of his life back in North Korea. On crutches, Ji Seong-Ho attended self-criticism sessions and was expected to publicly report on his and other people's crimes of listening to foreign broadcasts or watching films. "We were constantly told to report people who had illegal radios, and that if you had one, to turn yourself in, and that they'd go easy on us. The regime despised the radios because that was the way people heard information about the outside world . . . People who were caught listening to radios were treated and punished as spies. But despite this frightening environment, people still listened to radio broadcasts."

His friends listened to radios, but Ji Seong-Ho never did while in North Korea. "I was busy living, surviving, you know. I didn't report on anyone." Closeness among young friends is something that the regime, no matter how harsh a regime, cannot strip away. Among close friends, radio programs, songs, and movie plots were secretly yet excitedly discussed. They taught each other Korean pop songs, just as young friends do all over the world.

Despite his love for his family and friends, Ji Seong-Ho realized that his disability created a cement ceiling for him. Escaping North Korea was his only way to a better life. On his last night in North Korea in 2006, Ji Seong-Ho, his younger brother, and his father took shots together. In a society where men are to never express emotion, the three men wept.

The next day, twenty-four-year-old Ji Seong-Ho and his brother crossed the Tumen River. Without a plan, and certainly without cash to bribe guards to look the other way, they swam and splashed their way across the river into China. At one point in the river, Ji Seong-Ho lost his footing, but his brother grabbed him by the hair and dragged him across into Chinese territory. With wooden crutches that his father made for him, Ji Seong-Ho embarked on a six-thousand-mile journey through China then into Laos, Myanmar, and Thailand. Throughout this arduous journey, he lamented his wretched birthplace and desperately prayed to a larger spirit, vowing that he would work to make sure that no one else would have to live through his experience.

In July of 2006, Ji Seong-Ho arrived in the Republic of Korea. His greatest wish until that point was to have a prosthetic arm and leg, a wish that was fulfilled by the South Korean government. Wanting to relay the news to his father, he contacted people in his North Korean neighborhood through illegal cell phones, but learned that his father had passed away. After he and his younger brother escaped, his mother and younger sister had followed. His father was last to try to defect, but he was caught, detained, and then interrogated by intelligence officers, who demanded to know where his children had gone. Refusing to reveal that his three children and wife had defected to South

Korea, his father, a party member of the state, was tortured to death. There was chatter in his neighborhood that since he had no family left, the officials had put the beaten corpse of his father in a wheelbarrow and dumped the body in their empty house.

After mourning his father's fate, Seong-Ho channeled his grief into founding an NGO called Now, Action, Unity, and Human Rights (NAUH) that has rescued more than a hundred North Korean children, persons with disabilities, and vulnerable women and brought them to South Korea. Furthermore, since North Korean people are cut off from the outside world, he broadcasts radio programs into North Korea with content that ranges from news and culture to original radio dramas. He truly believes that the combination of street markets and access to outside information will spark and sustain changes inside his former country.

So what information does he send in? He has two radio shows that broadcast into North Korea through Radio Free Asia and the Far Eastern Broadcasting Corporation. Rather than bashing the North Korean government, he broadcasts radio programs that simply describe South Korean society and other parts of the world, and leaves it up to the listeners to come to their own conclusions.

One particularly shocking fact that listeners picked up on was that defectors who settled in South Korea lived in Seoul, the capital city. Only North Korea's crème de la crème live in the capital city, Pyongyang. The idea that defectors, who typically come from the lower social classes in North Korea, can live in a foreign country's capital city, one that is far more beautiful, convenient, and rich than Pyongyang, surprised most listeners. They were also shocked to learn that defectors can go to college, regardless of their age, upbringing, or financial situation. In the North, only the children of the elite can go to college. Listening to how Ji

Seong-Ho, a boy with severe disabilities who had begged other impoverished North Koreans for food, was now settled in rich South Korea—where he was treated with dignity, directing an NGO, and going to university—actually motivated an entire family to escape from North Korea. The family ended up meeting Ji Seong-Ho in South Korea to thank him and explain that their child had always wanted to attend college, but given their low Songbun status, it was never a possibility. The father, after hearing Ji Seong-Ho's story, decided to risk his and his family's life to escape and give his precious child a brighter future.

The most popular radio programs tell about the lives of North Korean defectors who have settled in South Korea. Seong-Ho's shows target North Korean youth, the "*jangmadang* generation" (street market generation) that knows that they can eat candy only if they have money enough to buy it on the market. Kids today in North Korea no longer wait in vain for bi-annual distributions of candy and other sweets by the state.

Rather than duplicating the North Korean government's method of communication, which is to force-feed its people the state's narrative, Seong-Ho wants people to come to their own conclusions. "Rise up, demonstrate, risk death to achieve freedom!" is not a message he wants to convey explicitly. He does not think that it would resonate with young people anyway. Rather, he wants listeners to have "aha!" moments. And since the radio program is targeting youth, it has to be entertaining. So Ji Seong-Ho has young North Korean defectors converse about concepts within the context of daily life. For example, would a chicken restaurant or a bakery make more money? If a chicken joint is going to make more of a profit, then where should the restaurant be built—in the suburbs, or downtown? How will the restaurant attract customers? By raising these questions in his youth radio program, he aims to teach North Koreans the basics of capitalism, skills for sustainable survival, and critical thinking.

During our most recent conversation, Ji Seong-Ho's Samsung smartphone kept vibrating, so he pulled it out of his pocket to see who was calling. Turning the phone screen to face me, he says, "It's a Chinese number. I'm getting a call from North Korea."

"Please pick up your call. I can step out if you'd like," I said.

"No, no. It's all right. He'll call back later when he can," he responded. I noted the casual nature of his handling the phone call, and realized how frequently he receives such calls. The novelty of receiving calls from contacts inside North Korea has worn off for Ji Seong-Ho, as well as other activists and North Koreans in South Korea. North Korea truly is not as sealed off as it once was.

4 THE DIGITAL UNDERGROUND

The global rise of technology certainly has not passed by North Korea. Although the government's relentless efforts to shield its citizens from outside information remain effective, North Korea's illicit information networks have benefited from recent innovations in technology. While Park Sang-Hak and his colleagues send in tall, cylindrical balloons filled with hard copies of freedom messages, other activists are driven by the same mission—liberating North Koreans' minds—but disseminate information through cellular networks, content-filled USB drives, and more.

THE PHONE AS A LIFELINE

In 1998, Nehemiah Park, whom we met earlier in the book, defected from North Korea. He is currently a graduate student in South Korea, working odd jobs to save cash to send as remittances to his family, all of whom still reside in North Korea. Several years ago, he sent cell phones to his family so that they could call him.

"Son, is that you?"

Recognizing the weak, shaky voice on the other line, Nehemiah immediately hangs up the phone with the intent to call his mother back using Skype, which costs only 1.1 cents per minute. His family uses this system of calling, hanging up, then calling back in order to keep Nehemiah's phone bill down. Additionally, they keep their phone calls to one or two minutes in order to minimize the risk of detection by the North Korean authorities, since it is illegal to make international phone calls.

Nehemiah calls his mother back and asks how she's doing, to which she always responds, "We're alive." He then listens to the items that his mother will ask him to send. These items range from medicine and clothing to DVD players and Japanese laptops. Despite the North Koreans' hatred for the Japanese as their former colonizer, North Koreans like Japan-manufactured electronics because they are sturdy. Nehemiah scribbles these items down while carefully eyeing the number of seconds he has been on the phone with his mother. When the phone call reaches around a hundred seconds, Nehemiah starts saying goodbye. His mother cannot risk getting caught by the authorities.

Tools and systems to detect and track down international phone calls made inside North Korea are becoming increasingly accurate and more widely used by authorities. For example, German-manufactured cellular-activity detection machines are used in many regions to track down within minutes the location of North Koreans making international calls. So Nehemiah must keep his calls under two minutes, though others use their discretion and make longer calls.

Nehemiah looks at the list of items that his mother has asked for this time—medicine, clothing, women's cosmetics, and an English dictionary for his cousin—and starts to purchase them online. After the items are delivered to his home, Nehemiah will wrap each in several layers of plastic and zip-top bags in order to waterproof them. The smugglers who are going to swim across the

Tumen River to get these to his family will most likely get the package wet. Nehemiah calls a friend in China who is a Joseonjok (an ethnic Korean who has Chinese citizenship), and who will work with the North Korean smuggler who will ultimately deliver the items to Nehemiah's family. Nehemiah goes through his Joseonjok friend because he no longer wants anything to do with North Korean smugglers directly. "You never know when they'll snitch or take off with the money," Nehemiah tells me. Nehemiah takes the liberty to add to this "care package" items that he thinks will be good for his family—books, an audio Bible that he personally recorded with a North Korean accent so that his family members would feel more comfortable listening to it, and magazines—and hopes that his family pays some attention to this information.

Nehemiah's Joseonjok friend refuses to take any commission, so sending this care package via a smuggler costs Nehemiah a flat fee of one hundred American dollars. The smuggler will strap the items in a waterproof sack, swim across the river, and bribe the guards on the North Korean border to let him pass into North Korea. These are guards with whom the smuggler has carefully built relationships over time. Smuggling goods is highly punishable, and letting people pass through the North Korean border, rather than shooting them, could get the border guards killed immediately. But North Korea is a country where money can solve any problem and can save lives. Given the failed Communist public distribution system, people are desperately turning to money, connections within the informal black markets, and any stroke of good luck to survive.

After Nehemiah's family receives the requested items, his mother calls to go over what they received to see if the smuggler's sticky hands got onto any of the contraband that Nehemiah sent in.

"An English dictionary."

"Yes."

"Chinese DVD player."

"Yes."

"Tuberculosis medicine."

"Yes. Oh good, that's still there."

"Two cell phones."

"Wait, I sent three. Check again."

"My son, there are only two cell phones."

"Dammit, I sent three. Those are expensive, too! OK, that smuggler ran off with a phone. We'll go with someone else next time. Let's continue. What else do you see in your care package?"

In addition to sending goods, literature, and dictionaries through smugglers, Nehemiah also shares information about world politics as it pertains to rice prices on the North Korean market. When there are big spikes in international humanitarian aid going into North Korea after diplomatic talks, Nehemiah tells his mother not to buy rice on the black market because prices will decrease for a while. On the contrary, when international sanctions stiffen, he advises his mother to buy rice because the prices will soar. Information that helps Nehemiah's family survive is always welcome. Information that is critical of the North Korean regime is too dangerous to listen to, so Nehemiah's mother insists that he not share any of that. Nehemiah's frustration is obvious, as his family refuses to change their fate by defecting.

An estimated two hundred to two thousand calls are made between North and South Korea every day, despite such communication being illegal in both countries. These calls are usually how families keep abreast of each other's lives. People in North Korea may ask their relatives in the South for financial assistance.

Some calls are of course used to arrange for defections. International phone calls are also increasingly being used for business and trading purposes. But subversive topics are usually not discussed in any international call in case the calls are tapped or leaked.

Nehemiah shares information with his family that is helpful to them, yet nonpolitical in nature, since his mother is too scared even to learn of outside politics. He realized the importance of relaying relevant information in 2009. On November 30, 2009, Pyongyang announced a surprise currency reform, whereby all citizens were required to exchange their North Korean currency for new currency that was worth only one-hundredth of the original currency's value. The regime limited the amount of old currency that each citizen could exchange to 100,000 to 150,000 North Korean won; all additional old notes that people had at home were deemed useless. At the official state rate, 100,000 North Korean won was valued at $690, but the black-market exchange rate valued the same amount at $35.

Rail stations were filled with "uncontrollable crowds" of people racing home to swap their money with underground currency exchangers. Nehemiah hadn't thought of telling his family about this currency reform that the North Korean government had instituted. Just having received the annual remittance that her son sent, Nehemiah's mother had exchanged the $700 she received into North Korean currency just days before the currency reform was announced. The money Nehemiah had sent became valueless overnight. Having learned the hard way, he now tries to tell her relevant information that helps her, assuring her that the information he's sharing with her is not political or subversive.

Nehemiah's family calls him with a cell phone that connects to the Chinese cellular network. On this particular one-minute call, the family asks for money, as they sometimes do. This time, they ask him for $700. They give Nehemiah a phone number to call to request a bank account to which he can send his money. Though he wants to talk to them for much longer, Nehemiah hangs up at the sixty-second mark. Nehemiah then calls that number and tells the stranger on the line that he got a call from someone (he uses a pseudonym to protect his parents' identity).

Strangely, every time he makes these calls to different numbers, the stranger on the other line is usually a woman, a Joseonjok woman. She gives Nehemiah a South Korean bank account, to which he wires $1,000. He then sends the woman a text message using Kakao Talk (a Korean smartphone application that's similar to Whatsapp), texting that he sent the $1,000. The Joseonjok lady then sends a message to a person living inside North Korea who runs a small underground financing shop. This person will then notify Nehemiah's family that the money has arrived. Nehemiah's parents, usually his mother, will then go to that individual's location, or the underground financial house, to pick up her $700 in Chinese RMB. The two middlemen take 30 percent of the requested money and split that commission.

For the past fifteen years, Nehemiah has been sending remittances to his family in North Korea through a complex network of Joseonjok businesspeople, as well as North Korean middlemen, brokers, and bribed guards. Despite the hefty 30 percent commission that the middlemen demand, Nehemiah continues to send $1,000 annually to his family to help make their lives just a little bit easier to survive. They use it for what Nehemiah describes as "living pay," which includes unexpected medical bills, winter clothing, and the occasional small birthday party.

Nehemiah is one of the thousands of North Korean defectors living in South Korea who send goods and remittances back to relatives who remain in North Korea, and who access large human, cellular, and technology networks to do so. More than 60 percent of the 29,900 defectors in South Korea send money back on a somewhat regular basis, which has created sophisticated networks and seamless operational flows that require merely twenty minutes to send money to a family in North Korea. Indeed, approximately $12 to $20 million is sent to North Korea by defectors annually despite both North and South Korean governments criminalizing this act. "It doesn't matter if you're a poor student or working. Most defectors send about $1,000 to their families inside North Korea if the families are alive."

Young defectors have made the following simple calculation for me. Minimum wage in Seoul is currently 5,580 Korean won, or about $4.90. Without thinking about taxes and other factors, a North Korean defector who works a minimum-wage job needs to work 204 hours to save $1,000 to send to their families. If one works ten hours a day, five days a week, then a defector can achieve this annual remittance goal in a single month. It, of course, usually takes longer than a month to save $1,000 because people have to go to school, spend money on living expenses, and so on. But most young North Korean defectors I met over the years don't blink an eye over this. Sending cash to their families is seen as an unquestionable duty that they need to fulfill.

Illegal cell phone networks throughout China and North Korea, especially those located near the Chinese–North Korean border where the cellular connection from the Chinese towers is powerful, allow people to make these calls. But doing so is very dangerous. There have been cases where people who have been caught making international calls have been publicly executed. Elaborate machinery and systems that detect cellular usage force people to walk miles from their homes to make a call that lasts a few minutes, then walk a few more miles away from the location of the first call to make another call in order to avoid detection. Despite these challenges, however, these networks and North Koreans' use of them are proliferating.

CHRISTIAN ORGANIZATIONS AND THUMB DRIVES

In North Korea, the state views Christianity as an especially serious threat to the regime because the Gospel challenges the official personality cult that is the social and political foundation of the state. Children are taught that their hands will burn off if they ever touch a Bible. Repatriated defectors who admit to meeting Christians in China are punished much more harshly than those who say they haven't. It must be noted that Kim Il-Sung and his family were Christians. Kim Il-Sung's mother, Kang Pan-Sok, was a Presbyterian deaconess. Much of the state's foundational principles, text, and belief system have parallels to the Christian Gospel, Ten Commandments, and Biblical texts. And yet, while variations of small-scale shamanism have been tolerated, Christianity is outlawed because it has the capacity to replace a citizen's belief in the North Korean state.

Despite the state's hatred toward Christianity, Christian organizations work to provide humanitarian aid to people and to infiltrate the country's hardened borders. Nehemiah Park described a situation where he worked with Christian missionaries and North Korean smugglers to sneak in about ten thousand USB thumb drives loaded with audio Bibles, recorded with a North Korean accent, into North Korea. A defector friend told Nehemiah months after the USB-Bible drop that most of the thumb drives were erased and the empty USBs sold on the black market for cheap. But Nehemiah and his Christian missionary partners do not view their project as futile; this only makes them more determined to send in literature—religious, political, cultural—that could hook at least a few willing and curious minds.

The alleged fate of the ten thousand USBs serves as a reminder that information campaigns into North Korea are not linear experiments with the human mind, whereby a piece of outside information instantly and magically liberates a person who has been living under an authoritarian state with its omnipresent propaganda. There are and will be people who will resist outside information, rejecting it as false, or who simply prefer the realities they know. Furthermore, the types of information being sent in are a combination of content that people from the outside world think is beneficial and of interest to North Koreans and material that has been requested.

Some Christian missionaries who sent in the audio Bibles learned that, to no one's surprise, there was a much higher demand for Japanese porn movies than for Bibles, which, to people unfamiliar with religious text, may seem to be merely a series of stories with no context or grounding. Some defectors believe that they are best positioned to send in content because they know most about what their compatriots are interested in secretly learning more about. Defectors must be part of the process of selecting, crafting, packaging, and curating information being sent into North Korea. Otherwise, information campaigns led by do-gooders with noble intentions who lack hyperlocal knowledge could either be futile or seem paternalistic, which in turn would be counterproductive.

Some Christian organizations in North Korea are allowed in as long as they do not proselytize and as long as they follow all of the regime's rules. There are organizations and individuals who work inside North Korea in development, food aid, and education who strictly abide by all of the government's policies of not proselytizing while trying to exemplify Christian values of generosity, love, charity, and honesty in day-to-day interactions with North Koreans.

There is one well-known Buddhist organization called Good Friends, led by the Venerable Pomnyun, a Buddhist monk from South Korea, that works inside North Korea to provide humanitarian aid and has been doing so for over twenty years. There are also rumors that Mormon churches have established networks inside North Korea, though I have not been able to confirm this claim. Christian organizations remain the most visible type of religious organizations in this field.

THE WORK OF KIM HEUNG-KWANG AND NKIS

Months after his release from the labor camp, Kim Heung-Kwang and his family defected by crossing into China and then arriving in South Korea, where they were granted asylum. What is so extraordinary about Kim Heung-Kwang's story is how a mere couple of banned books and a television drama convinced a man so entrenched in the North Korean system to defect. After serving his country by shielding its citizens from outside information, Kim Heung-Kwang decided to "switch sides." From being a North Korean gatekeeper of information to a seeker of information, Kim is now the executive director of North Korean Intellectuals Solidarity (NKIS), a Seoul-based NGO that strives to disseminate information into North Korea despite the regime's vehement disapproval. His organization collaborates with other North Korean defectors living in South Korea who used to be part of the elite class. NKIS works tirelessly to develop hardware, software, and information programs to send into North Korea via brokers and allies across China and into North Korea.

Kim Heung-Kwang explains his mission: "Films are films. I only knew parts of South Korea through films. I wanted to show North Koreans what the good life was. I want to send details of the basic conditions of life in South Korea through digital magazines and footage via USBs. For example, you turn the tap all the way to the left and there's a consistent source of hot water."

Kim regularly takes his smartphone camera and films his ordinary life. Walking through the aisles of E-Mart (Korea's upscale version of a Wal-Mart), he will capture the sheer number of options that consumers have for toothpaste, cookies, other types of food, clothing, and home goods. He chuckled when he said that he also filmed the aisle with countless options for pet food, pet toys, and pet clothes. "Pet clothes! What the heck [are those]?" He wants to share with North Koreans what real life is like for ordinary people living in Seoul.

For several years, DVDs have been the preferred means to sneak movies and shows into North Korea. As purchases of second-hand DVD players manufactured in China became more prevalent, the demand for illegal DVDs rose accordingly.

Over time, DVDs became dangerous for the merchants whom he would commission to sneak them across the border. More of the people he hired were getting caught, questioned, and detained, and consequently few merchants were willing to take on this risky job. NKIS had to come up with more creative ways to circumvent the dangerous security constraints. One of the technologies they created was the stealth USB, which "sleeps" and shows 100 percent empty space on a USB for a programmed period of time. The USB then "awakens" and downloads its contents onto the computer. This way, if a middleman were caught at a border checkpoint or elsewhere, he could insert the USBs into the authorities' computers and have them appear empty. (I am omitting any meaningful details on how these USBs are created, for obvious reasons.) This is only one of an increasing number of creative and clever technological methods that groups are creating in order to get more information into North Korea in a safer way.

Smuggling businesses run by North Koreans naturally facilitate the movement of information across the North Korean–Chinese border. These individuals make trips into China and are able to do so by bribing willing guards to turn a blind eye when the smugglers are moving back and forth. North Koreans demand smuggled electronics like laptops, or "notebooks" as Koreans prefer to call them, from China. A defector told me that sturdy electronics are important because North Koreans do not throw things away; if something is broken, they will figure out a way to fix it, and low-quality electronics are not as easily fixable.

Human smugglers are one way of getting information in. Another more rudimentary way is to wrap disks or drives with multiple layers of plastic bags, tie them with a rope, and slide the packages across the river. So too is hiding them in different parts of trucks, although not too many copies can get in this way. Tires are another way. Flash drives are wrapped in a few layers of plastic bags, stuffed in cigarette boxes, and then tied to the inside of tires (sometimes, without the cigarette boxes), and then someone from the Chinese side of the border will fling the tire into the river and run or hide. The clever dissemination options—albeit at a small scale—are endless.

Kim Heung-Kwang has been publicly and viciously condemned by the North Korean regime in the country's KCNA news, which has published articles of a mission to chop and dice

Kim's body as a chef chops and dices vegetables. Like Park Sang-Hak and other defectors, he has been the target of attempted assassinations as the North Korean government has tried to stop his subversive work: when death threats via KCNA and in the Pyongyang newspaper failed to deter Kim Heung-Kwang, the North Korean regime sent spies to assassinate him. After South Korean intelligence foiled the attempt, the South Korean government put a twenty-four-hour security detail on him.

These manhunts, which are designed not only to eliminate people inside North Korea who are guilty of consuming foreign information, but also to kill defectors living outside North Korea, reveal just how threatened the North Korean government is by information campaigns. The North Korean government consistently places Kim on its public defector assassination target lists, and as of September 2014, he was number two on their list.

The threat of death doesn't discourage Kim. He believes that "external information is North Korea's Achilles' heel, [and] that [it] will be the major force to speed up the breakdown of the current North Korean regime."

EFFORTS BY PARK SE-JOON AND THE NORTH KOREA STRATEGY CENTER

Dr. Park Se-Joon now works at the North Korea Strategy Center—a center founded by Kang Cheol-Hwan, who spent ten years in Yodok political prison camp and ended up escaping in 1992. Founded in 2007, this defector-led NGO works to "bring awareness of North Korea's human rights conditions and bring changes for freedom in North Korea." One of the main areas of focus is to "promote access to information through media dissemination in North Korea to raise public consciousness of human rights and democracy." The four thousand USBs and forty thousand

DVDs they sent in include entertaining films, documentaries, news articles, defector testimonies, and the offline version of the Korean Wikipedia. By hosting focus groups with recent defectors, NKSC works to send in content that is both enticing and edifying; they also conduct brainstorming sessions with university students and companies across the United States and elsewhere to help their operation expand and become more effective.

Kang Cheol-Hwan recently shared that his organization made the strategic decision to send USBs and other media through the Chinese–North Korean border quietly and covertly to induce change inside North Korea. His organization prefers this over sending airborne balloons, a method that attracts unnecessary public attention and so can quickly incur the wrath of the North Korean government and endanger South Korean national security. Whenever such balloon launches led by other groups are announced prior to their launches, too, activists and residents who reside near the DMZ protest because they are geographically the closest South Koreans, and so would bear the brunt of any military retaliation by the North.

JEONG GWANG-IL: FROM YODOK TO INFORMATION DISSEMINATION

Business was good for Jeong Gwang-Il, a former North Korean army veteran who had moved on to managing a big trading company. But in 1999 he was arrested for contacting South Korean people and was accused of being a spy for the South Koreans against the North. After being forced to make a false confession, he was sentenced to Camp 15—Yodok, one of the infamous North Korean camps for political prisoners. When he entered the Hoeryong City Security Agency for his interrogations, he weighed 75 kilograms (165.6 pounds). But after nine months of questioning in the underground cell of the security agency, where the guards broke all his teeth (leaving him toothless for four years), repeatedly beat him with a thick wooden club, and used "pigeon torture" to prevent him from sleeping, his weight dropped to 38 kilograms (83.9 pounds). He and other political prison camp survivors explain "pigeon torture" this way: "[My] handcuffed arms were tied at the back to a pillar, [so] I could [neither] stand up or sit down. [My] shoulders became paralyzed in a day, bones seemed to break through the chest, and the whole body [became] paralyzed."

Jeong Gwang-Il spent three harrowing years at Yodok, where most inmates are considered alleged political enemies of the North Korean regime. Droves of prisoners arrived every week, many of whom had been forcibly repatriated from China after being caught by Chinese police. After his release from Yodok, Jeong Gwang-Il defected from North Korea on April 30, 2003, and arrived in South Korea on April 22, 2004. Since then, he has been working toward the abolishment of prison camps. A few years into working for an organization called Free the NK Gulag, he began sending USBs with South Korean dramas loaded on them into North Korea.

When we met, Jeong spoke in a very matter-of-fact manner. He's a charismatic and engaging man, with a warm smile that has an affirming affect. He said, "Honestly, the North Korean people do not even know what love is. They do not know how to express love. Even when I arrived in South Korea and saw young couples expressing love for one another on the streets, for example, I disliked seeing that. Why? Because I was seeing it for the first time. North Korea is not a place for human beings to live in. So that's why we send dramas in to show a more normal view of South Korea. In South Korea, younger people like to

높이 60 cm

비둥기 고문

A drawing of pigeon torture sketched by Kim Kwang-Il, a former prisoner in a North Korean political camp. His drawings were submitted to the U.N. Commission of Inquiry on Human Rights in the Democratic Republic of Korea. Drawing by Kwon Hyo-Jin. Submitted to the UN Commission of Inquiry on Human Rights in the Democratic Republic of Korea by former prisoner Mr. Kim Kwang-Il.

watch dramas or romantic dramas and young men like to watch action flicks. It's the same thing in North Korea. Because they're humans, too. So we began to change the perception of the North Korean people [by] sending in outside media and information."

Jeong Gwang-Il later joined the North Korea Strategy Center, where he was tasked with sending USBs into North Korea. Given his experience, he recently started a new organization called "No Chain: the Association of North Korean Political Victims and Their Families," which works to raise awareness of the grievances experienced by political prison camp victims and their relatives. He works closely with Henry Song, a Korean-American who has been a relentless, selfless North Korean human rights activist for over a decade and is probably one of the most beloved activists by defectors. One project Jeong Gwang-Il completed was a report containing the names of 180 prisoners who were being held in Yodok, which he released. Included in his list of names was the name of the vice minister of the North Korean Ministry of Post and Telecommunications. He said, "You ask how I know that? How can a guy like me know a guy like him, a vice minister? Because we were in Yodok together at the same time. It's simple."

"The regime criticized me publicly for the third time this year alone," he told me while sipping on his Americano at an over-priced Seoul cafe. He bought me the same beverage. "They called me human scum, trash, and threatened to kill me again. In any case, it's not like I'm scared by these threats and attacks. All their threats are on their site, the Uriminzokkiri."

"Aren't you intimidated?" I asked. I ask this of every North Korean defector who is involved in this line of work. He responded: "If I were scared or intimidated by them, there is no way I would be doing this work in the first place. Last year in October, when participating in events at the U.N., I came face to face with North Korean diplomats there. Nine North Korean diplomats turned up at a session on North Korean human rights, and at first I was a bit flustered. But I mustered up the courage to ask them directly, 'Why am I labeled human scum and trash? Why do you guys call me trash?' The regime is reacting against me even more harshly now."

The North Korean government is well aware of Jeong Gwang-Il's frequent trips to China. The North Korean embassy in

Beijing provides information to Chinese authorities on select defectors, including activists like Jeong. "I guess they knew I was coming to China. So they're obviously trying to prevent me from going to China, but that won't stop me. I'll continue to go to China to do this work," Jeong said.

This courage, dedication, and resilience infuses the important work of sending information into North Korea, which has been further energized by Jeong's wide networks of supporters, brokers, and creative methods of sneaking in hardware. One video his organization created and sent into North Korea, *Answer Me,* features a series of people who were imprisoned, beaten, and silenced before defecting. Jeong Gwang-Il rhetorically asks the listener in each case: "Why was this high-ranking official sent to Yodok?" As Jeong explains, "Of course the regime had no answers for this. They just criticize me, and argue past me." Sim Chol-Ho, the vice minister of the North Korean Ministry of Post and Telecommunications, was allegedly sent to Yodok for criticizing the North Korean intelligence apparatus, but the charge cannot be confirmed.

Another video Jeong produced with Open Radio pertains to capitalism. Titled *Capitalism through the Eyes of the Defector,* it is designed to explain to North Koreans why taxes are important since the socialist system technically has no taxes and offers free education, free healthcare, and so on. "The roads in North Korea are just terrible," Jeong says while clucking his tongue. "Just awful. Taxes [are needed] to pay for paved roads!" He described an increase in complaints to local authorities about economic conditions in the country. Many of the grievances pertain to their particular situations, but knowledge of the outside world has given North Koreans points of comparison that heighten their frustration.

So, there's a sense of complaint and discontent rising to the top, and [it is] vocalized because there is no tangible mechanism by which people's lives can improve. Complaints are growing in their minds. In South Korea, if you work for a day, you get paid at a minimum of $50 [minimum wage in South Korea is $4.90 per hour]. With this money, you can buy 15–20 kilograms of rice on the black market in North Korea. This is a month's worth of food. If you work for two days in South Korea, this gives you enough money to eat happily and fully for an entire month in North Korea. Not only rice, but vegetables, condiments like soybean paste, soy sauce, sesame oil, things like that. So if you take South Korean minimum wage and apply it to North Korea's situation, this is what you get. Of course in South Korea, this is not the case. Most people don't eat on daily wages. People do not calculate their daily wages and convert it into daily meals. Well, maybe some do. But not most. So as North Koreans are learning more about how other people live, and they start to compare themselves to others, their grievances start to form and they start organizing and testing these thoughts in their mind.

Of course airing personal economic grievances with language carefully laced with self-deprecation among trusted friends is not going to spark a revolution in a big way any time soon. But, as Jeong says, "This is how sparks can ignite and eventually lead to democratization. Self and situational awareness coupled with discontent is the beginning of a long, arduous process."

Anecdotes and footage smuggled out of North Korea show graffiti in Chongjin where someone wrote "Down with Kim Jong-Un" on the wall of a university building. This was absolutely unthinkable in the past—making derisive comments about political leaders is no joke or prank. But Jeong and other older defectors who have lived through Kim Il-Sung and Kim Jong-Il's leadership believe that though unorganized and unstructured, the discontent that is quietly brewing in big pockets of the population is significant.

Knowing one's audience in North Korea is important for another reason. "Regarding the media, some people in this line of work just send whatever South Korean media they find and send it in. But this will not work; it's not the way to do it. The media formats in North Korea are different from China and South Korea. The TV format is PAL in North Korea, whereas in South Korea, the TV broadcast format is NTSC. If NTSC files are sent into North Korea, there are issues with playback. For example, the sound may play, but no images will show. The subtitles may come out, but no sound. Or the color may come out in just black and white. Files must be converted into PAL format, but some people don't realize this. Obviously, there are various methods of physically sending in information. Many DVDs were sent in. There are some drawbacks regarding discs but also benefits. There are many machines and DVD players in the market for people to buy for a good price. Around 2012, USBs became more popular items to sell and circulate."

These days, Chinese-manufactured MP4 players are widely used, so SD cards have been the more recently popularized method of distributing content. MP4 players are small, and the batteries are rechargeable with battery power lasting for about two hours at a time, so people can watch movies on the small screens. According to Jeong Gwang-Il, "Notetels are for bumpkins."

A Notetel—a word that combines a basic notebook (or a laptop) and television—is a popular Chinese-made portable media player that has ports for USBs and SDs, can also play DVD discs, and contains both radio and TV tuners. Notetels can be charged with a car battery, which is helpful since North Korean households do not have uninterrupted access to electricity. At about 300 Chinese yuan, or $47.20 in U.S. dollars, they became widespread, cracked down upon, and then legalized in 2014 with the stipulation that they had to be registered with the local authorities. Some owners of Notetels may actually watch state-sanctioned material, but more curious individuals load both a North Korean DVD and a South Korean USB drive onto their Notetel, since the USB drive can be easily pulled out and concealed if necessary. If the authorities burst into a person's home, checking for the heat on the machine, he or she could easily make the case that the Notetel was warm because it was playing the North Korean DVD. Sokeel Park, research director at Liberty in North Korea, stated: "They [Notetels] are so popular because they are perfect for overcoming the twin barriers to foreign media consumption: surveillance and power outages. If you were to design the perfect device for North Koreans, it would be this." Park further explains: "People inside North Korea sell USBs for money. If these USBs get to the huge market in Chongjin, for example, you could be sure that the USBs will spread all across the country like in Hwanghae Province, Wonsan, and Hamhung. Our sources tell us what they want to sell, and we get it for them."

I have heard this before, that marketeers inside North Korea contact activists like Jeong and ask them for specific movies and dramas they want to sell. I asked Jeong Gwang-Il how this works, given the incredible difficulties around communicating with people inside North Korea, especially around such a sensitive topic.

"Hold on, look. I'm trying to show you a text conversation with someone in North Korea." He pulls out his Samsung

Android phone and opens his Kakao Talk app, the most popular South Korean messaging app that also allows free international phone calls. With over 130 million registered users and 3 billion messages sent and received every day, North Koreans and Chinese middlemen have not been left in the dark. He pulls up a chat with a North Korean businessman who lives inside North Korea (the businessman used a Chinese name for his Kakao Talk ID) with a cartoon as his profile photo. As he allowed me to scroll up and down to read their text exchanges, I was amazed by how specific and recent some of these drama titles were. One of the messages had an enumerated list of ten drama and TV show titles—most were in Korean, while one was in Chinese and one was in English.

"Our sources inside North Korea figure out what their customers want to watch. What dramas to send by title. We get the texts and fulfill their orders, basically. Look at these TV show and drama titles. I mean, I have no idea what some of these shows are, and I *live* in South Korea!" he exclaimed.

He saw that I was amazed by how demand-driven this enterprise was, and was amused. "What, you don't use Kakao app?" he said. "It's different from the past because now, it's all demand-based. At least for me. And it's super specific. I'll get requests by the drama episode number! Sometimes a 16GB USB is too small to contain all the episodes, so I'll have to divide the different episodes into multiple USBs, but then I can't ensure that the same viewer will receive all the USBs from the same stock."

In his case, and that of some others, the activist fundraises and operates as an NGO to provide these media in different forms. They are sent into North Korea through smugglers—usually Chinese or Joseonjok—and are sold to vendors at street markets who then mark up the prices to sell to individual buyers who frequent the markets. As a defector, he aims to bring big ideas to his former countrymen in North Korea, but everyone else in the distribution network is motivated by profit. The profit-driven nature of foreign media distribution networks provides for the stable distribution of media from NGO offices in South Korea to North Korean homes. "If I send 100 USBs and SD cards loaded with movies and shows, I tell the middlemen who help transmit the stuff, which is our ultimate goal, to sell them. Selling them is the fastest way to disseminate the USBs and SD cards. The free market system will work best. If these USBs are just given away inside North Korea, it won't work. People will be suspicious and wonder why they're being given out for free. North Korea is an extremely free market system."

Much more political content is also sent in. There was recently a video made showing or narrating the deaths of dictators like Hitler, Stalin, Ghaddafi, and Ceaușescu, which of course alludes to the possibility of how Kim Jong-Un's life may end. The historical drama about the first prime minister of the Chosun dynasty, Jeong Do-Jeon, was sent in and was apparently very popular among older men.

"Look, I'm your father's age. I was born way before you were born," he tells me. "I lived through the Kim Il-Sung and Kim Jong-Il era, but not Kim Jong-Un era. It's different these days. Nowadays, people in North Korea will refer to Kim Jong-Un as just 'Jong-Un,' like he's their buddy. This was something unimaginable in the past! 'Jong-Un said this, Jong-Un did that.'"

In Korean culture, only peers of the same age who are comfortable with one another, or elders who are addressing younger people, use given names. Even so, elders who are addressing a younger person past a certain age will add a suffix like "-ssi" to show respect. If a new acquaintance were referring to me, for example, regardless of his or her age, he or she would refer to me as "Ms. Baek" or "Jieun-ssi." My parents, older relatives, and good friends, however, would call me "Jieun." So for citizens to refer to their supposedly divine leader by his name shows a complete lack of reverence.

Jeong Gwang-Il continues: "Even if the media we send in is confiscated, that's fine. Why? The security agents end up viewing the stuff. Whoever sells it, buys it, borrows it, loans it out, confiscates it, sells it, doesn't matter. It's all meant to be seen."

Watching outside materials is slowly opening the minds of viewers inside North Korea. This is undeniable. But most people do not automatically want to defect after watching a movie or two. Most people escape North Korea because they simply want to live a better life. People who leave for political reasons are few and far between. People's relationship with the North Korean state and country is complicated, regardless of how well fed or underprivileged they are. Ideological brainwashing happens on a daily basis, throughout the day, and has been happening for generations. This type of ideology, coupled with fear, cannot be reversed by watching a single drama or two. Additionally, defecting from North Korea is a clear act of betrayal, and citizens are extraordinarily reluctant to betray their country and endanger their families.

LEE JOON-HEE: VIEWS FROM THE YOUNGER GENERATION

Every time I see Lee Joon-Hee, he has his head buried in a book written in English. He's studying political science at a South Korean university and tries to study everything in English to prepare for a year abroad in the States. By watching him interact with young girls around his campus and at restaurants, I can tell he's a little flirtatious. Young female students steal glances at him when he walks by. He's on the taller side, lanky, and has thick black eyeglasses that frame his face. He has recently gotten a trendy "wave perm" that's popular among South Korean male students. Not accustomed to his new hairstyle, he used his left hand repeatedly to sweep his bangs to the side. Joon-Hee's school friends, who are also from North Korea, mischievously whispered to me, "He's what South Korean girls call a 'cool boy.'" Over time, I picked up on what a "cool boy" connotes in South Korea: a decently attractive male who is aloof and ignores the flirtations of girls while flirting back.

Born in 1990 in Hyesan, Ryanggang Province, Joon-Hee spent his first twenty years living what he describes as a "pretty normal, low-key life." He describes his home town as a hub for smuggling, trade, and market activity. Nonchalantly, he shrugs and says, "It's just an ordinary market city. Hundreds of different stalls. Before Kim Il-Sung died, I think our city was okay, but I don't remember because I was a baby. Once he died in 1994, all the state-related infrastructure crumbled. All I remember since being a toddler is how my city ran on markets." Within the street markets are black markets, where items like the MP3 and MP4 players that Joon-Hee bought were purchased. A guide would walk them over to someone's house or another nearby location to show them the sensitive merchandise. South Korean music and films were his preferred means of entertainment.

Joon-Hee's mellow and undramatic personality characterizes the way he describes his life back in North Korea. But his intelligence and nuance are cutting. "Obviously, each person's life is different. But what I observed is that I rarely thought about the government, especially before middle school. I guess unless you're really smart or belong to an elite family, a young person doesn't think too much about their government. I mean, did you?"

His question caught me off guard. I have been studying political science and public policy since college, but as a middle schooler, I rarely thought about politics. I didn't even know who my Congressional representatives were. Joon-Hee's question pointed to the common trait of young students—lack of interest in their government, illiberal or not. They just want to have fun with their friends, and do as little homework as possible without getting in too much trouble.

"Children of common people, at least in my town of Hyesan, had no interest in politics or broader economics other than how much money their parents gave them to buy stuff. As young students, we just lived in society's margins and tried our best to not get in trouble while doing everything we wanted. The key was to not get caught. We memorized North Korean history and the Kim family's history. It was boring and I really didn't want to do it, but my lack of interest wasn't an active political statement. I just didn't want to study. Who does, especially when they're young?"

Joon-Hee's grandfather used to call Kim Jong-Il by name, which is considered extremely disrespectful in Korean culture. "My grandfather would sit there and talk about how that bastard has to die. My parents talked a lot about Deng Xiaoping and said 'we need to liberalize, like Deng.' I was shocked, but didn't ask any deep questions. But at a young age, I observed that such a culture of disrespect towards the Kims was possible. I also knew there were incredibly strict rules around respecting the government. It boiled down to being smart about not saying the wrong things in front of the wrong people."

After watching films, he realized the dramatic gaps between South Korea and his own country. "Everyone in my town knows that South Korea is significantly wealthier than North Korea. We all know that Japanese goods are durable. But no one raises these issues in class, of course." The questions that Joon-Hee mulled over were related to why North Korea was so poor, but such questions did not tie into criticism of the government or his political system. The questions in his mind stopped at economic grievances. He once asked his parents that if the Dear Leader was so generous and loving, then "why don't I go and meet with the General? I need to have a chat with him. Won't he say yes if I asked?"

His parents shut the idea down immediately. When he pushed back, they responded by stating simply that he would not be able to obtain the permits required to move past the checkpoints from Hyesan to Pyongyang. He dropped the idea.

By watching films and by being able to compare the dual realities—the one he was living in real time, and the one he was being taught in school—Joon-Hee's thinking started to change. "But"—he was quick to preemptively measure his response—"a change in thinking about the regime does not mean it's radical change. Since I live in South Korea and can speak freely, I have acquired the language, the terminology, and the ability to critically think and question things on my own. Most defectors do. But in North Korea, even if you observe differences between reality and school textbooks, you really can't think about it. You don't have that ability."

While Joon-Hee was growing up, his parents' friends would gather and often refer to the four dragons of Asia: Singapore, Hong Kong, South Korea, and Taiwan. Joon-Hee says everyone in his vicinity knew that North Korea was objectively and comparatively poor. "But even with that information, there's no plan. People, at least those I knew, did not seem to link a grievance with action. The thinking simply stops there. So, like pigs, people are content with the options available to them. People just do not question or push the system too much. Maybe it's because we've been trained since birth not to question, or else we face grave consequences. I was one of those people, too."

Joon-Hee, like his peers from North Korea, has developed a keen sense of the differences between official rules and the unofficial, unspoken norms. Just like others, he was very aware of the need to bribe officials to get by. His mother bought produce from rural areas and sold them at marked-up prices in the Hyesan markets. Since produce changes by season, she would sometimes sell pine seeds, sesame oil, and at other times mushrooms and frogs. If the items she was selling were tolerated by the authorities, she would sell the goods to merchants who would then sell to consumers. Merchants would sometimes ask her to hold on to her inventory to ensure that their stock didn't build up. If the goods she was selling were illegal, she would sell directly to consumers.

This ability to navigate the world of unspoken rules in such a restrictive society translated into romance and dating for Joon-Hee. In North Korea, there are strict social norms controlling public and private behavior between the sexes. Similar rules exist in South Korea and other East Asian nations, but are growing increasingly obsolete. When discussing the novelty of American and Korean films, we broached the topic of romance and intimacy in the films. I asked him, "What did you feel when you saw the kissing, the holding hands, and the other stuff in the films?"

Without skipping a beat, Joon-Hee said coolly, "In my home town, and probably for the rest of the country, people can't hold hands during the day. It's considered rude and obscene to hold hands in public, even for married couples. But at nighttime, there are no limitations. I guess there's *some* benefit to North Korea not having sufficient electricity. It's so dark at night. When it comes to romance, love, and attraction, there is no nationality. There's a soul. That's the only similarity." Talk about a silver lining.

Joon-Hee is underscoring the point that North Korean young adults in his generation are more willing to break political, social, and cultural rules to serve their interests. When I speak to men and women born in the 1950s, 1960s, and 1970s, the idea of public (or even private) displays of affection is considered preposterous. Romance between teenagers during their time was unthinkable. Now, boys like Joon-Hee say there are no limits.

KIM HA-YOUNG: THE IMPORTANCE OF FRIENDSHIP NETWORKS

"I watched a lot of Hollywood movies, Korean movies, and Korean TV shows at home. I watched all the Bond movies—both the American and British series—and all the Disney movies." Ha-Young squeezed both eyes shut and swept her arms across the air to gesticulate that she had watched all the Disney movies. She then started to rattle off Disney titles and counted with her fingers. "OK so I watched *Sleeping Beauty, Cinderella, Snow White, Tarzan, Prince of Egypt,* and what's the one with the elephant?"

"*Dumbo*?" I offered. I haven't watched Disney movies for over fifteen years, and it was obvious that this North Korean girl had watched a lot more Disney movies than I had.

"Yes! *Dumbo.* Oh, and *Cinderella,* the second one. *Dreams Come True.*"

I was born an hour away from Disneyland, but I didn't even know that there was a sequel to *Cinderella.*

"When I came to South Korea, I searched for the third *Cinderella* and watched it on YouTube. I heard about the third *Cinderella* in North Korea, but didn't have time to watch it. Oh, of course, I watched the Harry Potter movies. All of them. For Korean materials, I watched *Autumn in My Heart.* I remember I was nine years old. That was 2000. Everyone watched that one. There was a drama called *Stairway to Heaven* that was released in 2003. I watched that that same year." Ha-Young beamed, proud that she was up with the world's entertainment trends, a freedom that underscored her well-to-do background.

Walt Disney once said, "Animation offers a medium of storytelling and visual entertainment which can bring pleasure and information to people of all ages everywhere in the world." Ha-Young and other North Koreans certainly were not beyond the reach of Disney's universally appealing animations that narrate the human spirit. Even Kim Jong-Un was intrigued by the world of Disney.[1]

Ha-Young continued, "*The General's Son.* You probably don't know that because you're American, but that was a hit. There was a drama called *Affection.* Oh I have to tell you. The most shocking movie was an adult movie called *Birdcage Inn.* It's a South Korean film about a college girl who is poor so she prostitutes. She ends up sleeping with the dad and the son, and it's all really twisted. But there's so much . . . you know. My parents would watch these kind of movies while I was asleep or out of the house. But one time, I woke up in the middle of the night and they were watching the movie in the same room I was sleeping. I couldn't fully open my eyes, or they'd turn it off. So I pretended to be asleep, occasionally move sleeping positions and pretend to mumble in my sleep. But I watched most of it. It was [my] first time [seeing] naked men and women. They still don't know that I did that. But it was so interesting! The most 'red' and intimate that North Korean films got was just hugging. Hugging is boring."

"Just so I understood you correctly, you're referring to sex scenes, right?" That was a bit forthright for her taste, because she blushed, covered her mouth with her right hand, and nodded.

"I didn't have too much of a political mind back then, but I naturally thought about what I learned in my North Korean textbook, about how South Koreans run around naked and starving because they are so poor. We were taught that South Koreans don't go to school because they can't pay tuition, and they die on the streets because they can't pay for hospitals. But as I watched Korean movies and shows, I thought to myself, 'What kind of bullshit are the textbooks talking about?' I quickly realized that South Korea was more developed than North Korea."

Although she had these questions that contradicted her education, she was able to neatly categorize them in her mind and not think of them too much. She lived comfortably, and bribes kept her family fairly immune from legal or political trouble. The one thing she was most jealous of while watching all these films and shows was uninterrupted electricity.

"Since electricity production is so weak, you get a lot of blackouts, but if you watch Korean or American TV shows or movies, you see that lights are on at night. Even on the streets! It's bright. At night!" She repeated these phrases to emphasize how shocking this was to her. "Then I thought to myself Koreans and Americans must be able to watch TV twenty-four hours a day, seven days a week. I was so jealous of them for that. We learned that they were imperialist wolves, that they were always ready to attack our state. But when I watched TV shows, they were really funny, and very romantic."

She lingered on this point.

I didn't even know the term "romantic" when I was back in the North. There, if a man was good, we described him as "friendly" or as a "family man." But in these South Korean TV shows, men cleaned the house, did the laundry, gave their wives shoulder massages. They were so affectionate to their families. They were so sweet to their girlfriends. They carried their purses, even if the purses weren't heavy, and even carried the girls on their backs if they were wearing high heels so that their feet wouldn't hurt. This is absolutely unimaginable in North Korea. People gossip even if a couple is holding hands because it's promiscuous. Both before and after marriage. If an unmarried couple is holding hands, they're promiscuous and obscene. If a married couple is holding hands, they're considered too much, like they're showing off. So if a couple is "dating," they walk on the street with good distance between the man and woman. But in these South Korean dramas, you see couples on piggyback, linking arms, boys touching the girls' hair, and it was just amazing. My girlfriends swooned when watching tall, handsome South Korean boyfriends gazing [into] their girlfriends' beautiful eyes. We would run around, imitating the South Korean accent amongst ourselves.

Ha-Young and others like her are on the receiving end of the work of NGOs like Jeong Gwang-Il's work. She would go to the equivalent of a department store that sold clothes and home products.

There, you can quietly ask a young lady over the counter if they have "it." They always have "it." They sell films, Korean dramas, and Korean music. K-pop is so fun. You can get it there, but the really wealthy, connected families get them straight from Chinese brokers. Within a week of a drama episode airing in South Korea, Chinese businessmen rip off copies and sell it in North Korea. You buy these and then exchange DVDs or USBs with your trusted friends. We were constantly exchanging and rotating our copies. The more films a trusted network acquired, the more embedded we would all become in a spider web of film exchanges. With drama episodes, the rotation system worked as follows: Let's say that a drama series has 30 episodes, and three families are involved in the rotation scheme of this particular drama series. Family One would watch episodes 1–10 in a few days and pass them onto Family Two while Family One moved onto episodes 11–20. Once these two families were finished, Family One would move onto episodes 21–30, Family Two would move onto 11–20, and pass on episodes 1–10 to Family Three. Once Family One was done, they would pass on episodes 21–30 to Family Two, etc., and start a new drama series, and this system would continue and expand as families pulled in other trusted friends.

People shared only among close friends, and among friends who were financially well-off enough to bribe officials if they got caught. "If my family loaned a film to a poor family, and they got caught, they [would] inevitably give up our names to the officials and we'd get in trouble. We only shared it with *jjigae*-pants friends. Babies wear baby clothes called *jjigae* that have buttons at the bottom for babies who are on the brink of being potty trained. So *jjigae* pants friends refer to friends whom you've known since you were that young."

5 A NEW GENERATION RISING

The concept of "young" or "old" is different in North Korea than across its borders. Ha-Young tells me, "I left North Korea when I was seventeen years old. But that's not young. Once you turn eighteen, you graduate [from] high school, start a job, and enter society as a full-grown adult. North Koreans generally have suffered a lot, and need to be hell-bent on surviving. Only the strongest-willed survive. The North Korean 'youth,' as the world may call us, are quite mature." She continues to defend her position that seventeen-year-old North Koreans are adults because they have seen the ugliest parts of society and human nature that in other societies are usually hidden from people that young.

THE JANGMADANG GENERATION

Ha-Young is part of what is now widely referred to as the *Jangmadang* generation. *Jangmadang* in Korean literally means "market grounds" and refers to the black and gray markets that sprang up around the time of the Great Famine. North Koreans who were born in the middle of, or after, the famine grew up depending on the markets. That is, almost all defectors who are thirty-five years old or younger—an age group that makes up about a quarter of the North Korean population—bought their food and goods by shopping in the informal markets. They didn't stand in lines with ration tickets to collect their rations like their parents or grandparents. Such infrastructure no longer exists in most parts of the country.

There are a few broad characteristics that describe this new, young generation. First, they are capitalistic, individualistic, and more likely to take risks. They have found ways to make money to buy things they want on the street markets. Sokeel Park, director of research at the U.S.-based NGO Liberty in North Korea, states that the Jangmadang generation has "grown up on capitalism," with many of them engaged in business operations smuggling in and selling off fashionable items coveted by residents viewing illicit South Korean dramas.[1] He refers to these North Korean young adults as "native capitalists . . . because they didn't really experience socialism in its economic form at any point. They grew up and only remember capitalism. So their first nature is to be profit driven, materialistic, individualistic."[2] In other words, people of this generation are self-reliant, and do not rely on their government, because they don't remember receiving anything of significant value from the government. The token rations that they did receive were of poor quality. Lee Joon-Hee received just one thing from the state when he was there: school uniforms, which were handed out twice. "But they were too big. I didn't wear them because they were such poor quality, so my mom would go to the street market to buy the nice red scarves. The crap the state gave out was thin and wrinkled easily. The fancy, expensive red scarves that we would tie around our necks were nice and stiff. They wouldn't wrinkle or crease."

Second, North Korea's young adults have unprecedented access to foreign information—information that is unraveling what they have learned in school and through their youth leagues. All the young defectors I met have watched foreign films and shows and read books, and knew about the world outside North Korea before defecting. A researcher at the South Korean Institute for National Unification (KINU) who has been interviewing North Korean defectors for twenty years told me that she and her colleagues cannot remember a single defector from recent years who has not seen or listened to foreign media before entering South Korea. Of course defectors comprise a select demographic, but many say that even those who decide to remain in North Korea consume foreign media. Only a slim minority who are too scared, or are too poor to bribe officials in case they are caught, do not watch films.

When asked to estimate the percentage of people in their North Korean home towns who watch foreign films and access media, most defectors answer 70 to 80 percent. It's relevant to note, too, that 76 to 84 percent of all defectors settled in South Korea today are from either North Hamgyong Province or Ryanggang Province, which are provinces that border the North Korean–Chinese border and are assumed to receive the most foreign media broadcasts and materials.[3] Min-Jun, a recent young defector, says, "In our generation, young people get together quietly in each other's homes, put on South Korean K-pop on a speaker, and have a little dance party. We have no idea if we're doing it right, but we dance with the music on low. The government says North Korea is socialist, but that's not true. North Korea is capitalistic. You can solve anything with money. Truly."

Third, this younger generation is significantly less loyal to the state and its leadership. Much of their experiences with markets and access to foreign information contradict the propaganda they learn from the state, so younger people dismiss much of what they hear via the state radio, television, and newspaper, and from school officials. This lack of devotion to the state presents a clear challenge to the authoritarian government: either adapt their narrative and policies to meaningfully capture the younger citizens' loyalty, or continue to lose credibility and support among the millennials, whose influence, over time, will naturally eclipse that of the older generations. If it doesn't adapt to the times, Kim's government risks experiencing dramatic changes that it may not be able to control.

KIM HA-YOUNG, A TYPICAL NORTH KOREAN MILLENNIAL

Kim Ha-Young is a good example of a North Korean who is part of the Jangmadang generation. Young people in North Korea wear clothes with Western cartoons on them, sport shorter skirts than previous generations of women, quietly whistle South Korean pop songs, and use South Korean slang that they picked up from secretly watching movies. Some more rebellious youth might even add a flourish to his or her hairstyle that does not exactly fit into any of the eighteen state-approved hairstyles for women, or the ten state-approved hairstyles for men.

Hair dyeing was not allowed, but some kids with money who were also considered more "enlightened" would get their hair slightly dyed somewhere. When those students got caught during dress code checks at school, they would lie and say that their hair was naturally yellow because they used to be malnourished. Teachers would sometimes believe this and let the students off the hook, since hair discoloration from severe malnutrition was common, especially during the 1990s. Nail polish was also forbidden, but girls would buy clear nail polish and wear it. At school, all students would have to show their hands to their teachers as part of the hygiene checkups, and girls with polished nails would be disciplined. Long nails were considered bad hygiene, and nail polish was considered Western. Thick, chunky scarves were en vogue in numerous dramas, so girls would dig through second-hand accessories from China at market stalls to find the most stylish scarves. Same with ankle-length coats, the small girly backpacks with long thin straps, polyester blouses with big bows, sneaker wedges, boot cut jeans, cropped jackets, glittery hair bands, and even "beggar style haircuts" for girls that had a shaggy, jagged look.

In *Autumn in My Heart,* the female protagonist wears her stick-straight hair all the way back in a thick hair band. Like any fashion trend that appears in a popular new drama, as the drama quietly circulates among trusted friends, the trendy style would spring up in the street markets. If glittery hair bands were the trend, they would suddenly be available for sale. If a new perm was shown in the South Korean dramas, then stalls offering perms would appear in the street markets. Ha-Young went to the market and found numerous stalls selling second-hand jewel-lined hair bands. Hers were confiscated twice by a peer disciplinarian, but she went to the assistant principal's office each time and offered him a few packs of cigarettes in exchange for it. She promised each time never to wear it again, but was caught a third time. The assistant principal growled and threatened to snap it in half if she was caught wearing it again. Desperately wanting her pretty hair band back, she swore never to do it again, traded him for more packs of cigarettes, stuck it in her backpack, and wore the hair band as soon as she walked out the school gates.

South Korea and the West, particularly the United States, are no longer seen as purely evil among this generation. Trying a new fashion trend from across the border or secretly singing South Korean pop songs are signs that young people are breaking away from the state's strict policies around permitted behavior. North Koreans who were born during or after the Great Famine and have been exposed to widespread street markets have grown up in a society where complete dependence on the state for people's livelihood was just not the case. So although young North Koreans continue to follow state laws and pay respect to their leader, young defectors share anecdotes about how many of their friends back at home in North Korea make jokes about the leader behind closed doors. Most households, too, they say, are involved in market activity to survive.

More consequentially, the new generation of North Korean people who grew up depending on street markets and watching foreign films have a fundamentally different relationship with the state and their leader. Since they are savvy, young people know how to minimally follow the rules and skirt the less important ones. They are living in two realities—the official North Korean state-sanctioned reality, and the more capitalistic reality—and they are determined to continue to learn about the world outside North Korea.

Out of boredom and curiosity, Ha-Young watched films, which sparked her strong preference for foreign goods—and by buying foreign goods, she came inevitably to question the party line about the state and about the economic realities across North Korea's borders. I asked her if she ever felt strong loyalty to her former government, to which she replied, "Even when I was in school, of course we learned about Kim Il-Sung, his wife Kim Jong-Suk, Kim Jong-Il, blah, blah, blah." She rolled her eyes while referring to the Great Leader and Dear Leader, which revealed a deep irreverence that simply couldn't have been contrived. "We learned about the history of the Kim family. In school, we learned about their crusades, how they founded the country, and worked for the happiness of the people. Their personal history was what we learned in history class. It was all really boring for me. If Kim Il-Sung said something, we had to write that sentence—word for word—on the test. It was so stressful. I mean, we weren't even law students. Kids didn't like it and I really didn't like it. I hated studying in general. Also, all the Kim family stuff was so distant from me because they never directly affected or benefited my life. That's why my mom pulled me out of school every other month or so. She told me that all that a girl needed to do was to marry well and know how to count money at an early age. I picked up from my mom that ideology was not that important."

She was adamant that people like her had no interest in ideology or politics; they were just interested in making money, making a living, being entertained, and getting by. Ha-Young's lack of interest in the Kim family was not politically motivated; it was simply indifference. Neither she nor her neighbors ever received rations or money from the state. They were simply busy making a living. "They didn't take care of us, so why should we care about them? Whatever they did didn't matter to us. We simply didn't care."

Whenever her inminban (neighborhood unit) received top orders from the government, households reluctantly complied. More often than not, they received orders to provide supplies for the military troops. For example, soldiers stand patrol at the borders and usually lie on their stomachs atop frozen surfaces, with their guns in position. Ha-Young and her neighbors had to find rabbits to skin and would make hats, belts, or patches out of them to protect the soldiers' stomachs. Rabbit fur was a common requirement during the winter. The inminban leader would also collect a few dollars from each household to support the soldiers.

As Ha-Young explained, "Everything cost money and people really hated it. But since the inminban leader kept track of who hadn't contributed, we all had to. If someone continually refused, they would get called out at a public self-criticism session. So to avoid public shame, people would begrudgingly pay and curse under their breath. Some poor people would even steal from another home to make their contributions to the government. People complained to trusted friends about local policies. Everyone knew better than to explicitly complain about Kim Il-Sung and Kim Jong-Un, so their outlet was to privately air economic grievances to their friends."

A BREAKFAST CHAT WITH THREE YOUNG DEFECTORS

Sitting cross-legged with three recent male defectors who had graduated from Hanawon together just months earlier, the four of us sipped on Maxwell instant coffee and nibbled at Korean melons for breakfast while chatting about how newer, cheaper Chinese equipment was entering North Korea that allowed young, savvy people to circumvent North Korean laws.

Joo-Won has a muscular build and a tan complexion that gives away his background in construction work while in North Korea.[4] He is a twenty-two-year-old from Eunduk County, North Hamgyong Province, who defected because he was frustrated with the lack of opportunities available to him due to his mother's earlier defection. A road construction manager approached him with a work order dispatched from the state for a road construction job. Having no choice, he had to work with "people who were marked as socially low class like those who were repatriated from China, or thuggish people."

Min-Jun has already dyed and wave-permed his hair to jumpstart his assimilation process into a fashion- and image-obsessed South Korean society.[5] He is a slight eighteen-year-old from Kyungdan, Ryanggang Province, whose mother had defected years before, putting him and his family under increased surveillance. He was repatriated twice from China, and on his third try, after figuring out the ins and outs of hiding in China, had lived rather comfortably in that country. In fact, he was able to live without significant fear because he had purchased the identity of a dead Chinese boy and used his papers to get by. The Chinese parents never reported the death of their son so that they could sell his identity in this way, which is usually done through a broker. Buyers of the dead people's identities are sometimes North Korean refugees in China, like Min-Jun.

Woo-Jin is tall, very thin, and quiet, with an aura of dark melancholy. He rarely looks up from the floor, even when he's speaking to someone, and he says only the bare minimum. (The other defectors who met Woo-Jin in Hanawon whispered to me that he was a particularly downtrodden defector.) He is a twenty-three-year-old soldier who defected after serving for five years. While based in South Pyongan Province, he was sick and tired of the freedomless, monotonous lifestyle of the North Korean military, so he walked for two months to the Chinese–North Korean border and bolted. It is *extremely* rare for a soldier to defect during his duty because he is so intertwined in a web of surveillance and accountability. Woo-Jin says, "If you [cross the border while on military duty], unless you killed someone or committed a serious crime, you've probably lost your mind . . . But I did it." He may be an uncommon defector in that he escaped *during* his military service. But increasingly, young men and women inside North Korea are unwilling to enter the military. Like Nehemiah, they are finding loopholes to dodge conscription.

Joo-Won tells me that watching foreign films was common near the border areas because local authorities were more corrupt and were able to be bribed to look away. He estimates that 70 percent of people watch films at home, and most of his friends and peers procured cheap Chinese USBs with battery chargers. "Since we didn't have electricity, we charged our batteries using solar-powered chargers or our computers. There are also these special Chinese-manufactured televisions that can charge batteries or have DVDs or USB ports to them that are sold to North Korea." The older, "unfashionable" people in their towns would connect a car battery to their television to power their television, which was also connected to a DVD player. The younger folks figured out ways to obtain electricity. They knew what to look for in the markets.

Joo-Won and Min-Jun both were involved in unsavory activities, including self-described thuggish behavior, running from the police, and smuggling goods in and out across the Chinese–North Korean border for profit. To make cash, Min-Jun fixed trinkets and personal electronics. He smuggled people out from North Korea to China on two occasions, but then stopped because he thought the risk of getting caught was not worth it. Joo-Won and Min-Jun's casual cursing and harsh slang add to their rough edges.

Joo-Won shared: "I watched foreign films because they were interesting, but I was also involved in smuggling them. I have a distant relative who is like a freak—he was in the dangerous business of smuggling DVDs and then gambling away all his money. He didn't have a good bone in his body. If he sensed that the authorities were onto him, he would dump all of his inventory at my house. What the hell? Anyway, I got involved in smuggling this stuff. It's good money. People take so much risk to buy this stuff on the market, it's crazy."

Min-Jun chimes in, eyes wide. "Those inspector guys would come into our homes without any notice and just search everything. But we hid them well. In the winter, I was able to [do] a lot of smuggling, since the river was frozen. Smugglers on the Chinese side would layer women's tights and then stuff 500–600 CDs or DVDs into them, tie a sturdy rope to it, and then hurl it as hard as possible across the frozen river to their counterparts in North Korea.[6] The smugglers on the North Korean side of the river would slide cash to their Chinese partners in a similar fashion. Of course there would be some damaged CDs here and there, but one would throw them away in the pond."

Min-Jun and Joo-Won are part of a generation that takes more risks and seeks thrills. Both males and females engage in smuggling films and other media because it's lucrative. Since the demand inside North Korea is so high, innovative young people are figuring out ways to maximize the quantity of foreign media entering North Korea while minimizing their personal risk. Blank USBs and DVDs are legal, so there are some rumored underground businesses inside North Korea that will buy a single copy of a film, make hundreds of copies, and then sell them to marketeers, bringing in major profit. Joo-Won references a photo studio in his neighborhood that made thousands of copies of DVDs before employees were caught and were punished publicly. "They made copies of Chinese movies, American films, and even porn. During the day, the place was a legal photo studio and at night they secretly copied and sold CDs."

The stories that these young men and other defectors have shared with me bring to light a culture among young people, especially young people living along the border, in which they seek immediate gratification, and are willing to take risks, to push the limits of laws and authorities, and to live out of self-interest.

Min-Jun asks me, "Have you watched a 007 movie on *bingdu* [crystal meth]? *Bingdu* became popular again in my area among my peers and the police are going crazy, trying to go after the drug dealers. They're after the American films and *bingdu*." I have never consumed *bingdu*.

Min-Jun and Joo-Won nodded while chatting about how the new 007 movies were better because the nightclub fight scenes were more realistic, and the movie colors were more vivid. They both preferred American movies because they had more action scenes, whereas the South Koreans were "too sappy [in a way that] girls tended to like."

EVOLVING VALUES, PRINCIPLES, AND VOCABULARIES

Young North Koreans explain that while living in North Korea, they didn't have the words or even the conceptual context to express their grievances or questions. The feelings of hunger and some quiet grumblings certainly exist, but since it's too dangerous to explicitly discuss complaints, and students are not taught to ask critical questions, there is no easy way for people to work together to reconcile cognitive dissonances or iron out competing realities.

Once North Koreans arrive in South Korea, the process of being inundated with the world's information catapults them into the long and complex process of learning, acquiring, changing, and refining their values and their personal narratives. The benefit of hindsight, coupled with the attention that defectors' stories receive from mass media, gives incoming defectors the opportunity to craft their narratives in a way that is palatable for themselves, their new social networks, and sometimes public consumption. Much of the language and values centered on universal human rights and freedom are learned after people escape.

Some NGO groups give defectors media training with tips and tricks on how to expound on parts of a personal narrative that will deliver shock value for Western audiences.

A professor at a prominent Seoul-based university who wishes to remain anonymous states, "Every North Korean defector's story is contaminated by the National Intelligence Services' interrogation process before they even enter Hanawon. They naturally gain a bias of whatever to say to future interviewers." Another Seoul-based researcher observes that defectors who enter South Korea learn a language of victimization. Of course most of them experienced travesties that no human being should. But some, especially the older defectors, don't have such clean slates, according to this researcher. Some held elite positions and were complicit in maintaining the brutal system. A few worked in political prison camps and killed prisoners. It can of course be argued that they had no choice but to serve in those positions. But what about in China? Some women who were sex-trafficked later become brokers and traffickers for women who came after them. But once these women who have walked the line between victim and violator enter South Korea, they relinquish all sense of responsibility and claim full victim status. These concerns about innocence and guilt come from only a few researchers and scholars. But defectors have shared as well that the process of learning and incorporating new values into their changing value system is a confusing and challenging process.

THE TRANSFORMATIVE POWER OF INFORMATION

As we have seen, the power of outside information plays an invaluable role in opening the minds of North Koreans, especially the youth. Outside information changes the way people think. Something as simple as creating envy of foreigners in the minds of young North Koreans is important. There's a reason why young North Koreans are imitating foreigners' hairstyles, fashion, slang, and behaviors, and more information will drive more social and cultural changes. Not just movies and TV shows, but also documentaries, news, and other media that show North Koreans how other people live can be transformative for those on the inside.

Gwang-Seong arrived in the Republic of Korea on August 1, 2006. Every defector remembers the exact date that they arrived in their country of freedom. He still keeps in touch with his relatives in North Korea via their illegal Chinese cell phones, and his parents, who are also in South Korea, send money back to them. Gwang-Seong shared that he wants everyone inside North Korea to know that

as long as you have money and a passport, you can travel to any place on the earth that you want, experience cultures anywhere in this big world, and even study abroad in a different country. We all need to show North Korean people that these opportunities are possible. North Koreans need to know that every single one of them has human rights. Some critics believe that we're inciting rebellion by sending in outside information, but I don't think so. North Koreans can choose to revolt if they want. They can choose to start a revolution, they can choose to maintain the status quo, or they can choose something in between. All that outside information is doing is giving North Koreans more options. By showing them how people live in other places around the world, and revealing to them that the government is constantly feeding them lies, we're giving North Koreans a choice. North

Korean defectors and others who are human rights activists have the responsibility to do this.

But the role and effectiveness of outside information should not be exaggerated. Gwang-Seong captures the sentiments well: "Not a lot of people defect solely because of outside information. One could say that movies lack credibility. They're fun, they push people to think and ask questions, but that's it. It's possible for someone to go to China after watching a movie to pursue economic wealth, access much more information in China, and then decide to go to South Korea. But not too many people in North Korea decide to go to South Korea directly." His views capture the opinion that foreign information is a necessary, but not sufficient, component of creating positive changes inside the country.

YU-MI, GWANG-SEONG'S FIRST LOVE

"My life is not extraordinary or interesting. I just led a quiet, normal life before defecting to South Korea without big ideas or expectations." Yu-Mi's modest, soft-spoken words match her personality and demeanor. Delicate, feminine, and quiet, this young woman and I chatted in an empty classroom at her university in Seoul. Even with the fan on, it was hot, so I took my blazer off, tied up my hair with a rubber band that held pencils together, grabbed a pamphlet off of a bookshelf, and started to frantically fan myself. Quietly giggling, Yu-Mi looked down—probably embarrassed on my behalf for such boorish behavior —and said, "It's quite warm, isn't it?"

Her male classmates who are also from North Korea told me before my "girl date" with Yu-Mi that she is so pretty and has such soft facial features that not even the most discriminating eye could guess she's from North Korea. Inherent in their comment is the unquestionable understanding that in South Korea, especially among defectors, assimilating is a good thing. Hiding, covering, or changing any visible or audible signal that one is a defector from North Korea is desirable. It makes life easier for defectors in South Korea, where unfortunately, discrimination toward minority groups, especially North Korean defectors, is striking.

Yu-Mi was born in 1989 in Hoeryong City, North Hamgyong Province, and graduated from high school in 2007. She left South Korea's Hanawon Resettlement Center in the late spring of 2015. During her years at *inmin hak-gyo* (elementary school), she learned to play the accordion and played hacky-sack with her girlfriends. Jumping rope was another favorite pastime of hers. "We also went camping twice, once in the spring and once in the fall one year. Our friends and moms came with us and we used to run races, and play sports."

Yu-Mi, part of the Jangmadang generation, led a pretty trouble-free life, unlike the experiences of many defectors described in memoirs that are available for sale. She described her typical day for me.

In the morning, I'd wake up around 6 a.m. since we had school at 7:30. If I had homework I didn't finish the night before, I would take about thirty minutes to finish and eat a quick breakfast with my mom. I'd leave the house at around 7:15. We would gather in front of the school—we, the students—and march into the school together. Since my house was right in front of the school, it was easy for me to get to and from school. I would peer down from my window to see how many students [had] gathered in front of the schoolyard. I was sometimes lucky enough to head down around 8 a.m.! We would sing songs and each class of students would walk into the school together. Each class had about thirty to forty students. Class started at 8:00 or 8:30, I think, and would go on until noon. We had about a ninety-minute lunch break, during which I would head home to eat. Kids who lived far away brought lunch from home and would eat together at school, so sometimes I brought my lunch to school to eat [with them] because that was fun. During the winter, we had a wood stove and we'd stack our lunches on top to warm [them] up. The lunches on the bottom of the stack would burn or get too hot, while the lunches on the top of the stove would stay pretty cold. The trick was to figure out a way to get your lunch in the middle of the stack.

Around 2 p.m., we had more instruction time. Not actual classes, but just reviews of the morning's lessons, [then we] did homework and went home between 4 or 5. Students were allowed to go home only if we [had] finished our homework for the day. There were kids who had permission to only come to school in the mornings and head back home after lunch, but I stayed for the whole day. During the summer break in August, I didn't study. I just played. Went swimming in the river, and some vacation homework. I stopped doing vacation homework in junior high.

In high school, I joined the Youth Solidarity Group. When I was sixteen or seventeen, I joined the Red Youth Brigade, when my peers and I would go to some type of barracks and spend a week doing basic military training. We wore uniforms, like in the real military, fired rifles. Starting in about the fourth year of junior high (the equivalent to ninth grade), we started participating in Mobilization for Farm

Work, where the students would spend about forty days on a farm doing farm labor, including planting rice, doing different things with vegetation, pulling weeds, things like that. I was in charge of making meals for the students, which you would think is not that hard. But it was. I had to prepare three meals a day for thirty people, every day. I hated it.

After high school, she said only one or two students out of thirty in a class would go on to college. "It was so hard to go to college. And even if you graduated . . . hmm, what's the best way to say it? The college degree would be useless unless you had good political standing. For the guys it may have been different, but for girls, many got married right after graduating from high school. It was natural to see girls get married early, at like twenty-two. There is no great desire to go on to college, especially as a woman. If you get married, it's over—you don't work in the workforce. You're just going to be a housewife. So what's the point?"

A year after graduating from high school, Yu-Mi was assigned to work in a bank as an accountant among nine other accountants. Her company had about three hundred workers and she did the accounting for the money that her company had to raise to give to the state. Additionally, she was in charge of handing out monthly salaries to workers. She said, "Yes, I handed out official salaries, which was supposed to be a month's worth of living wages, but in reality, this amount couldn't sustain an adult for a single day. It was worth maybe a single meal. Before I left North Korea, the monthly salary of one person in my company was about 1,000–2,000 North Korean won. Back then, rice sold for about 5,000 North Korean won in the street markets. So with this monthly salary, a worker couldn't even buy a kilogram of rice. So we had a situation where people, especially men, had to work for a company or office [to which] they were assigned to make this pitiful amount of money. Around 2010, I saw more and more women working hard on the side to make ends meet."

As she worked, she found ways to obtain films to watch to fill her free time. About 70 percent of the films that Yu-Mi watched were Chinese. Starting in 2004, she witnessed more neighbors quietly going over to each other's houses to view foreign dramas together. With all the smugglers across Hyesan and Musan, she saw a surge in USBs and SD cards loaded with films, despite the crackdowns in her home town over foreign media consumption.

"The Chinese films were OK. I really liked the South Korean dramas, but I really felt like a sinner. The punishment was so much more severe if we were caught watching South Korean films versus Chinese films. When watching Korean dramas, we always had this nerve-wracking feeling, but despite the fear and anxiety, my friends and I kept on watching them."

With an ear bud, she would watch films with her family members with the volume really low. Even when using an ear bud, she was careful to keep the volume low in case any sound leaked out of the house. She would either hold the ear bud up so multiple people could watch together with their faces close, or, if she and just one other family member wanted to watch, they would use one ear bud each. She first used laptops to watch the films, but since they used up too much electricity, she turned to the North Korean Notetels. Even when taking such precautions, she wasn't always safe. A frightening encounter with authorities occurred

in 2005, I think it was around 2 a.m. We usually watched films late at night because that's when electricity usually was the most consistently available. My mom, dad, and I were watching the South Korean drama *Autumn in My Heart.* There was also an older lady—I called her grandmother—who was watching with us. It was actually she who had brought over the drama for us to watch together. I guess she wanted company.

Suddenly, there was a loud banging on our front door. People are not allowed to visit each other at such a late hour, so we tried to ignore it, but the banging got so loud, so persistent, and there were shouts of "Hurry up and open this door!" and we figured out exactly who it was. We heard there were crackdowns taking place. So my father quickly took the CD out, put in a Russian movie CD, and the grandmother and I slid under the cover and pretended to be sleeping. When my father opened the door, there were three or four inspectors from the inspection team. Usually, the inminban director accompanies these inspections, but she was absent. They marched in, and my father recognized one person immediately, so we thought we were going to have an easy inspection. But another member we didn't know stepped right up to my father's face and accused him of changing the CDs to the Russian film before we opened the door. They said they had some special detectors that identified our household as one that was watching South Korean dramas. Through intense pressure and threats, my father gave up the CD containing the episode of *Autumn in My Heart* that we were watching. As a compromise my father asked, "Can I just break the CDs here?" We all knew that if the CDs were confiscated and taken away by inspectors, they watch the CDs themselves and then trade or sell them. By offering to ruin the CDs on the spot, my father was gaining reverse leverage on them—by eliminating a source of side income that these inspectors could make off of the confiscated materials. But they agreed. I guess his extremely contrite attitude, and desperately promising to never watch foreign media again, let us off the hook. So my father destroyed the neighborhood grandmother's CDs on the spot. Since one of the inspectors was my father's acquaintance, this team let us keep our VCD player and television. Usually, such teams confiscate everything. We paid a huge "fine." A bribe, essentially.

Film swapping among really close relatives or close friends was common, not just for Yu-Mi, but among most people who watch films. Once people acquired films on the black market, they would ask trusted friends: "I have [such and such] movie, what do you have? Wanna swap for a few days?" After USBs became popular, people started quickly to make free copies of films on USBs. The only cost involved was buying the empty USBs. "Once USB copying came about, these films spread like wildfire," Yu-Mi said.

Like most people I've encountered who secretly watched films, Yu-Mi was struck by the environment, the atmosphere, and the city landscapes that the films presented. "We'd say, 'Wow, over there in the South, is that really how they live? They live that well?' And we'd have those thoughts. South Koreans also speak so beautifully, so elegantly. We would imitate the way the South Korean actors and actresses spoke amongst ourselves. The trend in speech, the hairstyle, all of it."

"Whenever you saw hairstyles in films, all the girls copied it. By seeing who did what hairstyle, I knew who watched foreign films. Can you believe it? Even I got a curly perm!" She giggled softly, thinking it was so ridiculous. Her hair had been dyed brown since she arrived in Seoul. "For the boys, there was a period when they would shave off the side of their heads, just like how the handsome South Korean actors wore their hair. I saw teachers come down on them so hard in class. They would scold them and grab scissors and cut the boys' hair in front of all of us. It was pretty funny, actually."

From my conversations with Yu-Mi, it was clear that she did not have any political motivations behind watching films. She was just a young girl, bored with the available media, who skirted rules to watch fun movies with her friends. But such an innocuous activity is what drove her to ultimately defect from her country. The change in mindset was not immediate or dramatic. She carefully copied celebrities' fashion—like any young girl does, anywhere in the world—and tried out some slang among close girlfriends. But she still liked her home town, and the way things were, no matter how hard things got. As she watched films, she thought to herself how nice it would be to visit the city in the film. But such wishful thinking did not translate into real desire for awhile. The barrier to exit—literally speaking—was too high. The role that films and outside information played in her life was not the main factor in her decision to defect, but it pressed the gas pedal in her decision to do so.

She frequently listened to state media and propaganda, but because she lived close to the border, she knew "what the reality was. We knew that the news broadcasts from the regime were all lies. I think most of us knew that what we got from the state were all lies." In addition all the products she used—hair products, cosmetics, kitchen equipment to help her mother cook, clothes—were from China. Without anyone spelling it out for her that China and South Korea were wealthier than North Korea, she was able to compare products from different countries and make her own inferences. People automatically compare such products and assume that their quality indicates something about the development level of the countries where they were made. She used the example of medicines to explain her thought process to me: "Even without films, it was possible for people along the border to figure out what the world really was like. Take medicine. American drugs were the most expensive on the markets, and the households that had the means purchased American drugs and vitamins to treat ailments. In the case of very sick patients, people simply did not get better using Chinese medicine. But if they used American pills, they would get better and when they did, we all realized that American medicine was really good. American cold and flu medicine was the best, I remember."

Without relatives in South Korea, Yu-Mi never imagined escaping there, even after watching South Korean films for so long. It was all just wishful thinking. There was too much risk involved, and too many unknown steps to take. Leaving the country was altogether just too much of a foreign concept. South Korea seemed to be an entire universe away from her town in Hoeryong. As a twenty-five-year-old woman, she was feeling pressure from her parents to get married immediately. She had never spent more than a month away from her parents, and was frightened by the idea of escaping North Korea on her own, but at the same time did not want to get married. "I didn't want to become another *ajumma* [married or marriage-aged woman]. I had a boyfriend, but we happened to break up around that time I was having these thoughts." The lack of opportunities frustrated Yu-Mi, and with absolutely no desire to get married, she jumped at the chance of sneaking into China.

Unlike many high-profile defectors who fled North Korea due to harrowing childhoods or a particularly dangerous situation,

Yu-Mi's reason had to do more with a sense that she could have a better life across the border. Increasingly, too, defectors are leaving for China not having thought as far ahead as going to South Korea, and end up in South Korea as one event leads to another.

Once Yu-Mi arrived in China, she contacted some relatives who hid her in their home for over a month. "The streets were so grand and impressive, the people looked relaxed, unlike North Koreans who always look on edge, and there was plenty of food to eat. I felt so free. I thought—wow, China is rich!"

Like other North Koreans arriving in China, Yu-Mi hid out of view due to fear that someone would report her as an illegal immigrant. Consequently, she quickly became bored and watched South Korean television. South Korean television was even more eye-opening than the dramas and films from South Korea that she had watched while in North Korea. The news shows, the popular "variety shows," the music videos, and even commercials were so fun and revealed a country that was much more developed than China. She began to seriously ponder the possibility of going to South Korea. Living in China, although she'd probably never starve, seemed suboptimal compared to going to South Korea because she had no legal identity. Consequently she would either always have to hide and would have to marry an otherwise unmarriable Chinese bachelor who couldn't find a Chinese wife—or she would eventually learn Chinese, work and make money under the table, and always risk the possibility of being repatriated to North Korea.

Through three brokers who moved her through China, Laos, and Thailand, Yu-Mi eventually made her way to Incheon Airport, at which point she went through the standard interrogation by the National Intelligence Service, and then spent a few months in Hanawon. Now that she's a full citizen of South Korea, she has bought a smartphone that allows her to stay in touch with her new friends, and most importantly, to stay in touch with her parents who still live in North Korea.

Her parents rent out a cell phone from a North Korean whose business is to rent out illegal Chinese phones by the minute to North Koreans who want to make international phone calls illegally. Sometimes Yu-Mi's parents send her text messages, but they usually call her on her phone for five-minute conversations. "They're simple phone calls. Just about how they're doing. They're curious about my life, my new friends, how I'm faring, things that all parents are always worried about. But they're not curious enough to experience [it] for themselves. They're going to stay in North Korea."

Even though Yu-Mi has been out of Hanawon for only two months, she has quickly learned how to use technology, communication, and informal networks to support her family who remain in North Korea. She found out quickly how to have her parents call her (not the other way around, since she doesn't know when her parents are planning to rent a phone), and also learned how to send remittances back to North Korea. She's already done it since leaving Hanawon: she took part of the government's settlement cash that she was given and sent it back to her parents.

Another trend that Yu-Mi quickly picked up was Facebook. She learned that "all the trendy, fashionable South Koreans had Facebook accounts," so she created one and within weeks had received a Facebook message from a name she recognized. It was a girl from her junior-high-school class. Trusting that it was the same person, the two childhood friends from North Korea set a place and time to meet in Seoul, and indeed, it was her. The friend connected Yu-Mi to three other defectors who were all part of the same junior-high class. One of the three was Gwang-Seong.

CHILDHOOD CRUSHES FROM NORTH KOREA MEET IN SEOUL

I asked Gwang-Seong, who looks and sounds like a Seoul native, if he had a small crush on Yu-Mi. His perm, thick black rimmed glasses, and Seoul speech fool even my friends born in Seoul—no one believes that he's actually from North Korea. I can't tell if he got a perm, or if his hair is naturally wavy, but I wouldn't be surprised if he got a perm because it's one of the main trends among young men in Seoul.

"Crush?" he smiled sheepishly. We were walking through his school hallway and passed his classmates who were practicing a dance routine as part of the school's hip-hop dance club. He waited until we passed his peers, and in English, he said, "She was my first *love*." "Love? Weren't you guys in like, middle school?" "Yeah. She was my first love." The sheer innocence, sheer joy, and happiness that enveloped his face and voice when he said that is unforgettable.

I thought about the odds that these two young friends would reunite again in another country. Gwang-Seong defected without telling anyone, including his friends. He arrived in South Korea on August 1, 2006. He actually was unaware that he was defecting because he was just following his dad's friend's orders. The friend told Gwang-Seong that they were going to China to see his dad. Years passed, and he received a phone call from a fellow defector friend who told him that his beloved Yu-Mi was in Seoul. It was time for the childhood friends to make up for lost time.

After Gwang-Seong arrived in South Korea, he visited Jeju Island more than five times and said, "Whenever I visit the sites where *All In* was filmed, I get goose bumps. The fact that I am standing in a place—the place I used to watch in secret, huddled in my room with the doors locked—sends electricity throughout my body." Recently he went to the United States and spent Christmas in Las Vegas with a generous family who invited him on their family trip. Although he didn't gamble, he fell in love with the glittery lights, the throngs of people in flashy outfits, and the sheer happiness he saw in lovers with linked arms, in laughing friends, and in families milling about. "A small dream came true. It was so cold. Wow. But I didn't care at all. The fact that the scenes I risked my life to watch on a small DVD player were right in front of me brought tears to my eyes. I had found true freedom."

"Standing in Vegas made me realize that whatever it is, if you don't give up and move forward, holding onto it strongly inside your heart, anything can happen. Any dream can come true. So this drama series, *All In,* became the medium that showed me that dreams can come true. Look at me, Noona. I made it to South Korea. I'm friends with you, an American. I found freedom."

WHY DON'T ALL FILM-WATCHERS DEFECT?

Jeong Gwang-Il explained why all North Koreans who watch foreign films don't defect:

No matter [how] unhappy people are with their economic situation, if they figure out ways to improve their lives and that of their families just a little bit, people stay. Most people don't want to betray their country. Some try to defect, fail, get arrested, and if they're not killed, they're publicly branded as political traitors for the rest of their lives, and their family members suffer as well. It becomes hard [for a person] to get married if [he or she] is branded a political criminal. Most don't want to take the risk and go through all that, so people just end up living where they are, even if they watch a lot of films and drama and consequently know that a better world exists outside their country's borders. Also, how hard is it to drop everything you know and have to leave a place where you were born, the only place you know? This is human nature. People don't always want to leave. Most people don't. Not because they actually believe that they're living in socialist paradise, but because they're human. North Korea is what they know. For the mid-level elites and the higher-ranking elites, they are determined to work the system, make money, do what it takes to rise in the ranks because if the system collapses, they go down, too, so they remain and support the regime. Maintaining the regime means survival for them and their families. It's that simple. It's all about survival.

In August 2014, in a Middle Eastern restaurant in the San Francisco Bay Area, I was having lunch with a few North Korean defectors and several Egyptian Americans, including my friend Wael Ghonim, who were creating a startup after having worked at big Silicon Valley tech companies. Over hummus, olive oil and zaatyr, and lamb kebabs, we chatted excitedly about the importance of technology and information in changing the landscape in North Korea. After all, technology played a pivotal role in the Egyptian revolution. (Sustaining the revolution is a separate matter.) I turned to one of the Egyptian engineers at the table and discussed his family's whereabouts. His mother was in Cairo. He's pretty well off, living in the Bay Area, so I asked why his mother didn't come to the United States. Why willingly stay in a place that's ridden with political upheaval, unpredictable riots, and spurts of violence?

I'll never forget what he said. "It's where she's from. Where she grew up. She's familiar with the streets, even if they're messed up now. She knows the vendors, the shops, the owners of the shops. Even if we could afford for her to move here to the Bay Area, she prefers to stay where she's familiar." He later shared with me that beyond vendors and comfort, his mother and other older Egyptians who have the means to leave Egypt end up staying because they do not want to give up their positions in their social networks and society. Despite the upheaval in Egypt, "things are not dire enough. The thought of leaving their place, their network, and starting over somewhere new is quite unthinkable, especially at her old age."

Fast forward to 2015. A Syrian American friend who has extended family in Damascus told me anecdotes of middle-class uncles who refused to leave Syria despite the ongoing civil war. "Of *course* they know that they can travel to different countries and leave all the chaos, death, and violence behind. They certainly can afford it. But how could they leave? Their roots are in Damascus. The air, the land, the dirt, the people, the chaos—all of it created the essence of who they are." Some of her family members left. But listening to the reasons for the uncles who refuse to leave their home town despite knowing that there's a better and much safer life for them outside Damascus reminded me of what Jeong Gwang-Il had said.

Although my friends' stories are not directly related or even perfectly analogous, I retrospectively noted an underlying common thread. Both parties' families know that there is a better world they could live in if they left their home towns.

But home is irreplaceable, even with the death, violence, and chaos that come with it. Of course some people defect from North Korea after watching films and starting to question their regime. But many don't. They know that life is better outside North Korea. Life is wealthier, easier, safer, and freer outside North Korea. But the dirt roads, street markets, human politics, social networks, anachronistic propaganda, hardships that force families to become close, and friends who become like family are all reasons that may collectively trump the pursuit of life elsewhere.

LIVING WITH CONTRADICTIONS

"Are you a Christian?" a prominent South Korean professor who has been interviewing defectors for over a decade asked me. He looked like a traditional professor: thick glasses, shirt sleeves pushed up his arms, dress pants that were a tad too large for him, and a few pens sticking out of his rumpled dress shirt. In his late sixties, he was constantly smiling, eager to pass on his knowledge to younger people.

"Yes," I answered warily, curious as to how this part of my identity would factor into our conversation about how North Koreans are able to believe in mutually exclusive realities.

"Have you ever done anything that the Bible and the Church does not approve of?"

"Why, yes," I said, growing even more uncomfortable.

"But you still believe in the Bible, and the Gospel. Even though you 'stray' from Biblical teachings here and there?" the professor rhetorically asked, still smiling. I don't think he is able to *not* smile. I nodded. "Think of North Koreans who believe in the state yet continue to watch foreign media in this way. They believe in the core tenets of their state, just like you believe in the Bible. They 'stray' from their expected behavior, secretly watching things they shouldn't. But they return to what they're supposed to believe, how they're supposed to behave, and although they have complaints about the state—just like Christians have complaints about the church—they continue to believe."

The professor's way of explaining this to me was very effective in helping me understand how North Korean people can continue to believe in such strict doctrine while viewing materials that contradict that very doctrine. This sweet, grandfatherly professor blushed as he continued with this analogy. "It's like a Christian, especially a Christian bachelor, watching . . . 'red scenes' to carry him over until he's married. Similarly, some devout North Koreans watch foreign films because they're bored, but they ultimately come back to where they're supposed to be. Loyal. Unquestioning. Sacrificial." So he was trying to establish that Christian sinners who still believe in the Bible and Church are analogous to loyal North Koreans who "sin" by watching foreign films but still ultimately believe in the power of the state, the juche ideology, and its leaders.

Although this is not a perfect analogy, it did help me to wrap my head around how North Koreans are able to believe in dual realities. Ultimately the more powerful, more visible, more present ideology trumps the isolated acts of taboo behavior that are inspired by curiosity, a desire to be part of social trends, the thrill of immediate gratification, and a fear of missing out.

6 IMPLICATIONS, PREDICTIONS, AND A CALL TO ACTION

The pockets of social and cultural change springing up across the most closed society on Earth are irreversible. North Korea as we know it today is not the one that Kim Il-Sung, Kim Jong-Il, or even Kim Jong-Un intended to create and sustain. Some joke that if Kim Il-Sung were alive today, he would not recognize the country due to North Korea's widespread private marketization and citizens' knowledge about the world outside its borders.

When members of an authoritarian state learn about the wider world, the implications are manifold. First, people learn to distrust the government and to skirt the rules to support themselves. Hypothetically, not a single citizen should be marketeering inside North Korea because the government is supposed to provide for all. But it is clear to many North Korean citizens today that they do not live in a socialist paradise, so the markets flourish.

Distrusting the government in turn fundamentally changes people's relationship with the state. Once North Koreans start questioning the state's propaganda and narrative, and realize that much of it is not true, many feel a profound sense of betrayal. Some defectors have shared with me that the betrayal is akin to what a Christian might feel upon learning that the Gospel was a fluke. They were lied to their entire lives about a political and value system.

Many North Koreans are at this stage, where they feel a need for self-reliance as well as distrust of the regime and its leaders. Some North Korean scholars who have settled in South Korea estimate that more than 75 percent of the population depends on themselves for survival, while 40 percent of North Koreans experience this type of distrust.

For any significant political change to take place, this distrust would need to develop into collective action—a significant challenge in North Korean society, because the government is ruthless about eliminating any group activity. Out of fear of politically motivated action, group activities that are not state-sanctioned are banned. Student groups, soccer teams, social gatherings at night, and overnight stays at other people's houses without permits are all prohibited. In addition to the logistical challenges posed by these bans, collective action is difficult because trust is difficult to cultivate and sustain. Since the regime has long fostered suspicion by planting snitches in neighborhoods and incentivizing the exposure of others, meaningful trust among North Koreans is difficult to create.

Another hurdle for North Koreans who wish to participate in collective action against the state is communication. Since all electronic and cellular communication is assumed to be monitored, communicating sensitive information is extremely difficult.

Despite these challenges, from the standpoint of encouraging North Koreans to eventually take collective action against their state, the flow of foreign information into North Korea is crucial. But another reason why the dissemination of outside information is so consequential is that it is the only reasonable strategy for creating pressure from inside the country to force Kim Jong-Un to reappraise his domestic and foreign priorities. If his state narrative, actions, and policies continue to become more antiquated, they will lose more and more true followers, and inevitably become irrelevant. Traditional Western diplomatic campaigns have so far failed to generate much meaningful pressure on the intransigent state. It's time to add a new strategy to push North Korea toward making positive changes, even if the onus for taking action falls on private citizens and civil society organizations.

Alternatives to information campaigns are not viable. Military intervention is too costly for cash-strapped governments, the estimated casualties are too high, and a reasonable end goal is difficult to picture. Assassination plots will not guarantee a country that better serves North Koreans. North Korea's regime is deplorable, but certainly stable. In addition, such hardline alternatives can lead to a destabilized regime with loose nukes along with millions of impoverished people, a situation that could spark a massive refugee crisis. Some of the world's most persistent and skilled negotiators have been testing various methods to entice, punish, and engage North Korea in addressing the great powers' top concern: nuclear disarmament on the Korean Peninsula. It's not working.

Leaving North Korea alone would also not be an effective strategy. Doing so would effectively give the regime license to proliferate with immunity and act however it wants toward its citizens and its neighbors, with no accountability.

Civil society organizations and possibly government-agency-powered efforts to increase the flow of information into North Korea may well be the most reasonable, sustainable, cost-effective, and peaceful way of creating positive change inside North Korea. Information dissemination is significant because

North Koreans are demanding it, and an informed citizenry has more data points from which to determine its future. Access to more information gives North Korean people the agency, self-determination, and knowledge to write their own future and destiny as a nation.

NORTH KOREA'S ACHILLES' HEEL

Often hailed as the "father of nonviolent struggle," "a revolutionary's best friend," and a "dictator's worst nightmare," political scientist Gene Sharp states that "dictatorships are never as strong as they think they are, and people are never as weak as they think they are." In one of his widely cited how-to books on how to bring down dictatorships, *From Dictatorship to Democracy: A Conceptual Framework for Self-Liberation,* Sharp writes that dictatorships "can be conquered, but most quickly and with [the] least cost if their weaknesses can be identified and the attack concentrated on them."[1]

I am not the only one who believes that Kim Jong-Un's regime is afraid of foreign information. All it takes to measure how threatened the Kim regime is by foreign information is to observe how vehemently its leaders react to foreign information compared to other external threats like sanctions, public condemnations, and even a U.N. resolution that recommends the prosecution of Kim Jong-Un and senior officials at the International Criminal Court for crimes against humanity. Diplomats who work the halls of the United Nations and North Korea watchers have grown to expect North Korea's regime to saber-rattle and make hollow, bombastic threats. But airborne balloons and other information campaigns really get Kim's cadre riled up.

In August 2015, North Korean soldiers planted three landmines on the southern side of the border, maiming two South

Korean sergeants patrolling the DMZ. Two mines detonated the first explosion, instantly severing both legs of a soldier. As his colleague tried to help him, another mine exploded, maiming the second soldier.

South Korea retaliated with a measure that they thought was equally, if not more, damaging to North Korea's morale than maiming two soldiers: turning on loudspeakers. This was the first time in eleven years that South Korea had turned on the loudspeaker propaganda broadcasts that target the North Korean military and nearby villages on the northern side of the DMZ. They had shut off the loudspeakers in 2004 as a gesture of goodwill toward North Korea when the two countries' bilateral relations were warmer.

North Korea's top negotiator called South Korea's actions of turning on their loudspeakers a "declaration of war." His colleague, North Korea's deputy permanent representative to the United Nations, called the broadcasts "psychological warfare." Although South Korean officials did not think that turning on propaganda loudspeakers was an act of war, they did recognize that psychological warfare is one of the most potent weapons they have to use against the Kim regime. For two weeks after the landmine explosions, South Korea played a continuous stream of not only messages critical of the Kim regime, but also news stories that North Koreans otherwise would not hear, and even K-pop. It is estimated that on maximum power, the loudspeakers' content can be heard as far as fifteen miles into North Korea. Jang Jin-Sung, a former North Korean propaganda official and poet, said the broadcasts are "akin to a peaceful version of the nuclear bomb."

This tactic of information and psychological warfare between the two adversaries dates back to the Cold War era, during which both Koreas blasted propaganda via loudspeakers and sent airborne balloons filled with messages to entice soldiers to defect to the other side. This enticement was particularly tempting to South Koreans in the 1960s and 1970s when North Korea was economically more successful than its southern counterpart.

South Korea ended up shutting off the loudspeakers in the 2015 episode after the North provided a semblance of an apology. Keeping in mind that North Korea is not known to make public apologies to any government, its expression of "regret" over the maimed South Korean soldiers speaks to the level of concern that the regime has about foreign information infiltrating its society.[2]

WESTERN CONCERNS ABOUT INFORMATION DISSEMINATION INTO NORTH KOREA

Access to foreign information is certainly not the silver bullet for positive regime evolution. Knowledge and enlightenment alone will not sufficiently empower North Korean citizens to face off with a heavily armed military whose government has no qualms about murdering swaths of its population.

But knowledge about the outside world is undoubtedly a necessary component that North Koreans need if they want to create change for themselves in the future. Sending outside information and media into this closed society is a good option for creating the conditions needed for the regime to consider incremental political changes. As stated previously, knowledge that contradicts what one has been taught sparks cognitive dissonance and internal tension. Then as one's mind broadens and views the new knowledge in a more open way, measuring it against actual experience, one begins to distrust the source of the original teachings—which in the case of the North Koreans would mean the government and the Kim family. Only after one distrusts the government can one take action against it.

Converting enlightenment and distrust of the North Korean government into practical action is a much more complicated line of work, but a couple of strategies seem promising. Increasingly, activists and scholars of nonviolent resistance movements have been taking an interest in the North Korean case and have started to work with interested defectors to think through tactics that could be localized in the North Korean context. For example, small public projects that are not political in nature but that a neighborhood can rally around can create a sense of collective power. Working together to create a well or improve a small road can give a small community a sense of empowerment that can translate into other actions later on. This could be a long game, and perhaps a long shot, but is one strategy that can be tried by willing parties.

In addition, a contingency of critics of the North Korean regime had hoped that the late Hwang Jang-Yop would have been a unifying figure, or at least the symbolic head, of a North Korean government in exile. For several reasons, however, including a fractured North Korean defector community, such a government in exile did not take root. In theory, the possibility of a repeat attempt at establishing an alternative government entity to Kim Jong-Un's system exists.

IS IT A FORM OF WESTERN IMPERIALISM?

Some readers may question whether sending information into North Korea enables and strengthens the self-determination or self-consciousness of North Koreans, or if it is instead merely another form of Americanization. Of course no one should live under a dictatorship, but is sending in American movies and books, and South Korean dramas, the solution to liberating an oppressed population?

The most ardent proponents of sending information into North Korea are North Korean defectors. When I ask defectors how they select what materials to send in, they often tell me that they try to recall what they had yearned to watch and read when they were inside North Korea, and then look for similar materials to send. America has extraordinary "soft power," and North Korean people's interest in the media and literature that Americans produce is hardly unique in the world. And yet it is not only American materials that are brought into North Korea; South Korean, Japanese, Chinese, and European content is also pushed in.

It's crucial to understand that there is widespread demand for foreign information. While knowing the risks, North Koreans are seeking, purchasing, and borrowing information for their pleasure and sometimes edification. It is paternalistic for organizations to not send information into North Korea, despite private demand, on the basis that the risks are too high for North Korean information consumers, or that it's a form of Western imperialism.

Some lessons could be drawn from loosely parallel situations in other totalitarian regimes where outside information dramatically changed an oppressed people's behavior. Consider, for example, the former USSR and East German regimes. People living inside the USSR or East Germany were sealed off from the outside world and were punished for seeking exposure to information outside their territorial borders. But once some people started learning about how people on "the other side" were living, they started to seek more information about the reality outside their borders. As many as 80 percent of East Germans had access to West Germany's radio programs before the Berlin Wall fell. Internal dissidents and outside defectors worked to help their fellow countrymen access more information through radio programs and the stealthy circulation of literature. While access to outside information inside these otherwise sealed countries may not have been the primary reason for their collapse, it certainly played a large role in eroding people's loyalty to their regime.

We probably cannot expect to see a revolution like the Arab Spring take shape inside North Korea. A "North Korean Spring" or "Pyongyang Square" demonstration is unlikely to take place anytime soon. Yet people's perception of their daily reality fundamentally alters when they are exposed to information about how others live. Every North Korean defector who has safely arrived in South Korea states that China seemed significantly more developed than North Korea, which naturally triggered questions about why North Koreans cannot live like the Chinese. Witnessing the living standards of South Korea only accentuated the difference between North Korea and more developed countries.

Some hold the view that working to give North Korean people access to foreign information is a misplaced effort. Such critics believe that given the oppressive measures of North Korea and their dismissal of international opinion, the government will have no problem cracking down on its people if it believes that outside information is truly getting out of hand. An analogy used to describe this sentiment is a mosquito net. On a summer day, a person may open a window to let the cool outside air into a hot room, but will put a mosquito net in the window to keep the unwanted mosquitoes outside. Similarly, the North Korean government may be metaphorically "opening a window" by begrudgingly and minimally tolerating some foreign information coming into North Korea, but may also be keeping a "mosquito net" in place to prevent unwanted, irreversible changes from taking place.

My response to such pushback is that access to foreign information is, and has been, in such high demand—stemming from curiosity or profit—that people knowingly risk fines, physical punishment, or even death to watch and circulate foreign information. As some people quoted in previous chapters have shared, a public execution was not a sufficient deterrent for watching and listening to foreign films—and if that is not a sufficient deterrent, I don't know what is. Maybe the regime has deterrents that are more harrowing, drawn out, and far-reaching than death, saved for a situation that Kim Jong-Un considers to be truly out of control. But the citizens inside North Korea are the ones who are making the informed decision to access foreign media and information. And what is undeniable is that people cannot un-learn what they know or quash their natural curiosity, even if satisfying this curiosity means looking and listening in a locked bedroom with the curtains drawn, under the blankets, with a single ear bud inserted into an ear.

ENCOURAGING CHANGE IN A FEAR-BASED CULTURE

An elderly gentleman who grew up in the Soviet Union asked me what role fear plays in North Korea. He didn't think that North Koreans lacked information; what held them back from doing anything meaningful past improving their businesses with foreign information was fear: the fear of breaking the rules beyond what was bribable, the fear of saying something slightly political that would be deemed unacceptable by the authorities and neighbors, the fear of getting arrested, and the fear of having one's family carted off. This man brought up a very relevant concern. Fear prevents people from trusting themselves and trusting each other, and from taking action in any situation, not just in North Korea. But it is indeed North Koreans who live under one of the most violent regimes in modern history.

Sokeel Park, director of research at Liberty of North Korea, writes about increases in shared, or socially complicit, disobedience that address the point about fear in North Korean society. Pyongyang has heavily invested in efforts to monitor all forms of associations in society, and to prevent the creation of any bonds of loyalty and commitment that are stronger than those between citizens and the state. But the economic and information-related changes taking place in North Korea mean that "disorganized resistance against the system's restrictions is the norm for ordinary North Koreans, and such everyday disobedience also increasingly happens across horizontal linkages and human networks operating outside of government controlled space." This means that whether or not North Koreans are aware of it, they are resisting the government by covering for each other, bribing one another, turning a blind eye if necessary, and breaking rules—all out of self-interest—to be part of a larger system of markets and the circulation of information.

North Koreans are more connected than ever, not only with the outside world, but also to each other via cell phones and human networks inside the country. Without realizing it, they are increasingly trusting others in their social networks, and strengthening the very horizontal social bonds that their government has invested so many resources in preventing.

Serbian democracy activist Srđa Popović coined the term "laughtivism" to identify strategies that employ humor, laughter, and mockery in nonviolent movements to undermine the authority of an opponent. "Humor melts fear," he declares; and it does so while building credibility and trust among participants. Humor was part of Popović's nonviolent tactics when he led Otpor!, the student movement credited for helping topple the Serbian dictator Slobodan Milosevic in 2000. Although a few jokes about Kim Jong-Un are not going to bring him to his knees, "laughtivism" certainly can be introduced to segments of North

Korean society among those who are interested in finding ways to chip away at government-manufactured fear.

GETTING INVOLVED

Access to information for North Korea's 25 million citizens in this digital age of instant communication and information sharing should be considered essential. Given that South Korea's population has 1.1 cell phones per capita and a 92 percent internet penetration rate, the absence of such access in North Korea seems all the more stark and unfair.

For anyone interested in learning more about information access in North Korea and other closed societies, or in getting more involved, there are organizations based in South Korea, in the United States, and across Europe that work specifically to send information into North Korea. There are various components to such a process—researching best practices from comparative situations, finding and/or creating technologies for dissemination purposes, creating and editing original digital content, fundraising, and more.

The very fact that the North Korean government is such a ruthless and relentless regime has encouraged activists in this area to become even more entrepreneurial, resourceful, and creative than they would otherwise have been to meet the demands of citizens living inside North Korea. Justice Michael Kirby, who chaired the U.N. Commission of Inquiry report on North Korean human rights, has been encouraging people who are interested in this topic of information access and broader human rights to "think outside the square of complacent formalism."

OTHER ENTITIES INVOLVED IN THE EFFORT

Nongovernmental organizations of varying sizes and capacities have been getting increasingly involved in sending information directly into North Korea, brainstorming dissemination tactics and low-tech ideas for easy consumption, and fundraising to garner support for related initiatives. "Hackathons" and brainstorming sessions among college and graduate students, engineers, and human-rights NGOs have been springing up at campuses across the United States. For example, the New York City–based Human Rights Foundation organized a Silicon Valley hackathon where engineers and computer scientists broke out into teams to generate ideas on how information can be sent into North Korea stealthily. Similar brainstorming sessions with diverse players are taking place across the United States and South Korea with the goal of generating more effective ways of sending information in. Ideas that have come up so far include using satellite, Bluetooth, simple computers, and shortwave radios in more clever ways. A tricky part of brainstorming and implementing such projects is that more often than not, these ideas cannot be publicized in detail, or at all, so as to prevent unintentionally tipping off the North Korean authorities.

Not all NGOs are equally capable, transparent, or performance-based in this field of information dissemination, as is the case in any other field. Some groups in South Korea and elsewhere are nicknamed "one man shows," where a strong defector figure, usually an older male, runs a small team. Democratic decision-making, leadership development, capability building, transparent usage of funds, performance measurement, monitoring and evaluation, and succession of leadership are issues that some defector-led NGOS are grappling with. Accountability is crucial for NGOs, especially for those that work on North Korean issues. A skeptic could accuse groups of exploiting the information void that shrouds North Korea and using funds irresponsibly. "It's North Korea, there's no way to measure results. Let's just put money into a black hole." Over the past two decades, mismanagement of funds by select NGOs has decreased support for South Korea–based NGOs more generally. But this problem is easing. With rapidly expanding internet-based technologies and social media, younger and newer groups popping up, and new ideas garnering international attention and support, NGOs have been becoming increasingly professional, innovative, and transparent. This shift is indicative of a larger generational divide among younger defectors and older defectors when it comes to the approach of raising awareness about North Korean issues. Some young people, especially those in college, harbor skepticism and even antagonism for older defectors whom they call "career defectors" by treating North Korea as a business. As one group of college students told me, "They're always on TV, and say so many shocking things to bring in money. Why can't they be more subtle?"

As with all difficult issues, disagreements and tensions surround the approaches that people take to help North Koreans. In addition to the generational differences in opinion, there are groups that want to internationalize North Korean issues and engage Americans and Europeans more, whereas still other groups want to keep it a strictly Korean issue and underscore ethno-nationalist sentiments. Overt versus covert projects, awareness-raising versus action-oriented initiatives, refugee rescue versus defector assimilation are some other organizational cleavages that diversify and complicate the small world of North Korean NGO work. Yet despite these differences, there is a shared mission among both defector-led and non-defector-led groups: more organizations are recognizing the critical value of information and media dissemination into North Korea and are getting involved in efforts to expand overall operations in this area.

The church has also played a significant role in raising awareness and funds and in taking grassroots action to help North

Korean refugees in China, as well as defectors who have settled in South Korea.[3] Many older Koreans who have been separated from their families often seek solace in the church through prayer and community. I'm sure that most readers who are of ethnic Korean heritage know of older Koreans who pray for unification, for reuniting with family members, and for the good health of loved ones whom they haven't seen for almost seventy years. Given the church's heavy role in the Korean independence movement and resistance efforts during Japanese occupation, it is part and parcel of South Korean politics, especially when it pertains to North Korea. Some churches, including Korean-American churches in the United States, have North Korean ministries that fundraise to send missionaries to China, give scholarships to defector students, and host lecture series about North Korea. North Korean prayer groups abound in churches and at some college campuses in the United States and beyond.

Many defectors convert to Christianity during or after their defection process, and some defectors have been sending audio Bibles into North Korea. But I do not know what effect, if any, this has on consumers, or if anyone is listening to audio Bibles at all.

NGO and Christian organizations' efforts to exploit weaknesses in the North Korean system are complemented by some governments' efforts to send information in. For example, the U.S. State Department's Bureau of Democracy, Human Rights and Labor put out several open calls for statements of interest and request for proposals, asking the public to send in proposals related to projects promoting democracy and human rights, including information-access campaigns into North Korea.

The British Broadcasting Corporation (BBC) unveiled plans in September 2015 to expand its popular World Service broadcasting initiative into more countries, including North Korea via shortwave radio. The plan is to broadcast a daily news program to North Korean listeners. Britain's diplomatic relations with North Korea would not protect North Korean listeners who decided to tune in, however—listening to foreign radio broadcasts continues to be a very dangerous activity for those living under the regime.

TAKING THE LONG VIEW

North Koreans who remain inside North Korea and those who have left all need time to digest, internalize, and think critically about the information they are gaining from films, TV shows, books, radio, and word of mouth about the world outside North Korea. No matter how much people learn in a short period of time, they need time to process and figure out what they want to accept, reject, or think about further.

If one were to believe mass media on this topic, all North Koreans who watch an American movie suddenly crave freedom by defection. But such a narrative is grossly oversimplified, and actually does a disservice to the nuanced process that many North Koreans experience whereby they come to terms with competing realities and try to neutralize the cognitive dissonance in their minds. As one North Korean student said, the idea that exposure to a single film compels them to leave their home town makes them "seem like brainless idiots."

Information dissemination campaigns are essential to sustaining the small changes in North Korea that are already taking root. People who have been in this space, however—both in North Korea and other closed societies—warn that such campaigns need to take place with a long-term game plan in mind. A one-time operation or a "rescue mission" mentality will backfire and sustain the status quo for longer.

CLEAVAGES WITHIN NORTH KOREA

Just as there are divisions among elites in other societies, North Korea has social and political cleavages. There is much discussion on this topic among scholars and others interested in North Korea. Elites in North Korea are divided according to (1) geographical region, (2) generation (people in their fifties versus seventies, for example), (3) policy orientation (for instance, whether they are pro-China or are focused on self-reliance), and (4) whether they are simply Communist Party members or die-hard military men. I write this only to relay the point that North Korea is not a monolith, and there is room for differences in opinion, even if such differences are not openly expressed by people in the government.

Similarly, scholars from North Korea and South Korean professors who study North Korea attempt to categorize the North Korean citizen population based on levels of loyalty. There is significant debate about how to group people, and what percentage of the population comprises each group. But a broad population breakdown forwarded by several South Korean professors who have been interviewing North Koreans and studying the country for over two decades suggests that about 25 percent are diehard believers in North Korea; about 25 percent are intellectuals and people who have traveled abroad who basically know how the world works but continue to remain loyal; another 25 percent or so of people don't care about anything beyond their own households and are able to generally get by; and about 25 percent of people quietly criticize the North Korean government and have grievances against the state.

There is, of course, no way to confirm or dispute these percentages with an in-country survey. But a combination of interviews with defectors entering South Korea and analyses of North

Korean news and events provides a general platform for such estimates. When asked, defectors across age groups will estimate that between 20 and 30 percent of North Koreans remaining in the country still fully believe in the state propaganda. Keeping in mind the need to caution against taking defectors' projections of their former country as fact, I find that defectors and people who study North Korea broadly agree on the range of North Korea's population who are still true believers. And what is undeniably true is that North Korea is not the monolith it once was thought to be under Kim Il-Sung.

WILL REUNIFICATION EVER HAPPEN?

Like many of the topics addressed in this book, the reunification of the two Koreas merits several tomes. But since the future of the country may be meaningfully changed by an informed North Korean population, a brief discussion of reunification is warranted here.

The possibility of a unified Korea will have far-reaching implications for both populations. Let's consider first the economics of it. Estimates for the cost of unification range between $500 billion and $1 trillion, most of which South Korea will shoulder. No one knows when or how unification will occur, but South Korea ought to be prepared with a strong balance sheet. The Asan Institute for Policy Studies in Seoul has been conducting large surveys in South Korea to capture the population's sentiments on various aspects of reunification. Their survey found that 48 percent of South Koreans would be willing to pay a unification tax, but there are differences in the levels of willingness to pay according to age. Just 34 percent of people in their twenties are willing to pay a unification tax, for example, versus 63.8 percent of people in their fifties.

Social integration is another area of tremendous concern. Despite the South Korean government's efforts to resettle North Korean refugees, most defectors are nowhere near full assimilation. Surviving in a cutthroat-competitive, individualistic society is difficult enough for South Korean natives. Most do not have the extra time or emotional resources to think about defectors, much less proactively reach out to them.

A South Korean–born woman who works for a well-known Seoul-based North Korean NGO often vents with me whenever we meet in person, or via Kakao text messages, of a struggle that she experiences as an activist.[4] During college, she walked past a North Korean human-rights photo exhibit held on campus and was hooked. After graduating from a prominent college, she worked for various North Korean human-rights NGOs and spends most of her work hours and personal time with North Korean defectors and fellow activists. Her college friends noticeably distanced themselves from her, and the few that stuck around said that they hoped she wasn't becoming a "Commie" herself. The young men and women who expressed such concern—seriously or in semi-jest—graduated from good universities and were otherwise socially conscious people. Even her parents, "who are always so busy volunteering at church," encouraged her to pursue another—any other—social issue. This activist complains, "Everyone's a hypocrite. This whole North Korean human rights issue is so heartbreaking but so damned politicized in South Korea."

Several professors at prominent Seoul-based universities who prefer to remain anonymous told me on separate occasions that after studying North Korea for twenty years in South Korea, they find it difficult to study their northern counterpart with objectivity, or at least to write and share their opinions publicly without bias. Given that North Korean affairs are inextricably linked with South Korean domestic politics, a South Korean professor's party affiliation will largely influence his or her written analyses and policy recommendations. This is of course a generalization and a phenomenon that is not unique to South Korea. But it is worth noting that North Korean issues are directly linked with South Korean politics and consequently shape academia, homegrown research, and debates.

If the 29,900 defectors cannot integrate with 50 million South Koreans, then the possibility of 25 million North Koreans integrating with 50 million South Koreans seems to be a distant reality. To address this concern on a small scale, student groups have sprung up on college campuses. Called *Hana* (literally meaning "one," connoting "We Are One"), the groups comprise North Korean defectors and South Korean natives and are intended to foster mutual understanding and friendships. They are essentially creating a miniature "unification" between members of the two Korean cultures. So far, however, there is no formula to scale up this model to include the entire Korean Peninsula.

Jeremy is the leader of his Hana group at his university in Seoul.[5] We met more than three years ago, and we have gotten to know each other well. I recommended Doris Kearns Goodwin's *Team of Rivals* to Jeremy years ago, and after reading it, he set his sights on becoming a lawyer. Law is his preferred weapon to fight the Kim regime and unify the two countries in the future. But for the time being, he runs his Hana group. He has his own business cards to pass out to new contacts. He proudly handed me one of them. "I designed it myself," he said with a huge grin.

I went to Jeremy's church, which has a North Korean defector congregation. The pastor herself is a North Korean defector. The order of the worship service was identical to services I've attended in the United States my entire life: worship songs, prayers, a sermon, the passing of the peace (greeting each other), and collection of the offering. But the content was nothing like what I've experienced before. The passing of the peace in this congregation was not an obligatory "hi, how are you" exchanged with the two or three people around me. Instead congregation members walked throughout the whole sanctuary, tightly hugging, kissing each other on the cheek, holding hands. There was an outpouring of emotions among this North Korean Christian congregation. After the service, too, everyone broke off into preassigned small groups for a weekly check-in. I accompanied Jeremy. Each of the ten people had a chance to describe the highlights of their week and list their prayer requests. Some topics that were broached in this forty-five-minute "check-in" were "Please pray for my mom, she's still in the prison camp in Chongin." "Please pray for my husband, his depression and suicidal thoughts are back." "Please pray for my children, they're outcasts in school because of their North Korean accent." "Please pray for me, my engagement is broken because my fiancé's parents found out I am from North Korea."

Jeremy's prayer request was for his Hana student group to be successful, and for North Korean defectors and South Korean natives to understand each other on campus, so that the two governments can learn from them. His resilience and optimism are hard to wrap my mind around, given his background. His father passed away early, his mother passed away in a political prison camp, and Jeremy himself spent a few years in a prison camp after being repatriated from China. One memory he has from China is of working at a beer joint, bussing tables. The Chinese owner knew that Jeremy was a North Korean defector, so rather than paying him for his service, the owner compensated him in beer, knowing full well that Jeremy could not complain or push back. Jeremy had no income; the only calories that this tween consumed for months was beer. He tells me, "That owner was one of the nicer ones. The other Chinese people who *really* exploit defectors just blow their cover when they're pissed off."

From time to time, Jeremy refers to the time he spent in the prison camp. I can't tell if I'm the audience, or if he's replaying bitter memories for himself to compare them to the reality he lives now. When he first entered the camp, he was terrified at the sight of emaciated prisoners with hollowed, lifeless eyes. They performed meaningless, backbreaking tasks from sunrise to sundown, and suffered from not only physical torture, but also excruciating mental pain. People whispered to him that they did not know what crimes they were being sentenced for. One day, he was sent to the prison "hospital" where people lay on wooden boards shoulder to shoulder. He saw people try to cultivate diseases in their own bodies to expedite their own deaths. At age seventeen, when South Korean males are studying eight to twelve hours a day preparing for their college entrance exam, Jeremy developed a "sixth sense" of predicting when somebody would die, based on their breathing patterns. He recalls thinking, "that man has about two more days left before he leaves this earth. I give that man over there no longer than a week." After a hospital bedmate would die, Jeremy did not report his death because he would be able to eat the corpse's food ration. He continued to sleep next to corpses and eat their food until nurses noticed the rotting bodies. He would then be tasked with carrying the stiff, cold, skeletal corpses out into the mass open grave. "When I first entered the camp, the smell of burning bodies was nauseating. The idea of it, the smell, everything. But around the time I left, a few years later, the same smell was enticing as barbeque. That's how hungry and screwed up we all became in the camp."

Jeremy is fairly content with his life in his new country. "In Seoul, things are pretty good. I never, ever go hungry, I have good friends, I have a church family. I am even in university! But like all other North Korean defectors, there's so much baggage, trauma, and just shit underneath my new identity. The Korean name I use is not the name I was given by my parents. I changed it a few times. If you poke at a defector a tad too hard, she or he will flip out. You get a few defectors drunk, and you'll hear insane stories that they try so hard to cover up, ignore, or forget about. North Koreans and South Koreans grew up so, so differently. Unification is the dream, yes, but hell—it's going to take work, as you can see." For several years after settling in South Korea, Jeremy didn't drink beer. The depressing memories of constantly being buzzed while hiding in China turned him off. We had our first Tsingtao only months ago, paired with Korean fried chicken.

When the Korean War ended, millions of Korean families were divided. One big, proud ethnic family was divided. So naturally, one of the central tenets underpinning the drive for unification in South Korea has been a desire to reunite with the country's brothers and sisters—literally and figuratively. But this ethnonationalist argument weakens with each immediate divided family member who passes away. The Asan Institute for Policy Studies surveys between 2007 and 2012 capture the attitudinal shifts; the significance placed on ethnic reasons for unification is rapidly decreasing with every age group.[6] Young South Koreans' interest in reunification overall has been declining. Eighty percent of South Koreans support eventual reunification, but fewer than 20 percent of South Koreans support immediate reunification.

Another aspect of unification is the North Korean regime with which South Korea will potentially reunify. Hypothetically, if Kim Jong-Un were to honestly and genuinely offer to reunite with South Korea tomorrow, would the South Korean government agree to it? Would the South Korean people agree to immediately unify with North Korea as it is now, with its nuclear weapons, large-scale and egregious human-rights violations, broken economy, and so on? If the answer is no, then I would venture to propose meaningful discussions about regime evolution—not necessarily regime change—before unification. It's a sequencing issue. Of course, given the geographical and political position of South Korea, the government cannot hold public discussions about North Korean regime change because this would inevitably aggravate North Korea and South Korea would bear the brunt of such provocations. But I believe that North Korean regime evolution is a critical prerequisite to the two Koreas' unification.

How will unification occur? Many dissertations, research papers, conferences, and both open- and closed-door conversations among public and private entities in Korea, China, and the United States have examined this topic. On whose terms will unification take place and what will a unified Korean Peninsula look like—two countries under one system? an abrupt collapse of one country leading to absorption by the other? a negotiated, incremental, and consensual reunification? Also, what roles will other states, especially China and the United States, play during and after unification? Various contingency plans have been drafted in the halls of universities, think tanks, and probably government agencies. But there is no clear answer because short of a regime collapse, both Koreas will have to consent, and to date, the overwhelming majority of discussions surrounding unification have not included the North Korean government.

Other open-ended questions about unification include:

- What will happen to North Korea's nuclear weapons, including those in their undisclosed nuclear sites? What about the possibility of loose nuclear weapons being sold to other rogue states or nonstate actors such as extremist groups?

- How will North Korea's 1.2-million-strong military, special forces, and secret police be integrated with South Korea's military?

- How can the expected mass southern-bound migration patterns of North Koreans into South Korea be managed and controlled, assuming that the demilitarized zone will be made safe for crossing?

- What will happen to the thirty thousand American troops in South Korea? If the countries unify, will the troops remain on the Korean Peninsula, further straining the United States' security relationship with China?

- How will the infrastructure of the two countries, including their transportation, communication, health, education, and political systems, be integrated?

- What will happen to North Korea's leadership and elite class? Will Kim Jong-Un or his successor be part of a unified Korean political leadership? And will he be sent to the International Criminal Court based on the United Nations' recommendation in 2014?[7] Will some elites be granted amnesty or punished for their crimes against humanity?

The possible benefits of reunification are astonishing. Whether North and South Korea are absorbed, collapsed, or integrated, unification might neutralize a significant security concern for South Korea, its neighbors, and the United States. The world theater would no longer have as a sovereign state what is arguably the most brutal authoritarian and rogue regime in modern history. The new nation, with over 80 million people, could become an economic powerhouse and a stronger middle power than South Korea is today. North Koreans are known to be extremely hard working and all are known to be literate.

It's difficult to know how the North Korean government and people honestly view and plan for unification, if at all. According to Asan Institute surveys, 47 percent of defectors in South Korea responded in 2014 that when they were in North Korea, they believed that the biggest reason to work toward reunification was so that the lives of North Koreans would improve. Nearly all defectors responded to government interviewers that when they were in North Korea, they believed they would benefit from reunification both as a nation and as individuals.

For something as nationally, regionally, and globally meaningful as Korean unification, I hope that North Koreans will be involved in the planning and process as much as possible before it takes place.

Ha-Young once told me over coffee, "People say mountains change in about ten years. If something as stubborn and mammoth as a mountain can change in a decade, the hearts of ordinary North Koreans can change. I'm sure of it. I'm living proof. I'm from North Korea. North Korea is my home, and I revere the soil that my family tilled. But I grew to embrace democracy over time as I settled in my new home in South Korea. It's hard, and lots of things are still confusing in a democratic country. But if mountains can change, humans can change. North Koreans are humans too, you know. Just like you, me, and the reader. North Koreans can and will adapt to newer, better circumstances. I'm sure of it."

APPENDIX

How Remittances Are Sent to North Korea

Step 1. The North Korean recipient, or "Receiver," calls the North Korean defector in South Korea, or "Sender," by using an illicit Chinese cell phone of her own or that she borrows. Alternatively, the Sender calls a remittance broker in North Korea, "Broker A" (someone with whom she has previously established contact), to find her relative nearby and tell the relative that a certain amount of money is being sent. The point of this initial phone call is to connect the Receiver and Sender and to determine how much money will be sent.

Step 2. Broker A contacts his business partner (usually a relative or very close friend) in China, "Broker B," to obtain Broker B's bank account information to give to the Sender. The bank is either a Chinese bank or a South Korean bank with a Chinese branch, because banks in North Korea cannot do business in South Korea.

Step 3. The Sender transfers money (usually $1,000) to Broker B's bank in China.

Step 4. Broker B confirms that the money has been deposited via an online bank account and calls Broker A to notify him of the transfer. (Note that no hard cash has been transferred between China and North Korea during this transaction.)

Step 5. Broker A contacts the Receiver and tells her to pick up hard cash from Broker A's home, or some other stated location. The Receiver picks up 70 percent of the transferred amount, so if $1,000 was transferred, then she takes home $700. Broker A sits on a large amount of hard cash in his home. Since North Korean banks are not functional, and certainly cannot facilitate international transfers, this monetary system has been devised out of thin air. Approximately 30 percent of the transferred amount is taken out as commission. Since the broker inside North Korea is taking most of the risk, he takes more of the $300 than the broker in China. Hard cash is sent from Broker B to Broker A at a later time. Clearly, the relationship between Broker A and Broker B is one that has been established before and is one based on trust, since theoretically Broker B could just take the money and run. There are always bad apples, but these brokers would lose customers in the future if word got around that they had "lost" the deposit, or had simply taken off. The market for sending remittances to North Korea is limited, and the community of North Korean defectors sending money back is small. Word travels quickly, so brokers must be trustworthy and believable if they are going to run their businesses successfully.

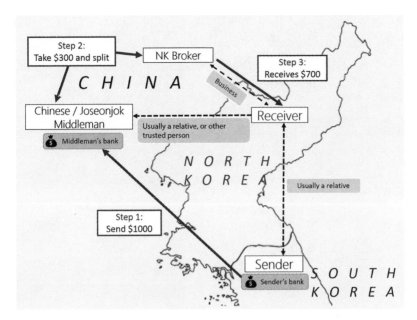

Simplified diagram showing how remittances are sent from South Korea–based defectors via middlemen to relatives living inside North Korea

Illustration copyright © 2016 by Catherine Myong

NOTES

CHAPTER 1. IMMORTAL GODS

1. The Democratic People's Republic of Korea (DPRK) is the state's official name, hereinafter referred to as North Korea for purposes of brevity. A more personal reason for referring to the country as North Korea rather than its official state name is my refusal to recognize, even nominally, the regime's self-declared democratic nature.

2. For more information on *juche,* please refer to Don Oberdorfer and Rob Carlin, *The Two Koreas: A Contemporary History* (New York: Basic Books, 2013); and Andrei Lankov, *The Real North Korea: Life and Politics in the Failed Stalinist Utopia* (Oxford, Eng.: Oxford University Press, 2013).

3. Created in the 1960s, an *inminban* is similar to a neighborhood watch unit and is organized by geographical area. Every North Korean is accounted for in an inminban unit of twenty to twenty-five families, and each unit is in charge of public works, of providing to the government the money and resources that it asks for, and for peer surveillance and monitoring for criminal activity and disobedient behavior. A North Korean woman usually heads the inminban units and is supposed to know everything about every person and household in her unit. The famine that killed so many people and left many people unaccounted for led to a less strict and functioning inminban system, although it is largely still in place. Kim Ha-Young describes her former inminban head as "so nosy that she even knew the number of silver and bronze spoons that my mom bought!"

4. Jasper Becker, *Rogue Regime: Kim Jong Il and the Looming Threat of North Korea* (Oxford, Eng.: Oxford University Press, 2005), p. 45.

5. Jung-Hyun Cho et al., "White Paper on Human Rights in North Korea, 2013," Korea Institute for National Unification, p. 282, available online at https://www.kinu.or.kr/eng/pub/pub_04_01.jsp?bid=DATA04&page=1&num=36&mode=view&category= (accessed April 3, 2016).

6. Ralph Hassig and Kongdan Oh, *The Hidden People of North Korea: Everyday Life in the Hermit Kingdom* (Lanham, Md.: Rowman and Littlefield, 2009), p. 7.

7. North Korea's State Administration for Quality Management, *Kimjongilia,* vol. 1: *Plant in Full Bloom,* October 10, 2005, available online at http://www.naenara.com.kp/en/book/download.php?6+6003 (accessed March 15, 2016).

8. International Institute for Strategic Studies, *North Korean Security Challenges: A Net Assessment,* July 21, 2011, pp. 47–64, available online at https://www.iiss.org/en/publications/strategic%20dossiers/issues/north-korean-security-challenges-4a8d (accessed March 15, 2016).

9. World Bank 2013, "Armed Forces Personnel, Total. Source: International Institute for Strategic Studies," available online at http://data.worldbank.org/indicator/MS.MIL.TOTL.P1 (accessed March 15, 2016).

10. Korea Central News Agency, "Kim Jong Un Makes Speech at Military Parade and Public Procession of Pyongyang Citizens, Pyongyang," October 11, 2015, translation obtained from National Committee on North Korea, available online at http://www.ncnk.org/resources/news-items/kim-jong-uns-speeches-and-public-statements-1/kim-jong-un-makes-speech-at-military-parade-and-public-procession-of-pyongyang-citizens (accessed March 15, 2016).

11. The Korea Institute for Defense Analyses (KIDA) is a South Korean government-funded policy think tank that reports to the Minister of Defense. KIDA-produced estimates about North Korea's military expenditure and capabilities may veer on the conservative side.

12. South Korea's Ministry of Unification, Understanding North Korea, 2012, p. 113, available online at http://eng.unikorea.go.kr/content.do?cmsid=1817 (accessed March 15, 2016).

13. Ibid., p. 112.

14. North Korea is the only country to withdraw from the Treaty on the Non-Proliferation of Nuclear Weapons, commonly known as the Non-Proliferation Treaty (NPT).

15. Full text of a speech by Kim Jong-Un given at the March 31, 2013, plenary meeting of the Central Committee of the Korean Workers' Party,

available online at http://www.ncnk.org/resources/news-items/kim-jong-uns-speeches-and-public-statements-1/KJU_CentralCommittee_KWP.pdf (accessed March 15, 2016).

16. David Sanger, "U.S. Commander Sees Key Nuclear Step by North Korea," *New York Times,* October 24, 2014.

17. The title of the short video clip of this girl on YouTube is "North Korea: Starving 23-Year-Old Homeless Woman (Rimjin-gang/ASIAPRESS)," available online at https://www.youtube.com/watch?v=Xh4CtTGAzKw (accessed April 3, 2016).

18. David Hawk, *The Hidden Gulag: The Lives and Voices of "Those Who Are Sent to the Mountains,"* 2nd ed. (Washington, D.C.: Committee for Human Rights in North Korea, 2012), p. 29.

19. For further reading on North Korea's brutal prison and detention facilities, refer to the Committee for Human Rights in North Korea's *The Hidden Gulag* four-part series, available online at https://www.hrnk.org/publications/hrnk-publications.php (accessed March 15, 2016). North Korean defectors who were imprisoned for years in prison camps have spoken and written about their experiences. Ahn Myong-Chol is a former prison guard at several political camps who later defected and also has written about his experiences working in camps.

20. Kang Chol-Hwan wrote a memoir titled *Aquariums of Pyongyang: Ten Years in the North Korean Gulag.* Originally published in French in 2000 then translated into English in 2001, Mr. Kang's book is one of the first widely published accounts of the North Korean prison system.

21. These forced repatriations of North Korean refugees by Chinese authorities are illegal according to international laws, so the "Friendship Agreement" between North Korea and China is in conflict with these laws.

22. In December 2013, Jang Song-Taek was executed by the orders of Kim Jong-Un. This news shocked North Korean watchers because as the son-in-law of Kim Il-Sung and the uncle-in-law of Kim Jong-Un, Jang Song-Taek was considered to be a key policy adviser to the young leader. In December 2013, he was abruptly accused of counter-revolutionary activity, stripped of his senior posts, expelled from the Workers' Party, and his name and images were removed from official media. On December 13, 2013, North Korean state media announced that he had been executed.

23. U.N. Commission of Inquiry on Human Rights in the Democratic People's Republic of Korea, *Report of the Commission of Inquiry on Human Rights in the Democratic People's Republic of Korea, 2014,* available online

at http://www.ohchr.org/EN/HRBodies/HRC/CoIDPRK/Pages/Reportofthe
CommissionofInquiryDPRK.aspx (accessed March 15, 2016).

24. Jang Jin-Sung, *Dear Leader: Poet, Spy, Escapee; a Look inside North
Korea* (New York: Atria Books, 2014), pp. 48–49.

25. Defectors have said that some North Korean households are able to
catch South Korean television programming in Kang-Won Province and
South Hwangae Province, two provinces that are geographically closer to
South Korea than other regions.

26. "Orascom Suffers Static in North Korean Venture," *Wall Street
Journal*, January 1, 2016, available online at http://www.wsj.com/articles/
orascom-suffers-static-in-north-korean-venture-1451628004?cb=log
ged0.7525846343487501 (accessed March 15, 2016).

27. Yonho Kim, *Cell Phones in North Korea: Has North Korea Entered the
Telecommunications Revolution?* (Baltimore: U.S.-Korea Institute at SAIS and
Voice of America, 2014), p. 11.

28. "Public Executions Seen in Seven North Korean Cities," *Korea
JoongAng Daily*, November 11, 2013, available online at http://koreajoongang-
daily.joins.com/news/article/article.aspx?aid=2980240 (accessed March 15,
2016).

29. "Three Executed for Watching South Korean Shows," DailyNK.
com, September 11, 2015, available online at http://www.dailynk.com/
english/read.php?num=13459&cataId=nk01500 (accessed March 15,
2016).

CHAPTER 2. CRACKS IN THE SYSTEM

1. Jeju Island, off the southern coast of South Korea, is a popular vacation spot for foreigners and a top honeymoon destination for South Koreans.

2. *Podaegi* is a traditional Korean wrap-around blanket with straps that
is used to secure a baby around the mother's back.

3. Trade in global waste, whereby countries sell their waste to other
countries for further treatment, recycling, and/or disposal, is not a new phenomenon. Generally waste—especially hazardous waste—has been produced in wealthy countries and then been exported to poorer countries. In
1997, North Korea agreed to accept up to 200,000 barrels of Taiwan's
nuclear waste for tens of millions of dollars. Incensed at this deal, South
Korea pressured Taiwan to cancel the agreement. This is only one of
several instances in which North Korea offered, for cash, to import foreign

waste that is so polluted and toxic that other countries have refused to handle it.

4. Sandra Fahy's book *Marching through Suffering* (New York: Columbia University Press, 2015) has incredibly nuanced observations and descriptions of how North Koreans coped with the famine years by using nonpolitical behaviors and language that would not get them in trouble, but would convey their thoughts to their peers.

CHAPTER 3. "OLD SCHOOL" MEDIA

1. These names have been altered.

2. Intermedia, "A Quiet Opening: North Koreans in a Changing Media Environment," 2013, available online at http://www.intermedia.org/ a-quiet-opening-in-north-korea (accessed April 2, 2016).

3. More recently, in 2015, there are often designated personnel who exchange currency for buyers and sellers on the market.

4. "We Will Destroy Imjingak, in Its Entirety," Urikimzokkiri, June 26, 2013, trans. Sinui Kim and James Pearson, available online at http://human-rightsfoundation.org/uploads/NKthreatagainstHRF.pdf (accessed March 15, 2016).

5. Sanyo is a major Japanese electronics company.

6. When I was in North Korea in 2013, I went to the DMZ and struck up a conversation with a North Korean soldier. After telling him I was a Harvard student, he beamed with pride, saying that Koreans, indeed, were smart. He was impressed that I went to the second-best university in the world. When I asked him what the first was, he matter-of-factly stated, "Kim Il-Sung University."

7. Kim Dong-Shik was a Korean-American pastor who led several Christian missions to serve people, including North Koreans hiding in China who wanted to go to South Korea. Despite a series of unfortunate car accidents and rectal cancer, he persevered in his work. In January 2000, Kim Dong-Shik was abducted by North Korean agents in China, sentenced to a political prison camp, and tortured. It is believed that he passed away in a camp. According to his wife, Jung Young Hwa, his weight dropped from eighty kilograms to thirty-five kilograms and he died within a year. On January 28, 2005, twenty Congressmen and women from Illinois (including Barack Obama) jointly sent a letter to Pak Gil Yon, the North Korean Permanent Representative of North Korea to the United Nations, seeking a

full accounting of the pastor's fate. In April 2015, Pastor Kim's son and brother (both American citizens) won a $330 million judgment against the North Korean government, ordered by the U.S. Court for the District of Columbia. Shurat HaDin, a civil rights group based in Tel Aviv, served as the Kim family's legal representation. North Korea dismissed both the letter and the American court ruling, and it is highly unlikely that they will pay the damages.

8. FNKR is not the only NGO that ran into legal and financial challenges and charges. Although I heard several accounts of the accusations against FNKR, I'm in no position to make declarative statements on what happened, since I do not have all the details or information. But I do believe that it is important to hold all NGOs accountable and be constructively critical. There is a tendency to hold organizations pertaining to North Korea to lower standards, if any, because the country is perceived to be a "black hole." But like other NGOs that do humanitarian and civic work, organizations that do good work regarding North Korea should be held to common standards of accountability, transparency, benchmarks, monitoring, and evaluation. Otherwise, these organizations might intentionally or even inadvertently act illegally or unethically.

9. *Bowibu* is North Korea's internal intelligence unit. Although I will not go into detail here about its organizational structure, defectors, including the former poet Jang Jin-Sung, have described it as a governmental body so threatening and chilling that even hearing the word Bowibu could silence a crying baby.

10. Members of the organization intentionally do not capitalize the N in North Korea when referring to their group.

11. Han-Yong Yi, also known as Il-Nam Ri, was the son of Song Hye-Rang, who was the older sister of Song Hye-Rim, the mistress of Kim Jong-Il. Kim Il-Sung vehemently disapproved of Song Hye-Rim as Kim Jong-Il's partner, so after they had a child in secret (Kim Jong-Nam), the mistress's older sister Song Hye-Rang was tasked to raise her own children along with Kim Jong-Nam in a secluded village, so that Kim Jong-Nam's parentage would be kept secret from Kim Il-Sung and the nation. Han-Yong Yi was raised alongside, among others, Kim Jong-Nam, who made his claim to fame in Western media when he was caught at Narita International Airport using a fake Dominican passport to enter Japan to visit Tokyo Disneyland. This highly public and embarrassing account is largely blamed for Kim Jong-

Nam's falling out of favor with Kim Jong-Il to become the heir of the country. Han-Yong Yi's inside knowledge of the royal family, which he described and publicized in his memoir *Taedong River Royal Family*, made him a prime target of the North Korean regime. Although he changed his name and underwent cosmetic surgery to hide his identity, he was killed on February 15, 1997, eight months after the publication of his memoir. Although the murderers escaped, a North Korean spy who was later captured by the South Korean authorities confessed under interrogation that three colleagues had been sent to kill the defector "as a birthday gift for Kim Jong-Il." Kim Jong-Il's birthday is February 16.

12. Nat Kretchun and Jane Kim, *A Quiet Opening: North Koreans in a Changing Media Environment* (Tampa, FL: Intermedia, 2012), p. 10.

13. Camp 22 was shut down in 2012.

CHAPTER 4. THE DIGITAL UNDERGROUND

1. In July 2012, a series of Disney characters including Mickey Mouse, Minnie Mouse, and Winnie the Pooh danced on a stage while the famous Moranbang Band sang a North Korean version of "It's a Small World" and other Disney tunes. Kim Jong-Un and other generals were part of the clapping crowd. A Disney spokeswoman, Zenia Mucha, commented, "This was not licensed or authorized by the Walt Disney Company." See "On North Korean TV, a Dash of (Unapproved) Disney Magic," *New York Times*, July 9, 2012, available online at http://www.nytimes.com/2012/07/10/world/asia/kim-jong-un-appears-with-mickey-mouse-and-other-disney-characters-on-north-korean-tv.html (accessed March 15, 2016).

CHAPTER 5. A NEW GENERATION RISING

1. Quoted in Jihae Lee and George Swartz, "Jangmadang Generation at the Core of Change in NK," *Daily NK*, July 6, 2015, available online at http://www.dailynk.com/english/read.php?cataId=nk02501&num=13323 (accessed March 15, 2016).

2. "North Korea's Millennials Demonstrate Entrepreneurial Spirit," *NPR* broadcast, August 11, 2015, available online at http://www.npr.org/2015/08/11/431512111/north-korea-s-millennials-demonstrate-entrepreneurial-spirit (accessed March 15, 2016).

3. Approximately 40 percent of North Korea's population lives in these two provinces.

4. This name has been altered.

5. This name has also been altered.

6. A pack of one hundred CDs weighs four pounds, so five to six hundred CDs would weigh between twenty and twenty-four pounds.

CHAPTER 6. IMPLICATIONS, PREDICTIONS, CALL TO ACTION

1. Gene Sharp, *From Dictatorship to Democracy: A Conceptual Framework for Self-Liberation,* 4th ed. (East Boston, MA: Albert Einstein Institution, 2010), p. 25.

2. After expressing public regret over the South Korean soldiers' accident, North Korea backtracked and stated that expressing "regret" does not equate to making an apology, which implies ownership of the accident. Rather, they claimed that "regret" means "that's too bad."

3. In 1900, just 1 percent of all Koreans on the peninsula were Christians, according to estimates by the World Religion Database. Due to efforts by foreign missionaries and churches, today 29 percent of South Koreans are Christians. South Korea is also home to the world's largest Pentecostal church, Yeouido's Full Gospel Church. Of the 1.7 million Korean Americans, approximately 71 percent are Christians. Over the years, there have been controversies and accusations made against individual pastors and Christian groups, but I personally do not have comprehensive, conclusive evidence regarding any of these cases.

4. The South Korean–born woman asked to not be identified, but was adamant that I include her perspective.

5. Jeremy is his preferred English name. He adopted several names in English and Korean after leaving North Korea. Although "Jeremy" does not sound like an authentic Korean name, he asked me to use it.

6. Asan Institute for Policy Studies, *South Korean Attitudes toward North Korea and Unification,* January 26, 2015, available online at http://en.asan-inst.org/contents/south-korean-attitudes-toward-north-korea-and-reunification (accessed March 15, 2016).

7. In November 2014, the United Nations voted in favor of a resolution that condemned North Korea's leadership for human rights abuses and recommended the prosecution of Kim Jong-Un and other top officials in the International Criminal Court for crimes against humanity.

ACKNOWLEDGMENTS

There are so many people whom I would like to thank for being part of bringing this book project to fruition: first and most importantly, every person from North Korea who offered to do a recorded interview for this book, and who shared personal stories and insights with me over the years.

I want to express my gratitude to Jeong Gwang-Seong for spending the time to answer every question I had, for inviting me to spend time with friends from his home town, and for always being so generous in helping me get around Seoul. Thank you, too, to Kim Ha-Young, Ahn Yu-Mi, Lee Joon-Hee, and Jeremy for sharing so much of your lives with me and for helping me understand parts of North Korea through the eyes of millennials. Nehemiah Park and Ms. Esther, thank you for introducing me to so many of your friends who have resettled in South Korea over the years; it was illuminating to chat, hang out, and try to understand one another as fellow human beings with ethnic Korean heritage. Kim Seong-Min and Choi Jung-Hoon—your input was invaluable in understanding the motivation behind the founding of the first radio station by a North Korean defector to broadcast into North Korea. Thank you to Dr. Park Se-Joon for always adding nuance to conversations, and for pushing me to think more creatively on the subject of information dissemination. Mr. Kim Heung-Kwang, your friendship and collaboration on projects have been so encouraging, and I thank you for your trust. Mr. Ji Seong-Ho, thank you for sharing such a powerful life story with me and the rest of the world, and I am ecstatic that your Kickstarter campaign to expand your NGO Now, Action, Unity, Human Rights (NAUH) was successful. I sincerely am so grateful as well to those defectors from North Korea who shared their stories with me over the years but who asked to not be quoted or included in this book in any way. A special thank-you to Lee Kwang-Baek, Kwon Eun-Kyong, Kim Sung-Joon, and your colleagues at the Unification Media Group for sharing your creativity, passion, and persistence in your mission and vision with so many others.

Thank you to my research assistant, Catherine Myong, for stellar research, translations, and commitment to the project. Translations by Bo Seo, Rurie Lee, and Henry Song were invaluable. And a special thanks to Henry for connecting me with his colleagues and sharing with me not only his passion for these issues, but also his insights into the fieldwork of NGOs.

I will forever be grateful to Mr. Kang Chol-Hwan who sparked my interest in North Korea when giving a lecture at Harvard in Kirkland House when I was a freshman. Hannah Song, you're my role model and I thank you for setting the bar for being a truly compassionate and effective practitioner of human rights. Sokeel Park, I am indebted to you for sharing with me your research and unparalleled insights over the years of the changes quietly bubbling up across North Korea. You're simply brilliant.

Dr. Katharine Moon, you have become such a powerful mentor for me and I thank you for the personal and professional guidance you continue to provide me. Dr. Lee Keum-Soon, thank you for your bountiful knowledge and for sharing with me your experiences, all of which added complexity to this consequential topic.

This project would not have been possible without the generous support of the Belfer Center for Science and International Affairs at the John F. Kennedy School of Government at Harvard, which also provided an intellectually stimulating and open-minded environment to pursue my research endeavors. To my mentor and adviser Professor Graham Allison, I thank you for consistently pushing me to think bigger and more rigorously about foreign-policy challenges that I care most about, and for giving me the opportunity to commit to this research topic. Ambassador Stephen Bosworth, thank you for giving me the opportunity to work closely with you on North Korea and East Asia policy projects to deepen my understanding of this region. I am indebted to Professor Matthew Bunn for training me to analyze policy questions, and for broadening my intellectual horizons. Thank you for always checking in on my progress and for encouraging me through unforeseen challenges with the book project. Professor Michael Ignatieff, I will always be grateful for your walking me through the process of writing this book, and for your sharing with me your experience in writing your first book years ago. My sincere appreciation also goes to William Tobey and General Kevin Ryan for guiding me through the sections in this book that were particularly challenging for me. John Park, it has been so edifying and challenging to learn from such a nuanced thinker and scholar as yourself.

Thank you to Professor Carter Eckert, who taught me Korean history in college, and has been so actively supportive of my passions in human rights and other issues pertaining to North Korea and the Korean Peninsula. Ed Baker, thank you for sharing such beautiful stories with me about your time as a young member of the first class of American Peace Corps volunteers to serve in South Korea after the war. The memories you have shared with me of personally witnessing the growth of South Korea over the past several decades have personalized the historical and academic angles of this research.

Thank you to my best friend, Morgan Kelly Radford, and my dear friends Tracey Hsu and Sarah Yun for daily encouraging me during the grueling process of drafting and editing. To my partner, Isaac Lara, I will always be so grateful for your patience in reading through so many sections of the book and providing your feedback when I would, at times, lose my discriminating sense of what is common knowledge and what is novel. Thank you for keeping me focused.

Mom, Dad, Joon—no words can describe how unconditionally supportive you have been of my passion over the years that has temporarily culminated in this book project. Dad, thank you for always taking my frantic calls when I needed you to explain a historical concept, and for always, always reminding me of the humanity behind history, foreign policy, tragedies, research, and policy.

I want to particularly thank Katherine Flynn for sparking this idea of a book project and for walking me through this brand new process for me. Thank you to my editor, Jaya Aninda Chatterjee at Yale University Press, for being so meticulous and guiding me through the writing and editing process. Julie Carlson, thank you for fine-tuning the manuscript. You are tremendous.

Finally, thank you to the readers of this book for your interest. I hope this book will provoke and energize you to learn more about how now, more than ever, North Korean people are taking extraordinary risks to learn more about the world that exists outside of their universe, the universe that is North Korea.

INDEX

Illustrations and figures are indicated by italic page numbers.

Cheonan sinking (2010), 132

children: as defectors, xix, xxiii–xxiv, 147; forced to watch public executions, 62; *kotjebis* (homeless children), 37, 53–55, 70, 99; political ideology taught to, 11–12; self-criticism sessions for, 6–7; South Korean children collecting propaganda leaflets dropped by North Korea, 96

China: dead individuals, selling identities of, 191; defectors caught in and returned to North Korea, 109, 164, 191, 206, 234–235, 247n21; defectors crossing into and living in, xix–xxi, 26, 36–37, 131, 133, 140–146, 206, 234–235; as exporter to North Korea, 38, 69, 92–93; Gojoseon kingdom and, 1–2; Joseonjoks (ethnic Koreans) in, 105, 117, 152, 155, 171; military, 20, 21; North Korea alerting to presence of defectors in, 166–167; South Korea's influence on, 142, 206; trade networks as information source, 69, 89, 92–93

Choi Jung-Hoon: biography of, xiii, 71; defection of, 76, 118; punishment of his family in North Korea, 119; radio broadcasting by, 119–122; South Korean hiring him to find her father kidnapped by North Koreans, 72–76

Choi Uk-Il, 73–76

Chongin prison camp, 29

Chosun Monthly (magazine), 106–107

Christians and Christian organizations: analogy of North Koreans to Christians who stray from "true" faith, 61–62, 212–213; author as Christian, 18, 212; Bible distribution and, xvii, 152, 157–158, 228; churches with North Korean defector congregations, 233–234; grassroots action of, 227–228; missionaries in China, 228; number of Korean Christians, 252n3; permitted in North Korea under certain conditions, 158–159. *See also* religion and religious organizations

Chun Doo-Hwan, 83

CIA's *World Factbook*, xvii

civil society organizations. *See* nongovernmental organizations

clothing and appearance: black market sale of, 35; defectors asked to send, 151; foreign influence on, 81, 131, 203–204; hair coloring and hair styles, 186, 187, 203–204, 208; of *jangmadang* (millennial) generation, 187, 190; outside goods brought into North Korea, xvii; in prison camps, 29; rabbit fur for soldiers to wear, 189; school uniforms, 182; second-hand from China, sale of, 69, 92; South Korean influence, 142, 203–204, 208

coal mining, 136–137

cognitive dissonance, 60, 80, 89, 176, 194, 219, 229
Cold War psychological warfare, 218–219
collective action to precipitate political change, 215, 220
College Scholastic Aptitude Test (*Suneung*), xxv
Commission of Inquiry (UN), 34, *165*, 225
compassion-driven networks, xvii, *xviii. See also* nongovernmental organizations (NGOs)
computers. *See* electronics and electronic media; internet; laptops; USB drives
conscription. *See* military of North Korea
Corpse Divisions, 35–36
corruption. *See* bribe culture
cram schools (*hagwons*), xxiv–xxv
crime and punishment, 28, 30–33, 43–44; criminal enterprises fostered by North Korea, xvii; criticizing government or despoiling image of North Korean leaders, 13, 26, 30, 95, 167; crossing border from China back into North Korea, 143–144; defecting, xix–xx, 74, 94, 209–210; failure to discourage secret listening or viewing of foreign media, 82; failure to report defection or political crime, 33; family punished for crime of relative, 27, 56, 68, 94, 146–147; group punishment, 28, 29; guilt

by association, 27, 33; information-related crime, ix, 30, 42–44, 46, 62, 83–84, 91, 96, 145, 201, 229; peer-monitoring, 7, 33, 189–190, 215, 245n3; remittances as criminal activity in both North and South Korea, 156; smuggling, xvi; social punishment of political criminals, 209–210. *See also* executions; prison camps and detention centers
cult of personality, 3, 12–19, 110, 157
cultural change, 214–225; ability of humans to change, 239; economic grievances as sparks for, 168; irreversible nature of, 9, 214; *jangmadang* (millennial) generation and, 186; nonviolent resistance and, 220, 224–225; transformative power of information, xvi–xvii, 147, 196, 215–216, 219–220. *See also* awareness creating doubts and discontent; future scenarios
cultural norms: grassroots markets and, 9; romance, affection, and dating, 164, 177–181; to serve government interests, 4, 10, 177–178
curiosity as driving force, 50–52, 78, 91, 100–103, 188, 207, 222–223
currency: designated exchange personnel, 249n3 (ch. 3); exchange rates, 92, 154; North Korean reform of, 154

Daily NK (internet periodical), 97, 134

Dangun Waonggeom, 13

dead individuals, selling identities of, 191

"The Dear Leader." *See* Kim Jong-Il

death threats. *See* assassinations and threats of assassinations

defectors: as assassination targets, 102, 111–112, *113*, 162, 166; author's interviews and interactions with, ix–x; "career defectors" criticized by younger defectors, 227; children as, xix, xxiii–xxiv, 147; costs for South Korea to resettle, xxiii; family left in North Korea, effect on, xix, xxi, 7, 27, 34, 94, 119–120, 190–191, 209–210; family members who defected earlier helping other relatives to defect, xxi–xxii, 37; generational divide among, 227; highest ranking, 110, *113*; increasing numbers of, 26; language of victimization learned by, 195; life in South Korea, xx–xxiv, 37, 130, 194–195, 236; media training of, 195; missing students, investigation for, 57; North Korean provinces as home of majority of, 185; North Korean soldiers as, 108, 191; political thought not factor for, 174–177, 204; process of defecting, xix–xxvi, 229; radio broadcasts by, 104–105, 112–117, 121–122,

134; reasons for defecting, 36–37, 108, 197, 204–205; reasons for not defecting, 209–212; remittances to North Korea, 154, 155–156, 196, 207, 241–242, *243*; responsibility to those remaining in North Korea, 197; on reunification, 239; Seoul as residence of, 147; South Korean initial treatment of, xxii, 61, 105, 110, 115, 195; statistics on, xx; suicide rate of, xxvi; terms for, xi. *See also* China; crime and punishment; foreign information dissemination; South Korea; *specific defectors by name*

demand-driven networks, xviii, *xviii*, 170

Demilitarized Zone (DMZ), xix, 2–3, 50–52, 95–96, 106, 163, 217–218, 249n6

democracy without war, 118–122

Deng Xiaoping, 175

detention centers. *See* prison camps and detention centers

dictatorships, 217

digital underground, 150–182, 190; cell phones, as lifelines, 150–157; Christian organizations' use of thumb drives, 157–159; importance of, 210–211; Jeong Gwang-Il and, 163–173; Kim Ha-Young and, 178–182; Kim Heung-Kwang's dissemination of DVDs and stealth USBs, 159–162; Lee Joon-Hee and, 173–178; MP4 players, 169, 174; Park Se-Joon

elites in North Korea, 40, 64, 70, 101, 159, 195, 210, 238; divisions among, 230

E-Mart (South Korean store), 160

empowerment, sense of, 220

envelopes, Security Ministry opening of, 107

escaping North Korea. *See* defectors

espionage: North Korean defectors suspected of, xxii; *Songbun* category of spies, 8; South Korean spy, arrest on suspicion of being, 163

Eternal President. *See* Kim Il-Sung

Eun-Ji (defector), 86, 88

executions: for cell phone calling, 156–157; of defectors, 108; of defectors' family members, 119–120; for distributing illegal media, 43, 62; forcing children to watch, 62; public, 30–32, 55; for watching illegal media, 62, 223

Facebook, 207

factory workers, 64

Fahy, Sandra, 249n4 (ch. 2)

families: of defectors, xix, xxi, 7, 27, 34, 94, 119–120, 190–191, 209–210; hiring brokers to help relatives to defect, xxi–xxii, 37; memorial service for younger sibling, 120; of political prisoners, 8, 28, 33; punishment of three generations, 27; remittances sent to family members in North Korea, 154,

155–156, 196, 207, 241–242, *243*; reunification of those separated in Korean War, 106–107, 236; searching for family members, 106–107, 115. *See also* cell phones and smartphones; social classification system

famine. *See* Great Famine

Far Eastern Broadcasting Corporation, 147

fear-based culture, xvi, 45–47, 162, 173, 217; as barrier to reform, 215; encouraging change in, 223–225

Fighters for a Free North Korea, 94

films. *See* foreign films and media

fishermen: as defectors, 133–134; South Koreans abducted from boat by North Koreans, 72–76

FNKR. *See* Free North Korea Radio

food: access to, 55, 90; black market sale of, 35; international aid and, 93, 121, 153, 159; politicizing access to, 27; violations of human right to, 34. *See also* Great Famine; rice; starvation

foreigners visiting North Korea, 14–16, 50–52

foreign films and media: in black markets, xv–xvii, 89, 174; copying of, 193, 203; demand-driven enterprise in providing to North Korea, 170; distribution of DVDs and CDs, 160, 164, 169, 181–182; DVD players,

markets: free market system, 172;
grassroots marketization, 9, 35,
37–38, 214; importance of, 174,
183–184, 214; in Musan, 91–92;
selling to merchants vs. selling to
consumers, 177. *See also* black
market; street markets

marriage: North Korean wife as
monitor of South Korean
husband, 74; of North Korean
women living illegally in China,
xxi; pressure on North Korean
girls to marry, 189, 200, 205;
spouse keeping secrets, 79

Marxist-Leninist thought, 3, 4

media: control of, 10, 38–43;
reporting story of kidnapped
fisherman returning to South
Korea, 76; secretly operating
within North Korea, 24–25. *See
also* foreign films and media;
internet; *specific types of media*

medical treatment: access to
medicines, 53, 92, 138–139;
American medicines, quality of,
205; defectors' demand for, xxiii;
medical equipment, lack of,
53, 138

membership training (MT) events,
66–67

memorial service for younger
sibling, 120

middle class in North Korea, 70

military intervention in North
Korea, nonviability of, 216

military of North Korea:
conscription avoidance, 91, 191;
conscription requirements, 21;
defections of, 108, 191; defectors'
radio broadcasts targeting
soldiers, 116–117; in DMZ,
curiosity of, 50–52; expenditures,
20–21, 246n11; impact of
possible reunification on, 238;
"military first" (*Songun*) principle,
21; propaganda writer position
in, 101–105; public to provide
supplies for, 189–190; rank in,
101; Red Youth Brigade as
training for, 199; reunification's
effect on, 238; size of, 20

millennials. See *jangmadang*
(millennial) generation

Milosevic, Slobodan, 224

Minju Choson (newspaper), 39

Min-Jun (defector), 185, 190–194

mobile phones. *See* cell phones and
smartphones

Mobilization for Farm Work (North
Korea), 199–200

money transfers. *See* remittances to
North Korea

monitoring, 72, 215; *inminban*s
(neighborhood watch units), 7,
189–190, 245n3. *See also* crime
and punishment; household
inspections

monotony of daily life, 50, 56–57,
191, 204, 206, 213

Mormon church, 159

Mount Baekdu, 13

movement: freedom of, 27, 34,
100; unusual instances of, 90–91.
See also travel within North Korea

political thought, not influential for defectors, 174–177, 204

Pomnyun, Venerable, 159

Popović, Srda, 224–225

population of North Korea, xix, 251n3

pornography ("red videos"), 61–62, 158, 179, 193, 213

predictions. *See* future scenarios

press. *See* media

prison camps and detention centers, 27–28; books on, 247n20; Camp 22, 136, 251n13; life in, 114, 235, 247nn19–20; in North Hamgyong Province, 108; "pigeon torture" in, 164, *165*; reeducation labor camps, 28, 84; *Songbun* category of political prisoners and their families, 8; types of, 28; violations of human rights and, 34; workers in, becoming defectors, 195; Yodok (Camp 15), 28, 163–164, 166

profit-driven networks, xvii–xviii, *xviii*, 161, 172, 193, 222

"progress in tandem" (*Byungjin*) policy, 22

propaganda: balloon leaflet campaigns, 94–96, 102–104, 150, 163, 217, 219; *bbira* (propaganda leaflet), origin of term, 96; belief in, 60–61, 214, 231; contradiction by foreign information, 185–186, 196, 204, 219; false history and, 9–12, 24; Kim Seong-Min as

writer of, 101–102; living standards vs., xix, 140–141; loudspeaker broadcasts of, 102, 112, 218–219; sources of, 15–16; about South Korea, 11–12, 59–60, 122, 180; ubiquity of, 12. *See also* dual realities

protests: awareness of, in North Korea, 100; student protests in South Korea, 83

Proto-Three Kingdoms, 2

psychological warfare, 102, 218

public displays of affection, 164, 177–178, 181, 208, 234

Public Distribution System, 35

punishment. *See* crime and punishment; executions; prison camps and detention centers

Pyongyang, North Korea: cell phones in, 42; defectors from, 24, 52–54; elites in, 70–71; Great Famine and, 35–36; Kumsusan Mausoleum, 16–18; Mansudae Art Studio, 15–16; military parades, 23; North Korean leaders' statues in, 14–15, 17; quality of life in, 9; social status and residency in, 56; War Museum, 10

"A Quiet Opening: North Koreans in a Changing Media Environment" (Intermedia Report), 88

praying for children to score well on tests, xxv; praying to Christian God while in North Korea, 30; punishment for interacting with Christians, 30, 157; radio broadcasting of, 104; reverence to deceased North Korean leaders compared to religions, 17–18. *See also* Christians and Christian organizations

remittances to North Korea, 154, 155–156, 196, 207, 241–242, *243*

repatriation, 247n21. *See also* China: defectors caught in and returned to North Korea

Reporters without Borders 2013–2014 World Press Freedom Index, 38–39

Republic of Korea. *See* South Korea

resettlement and assimilation assistance for defectors, xxii–xxiv, 207. *See also* assimilation of defectors

resilience, x, xxvi, 66, 136, 167, 234

resistance. *See* disobedience and discontent

reunification of families separated in Korean War, 106–107, 236

reunification of North and South Korea, 231–239; benefits of, 238–239; cost of, 231; desire for, 51; issues needing resolution prior to, 238; prayer for, 228; regime evolution as precondition to, 237; social integration and, 232–236

revolutionary organizations (R.O.s), 122

Rhee Syngman, 2

Ri, Il-Nam (Han-Yong Yi), 129, 250–251n11

rice: costs of, 65, 153, 168, 200–201; from defectors, 124, 140; envelope seals from, 107; from South Korea, 121

Rimjin-gang (magazine), 24–25

risk-taking, reasons for, 49–50, 148, 193, 205, 221. *See also* survival, drive for

Rodonga Sinmun (Workers' newspaper), 39

Rodong Sinmun (newspaper): control of news in, 10, 39; on Han Hyon-Gyong's heroism, 1; on Kim Jong-Il as global fashion icon, 13; mobile phone access to, 42

romanization of Korean terms, xi–xii

R.O.s (revolutionary organizations), 122

rumors: as information sources, 87–89; of possible coup, 25

Ryanggang Province, 43, 72, 174, 185, 191

Ryongchon city, train explosion near (2004), 41

Sang Man construction company, 72

Scaparrotti, Curtis M., 23

schools. *See* education and schools

Uriminzokkiri (UMG website),
39–40, 44, 134, 166
USB drives, xv–xvi, 157–159, 163,
203; dividing show episodes over
multiple drives, 171; exchanging
among friends, 182; free
distribution regarded as
suspicious, 172; as popular
medium, 169, 192; sale for
money in North Korea, 170,
172; stealth drives, 160
USSR. *See* Soviet Union

victimization, language of, 195
videos: as foreign information
medium, 167; of starving
homeless woman, 25, 247n17
Voice of America, ix, 78, 97
Voice of Freedom, 97
Voice of Korea, 39
The Voice of National Salvation
(North Korean radio program),
123, 125
volunteer activities: defector
students in South Korea serving
food to homeless, 65–67;
information dissemination via,
225; Peace Corps in South
Korea, 256

wages. *See* income
War Museum (Pyongyang), 10
waste, trade in, 76–77, 91,
248–249n3
wealth, impact of, 9, 63–64, 71,
131, 180, 182. *See also* elites in
North Korea

weather forecasts, popularity of,
115, 133
websites. *See* internet
We Warn the Dictatorship (defectors'
radio program), 114
women: as breadwinners, 64–65,
68–69, 201; goals for North
Korean girls, 189, 200, 205;
military service of, 21; North
Korean women living illegally in
China, xxi; in prison camps, 28;
sex trafficking of, xxi, 195;
smuggling money into North
Korea, 36; starving and
homeless, 2010 video of, 25,
247n17. *See also* clothing and
appearance
Wonkwang University (South
Korea), 122
Woo-Jin, 191
word of mouth as source of
information, 87–89
Workers' Party (North Korea), 8,
20, 22, 104
World Bank: on Korean People's
Army, 20; on North Korea GDP,
xvii
World Food Programme, 93; report
(2012), 37
World Press Freedom Index
(2013–2014), 38–39
World Service broadcasts (BBC),
228–229
World War II, 2

Yang Jong-Ja, 74–75
Yanyi (Chinese border town), 74